D0843070

Invest with the Fed

INVEST WITH THE FED

MAXIMIZING PORTFOLIO PERFORMANCE BY FOLLOWING
FEDERAL RESERVE POLICY

ROBERT R. JOHNSON,
GERALD R. JENSEN
AND LUIS GARCIA-FEIJOO

New York   Chicago   San Francisco   Athens   London   Madrid
Mexico City   Milan   New Delhi   Singapore   Sydney   Toronto

2 3 4 5 6 7 8 9 0   DOC/DOC   1 2 0 9 8 7 6 5

ISBN: 978-0-07-183440-7
MHID: 0-07-183440-0

e-ISBN: 978-0-07-183441-4
e-MHID: 0-07-183441-9

Library of Congress Cataloging-in-Publication Data

Johnson, Robert, 1939-
    Invest with the Fed : maximizing portfolio performance by following Federal Reserve policy / Robert Johnson, Gerry Jensen, and Luis Garcia-Feijoo.
        pages cm
    ISBN 978-0-07-183440-7 (alk. paper) — ISBN 0-07-183440-0 (alk. paper)
    1. Monetary policy—United States.   2. Investments.   3. Portfolio management.
    I. Jensen, Gerald R.   II. Garcia-Feijoo, Luis.   III. Title.
    HG540.J644   2015
    332.6—dc23
                                                                            2015001180

McGraw-Hill Education books are available at special quantity discounts to use as premiums and sales promotions, or for use in corporate training programs. To contact a representative, please visit the Contact Us page at www.mhprofessional.com.

CONTENTS

ACKNOWLEDGMENTS

From Robert Johnson

Thanks to my coauthors Gerry and Luis. Gerry's wisdom, sage counsel, intellectual insights and friendship have greatly enriched my life over the past thirty years. Luis is the rare individual who combines intellectual firepower and quick humor. Anyone fortunate enough to spend time with Gerry and Luis are better people for having done so.

My dissertation chairman and friend Thomas Zorn along with Richard DeFusco continue to have a profound influence on both my personal and professional life. I learned a great deal from working with them. The most valuable lesson was that you could combine friendship and academic rigor. John Maginn and Donald Tuttle are consummate professionals and their influence has truly made me a better person. John and Don are each the embodiment of the gentleman-scholar.

Dean Anthony Hendrickson and my former colleagues in the Heider College of Business at Creighton University have supported this project. I was fortunate to work with individuals who recognize that business is an applied discipline—a simple concept that all too many business school academicians forget.

There are times in your life when you discover who your friends truly are. Thanks to Matt Scanlan and Jeff Lorenzen for their unwavering support during difficult times.

Most of all, thanks to my mother, Rowena, for inspiring me to continue learning throughout my life. She didn't have the opportunities that I have, but instilled early in my life a thirst for knowledge. I wish she had lived to see the publication of this work.

From Gerald Jensen

Thanks to my parents, Bob and Marilyn, who instilled in me the importance of hard work and doing the right thing.

I am forever indebted to my coauthors for making this book project both intellectually rewarding and enjoyable. Bob and Luis are both consummate academicians and true friends.

I acknowledge the influence of three professors that had a profound effect on me and who I have tried to emulate throughout my own academic career, Manferd Peterson, Thomas Zorn, and Roger Stover.

From Luis García-Feijóo

Thanks to my coauthors, Bob and Gerry, for their trust, guidance, and example; and for sharing with me their sense of humor. Thanks also to Richard Pettway and Jeff Madura for their advice, and for becoming my mentors without realizing it.

INTRODUCTION: FEDERAL RESERVE POLICY

I am afraid the ordinary citizen will not like to be told that the banks can and do create money. And they who control the credit of the nation direct the policy of Governments and hold in the hollow of their hand the destiny of the people.

Reginald McKenna,
chairman of the Midland Bank,
addressing stockholders in 1924

September 8, 2013, started with the global equity markets spiraling downward, languishing as a result of a confluence of economic data that were below expectations for a recovering economy. Suddenly markets all around the world reversed course and surged upward, restoring billions of dollars in global wealth in literally a matter of minutes. What dramatic event caused this remarkable reversal of fortune? Shockingly, it was the pronouncements of a single man. Thus is the power of the Federal Reserve chairman, in this case Ben Bernanke. On this particular date Bernanke's dramatic announcement was simply that of a delay in the Fed's planned

1

curtailment of its monthly injection of money. The dramatic global response to a seemingly innocuous announcement exemplifies the tremendous influence that the Fed has on the financial markets. The Fed chairman has been described as the second most powerful person in the world, second only to the U.S. president, and many would argue that this understates the power of the position.

Irrational Exuberance

The most memorable case of the market reacting to the pronouncements of a Fed chairman was the famous—or, if you are a stock market bull, infamous—"irrational exuberance" phrase uttered by then Fed chairman Alan Greenspan. In the course of a very dry speech (and for anyone who ever heard Greenspan speak, was there any other kind?), Greenspan interjected the following lines:

> Clearly, sustained low inflation implies less uncertainty about the future, and lower risk premiums imply higher prices of stocks and other earning assets. We can see that in the inverse relationship exhibited by price/earnings ratios and the rate of inflation in the past. But how do we know when irrational exuberance has unduly escalated asset values, which then become subject to unexpected and prolonged contractions as they have in Japan over the past decade?[1]

The immediate response to the Fed chairman was swift and dramatic. The U.S. market was closed at the time of Greenspan's speech, but as word of the remarks was disseminated around the globe, world markets started a free fall as investors became increasingly worried—some would contend panicked—that the Fed would soon raise interest rates to slow down the economy. Investors interpreted the remarks as a signal that the Fed would soon be tightening monetary policy. The Japanese market fell 3.2%, Hong Kong closed off nearly 3%, Frankfurt fell 4%, and London lost 2% of its market value. Upon opening the next day, the Dow Jones Industrial Average fell 145 points (nearly 2.3%) but subsequently rebounded and was off only 55 points that day. It is worth noting that Greenspan didn't say that the Fed would soon raise rates. The market interpreted his remarks as a signal that a rate increase was imminent. The phrase took on a life of its own, as Box I.1 describes.

Box I.1   The Irrational Exuberance of the Phrase Irrational Exuberance

The phrase "irrational exuberance" became part of the common lexicon. Nobel Prize–winning economist and Yale professor Robert Shiller wrote a bestselling book titled *Irrational Exuberance* in deference to the quote. In December 2013, a *Wall Street Journal* article reported that a Google search of the phrase "irrational exuberance" generated 2.53 million results.[2] The phrase was being used in various contexts to describe overenthusiastic or unbridled expectations. For instance, a scholarly paper published by the National Bureau of Economic Research with the title "Does March Madness Lead to Irrational Exuberance in the NBA Draft?" appeared in 2012.[3] The phrase even permeated popular sports culture as an article titled "The Irrational Exuberance of August Football" appeared on Profootballtalk.com.[4] The beer world has even been characterized as having fallen prey to unbridled expectations, as Greg Koch, CEO of Stone Brewing, was quoted as saying that "[the industry is] . . . in a time of irrational exuberance in craft brewing."[5] Bumper stickers

(continued)

---

appeared that read "I want to be irrationally exuberant again." You could even purchase T-shirts that said "I'm Irrationally Exuberant." Clearly, Greenspan's remarks made a dramatic impression in the financial markets and elsewhere.

Perhaps the most curious aspect of the power of the Fed and Fed chairman is the ability to move markets not only by what they say but by what they don't say. See Box I.2 for more discussion of the power wielded by the Fed chairman. In September 2013, many market participants and pundits expected the Fed to announce that it would begin "tapering" or reducing the amount of quantitative easing. The announcement was widely anticipated to take place immediately after the September 18 meeting of the Federal Open Market Committee. In the days leading up to the meeting, many speculated about both the timing and the amount of the presumed change in Fed policy. A week before the meeting, the *New York Times* ran a story with the headline "Fed Prepares for Change in Policy, and in Policy Makers."[6] To nearly everyone's surprise, the Fed made no such announcement, prompting *The Economist* to carry a story titled "The Federal Reserve Surprises Everyone by Changing Nothing."[7] The markets were heartened by the nonannouncement, and the Dow Jones Industrial Average rose over 800 points for the little over three months remaining in 2013.

Box I.2 Alan Greenspan: Rock Star

During his term as Fed chairman, Alan Greenspan clearly achieved rock star status. His utterances were covered on the front page of major newspapers—not the front page of the business section, mind you, but the front page of the entire paper. Any movement by the Federal Reserve was the lead story on the evening news, not simply the business news. Greenspan became one of the most recognizable people in the world and a popular culture figure. He was even profiled in *People* magazine with a subheading indicating that he "held the world's markets in his hands."[8]

Greenspan's celebrity is perhaps best exemplified by late night comedians such as Jay Leno and Conan O'Brien including references to Greenspan and the Federal Reserve in their monologues. *Saturday Night Live*'s Seth Meyers poked fun at Greenspan's testimony before Congress in a "Weekend Update" bit in October 2008.[9] Greenspan even made an appearance on *The Daily Show* with Jon Stewart. In fact, on his last day as Fed chairman, Stewart aired what was titled "*The Daily Show's* Irrationally Exuberant Tribute to Alan Greenspan."[10]

Upon retirement, Greenspan commanded fees of upward of $100,000 per speech. In fact, in the week after his retirement in 2006, Lehman Brothers paid him a cool $250,000 to address 15 of the bank's most important clients.[11] It is ironic that it was Lehman Brothers that did this—remember them?

As an example of his celebrity, a popular joke stated that when Greenspan went out for breakfast one day, he asked for a plain bagel without cream cheese. The waiter took his spartan request as a sign of hard times and called his broker with a market sell order. Suffice it to say that Greenspan's public actions were closely scrutinized, a far cry from the relative obscurity in which predecessors such as Arthur Burns, G. William Miller, and Paul Volcker toiled.

Although Greenspan may have been the first celebrity Fed chairman, the focus on who occupies the position has not subsided with

(continued)

the passing of the torch from Greenspan to Bernanke and in 2014 to Janet Yellen. For example, the announcement of Yellen's nomination as Fed chairman was the subject of breaking news announcements on CNN, in the *New York Times*, and in other news outlets. In mid-January, the website for *TIME* magazine presented Janet Yellen as the "Person of the Moment." The significance is that *TIME* is not a business magazine but a news magazine.

Similar to Greenspan commanding high speaking fees when he stepped down, Ben Bernanke was reportedly paid $250,000 for a 40-minute speech in Abu Dhabi at his first public speaking engagement after stepping down from the Fed. This is considerably more than the $199,700 he earned for the entire year in 2013 as Fed chairman.[12] The Fed chairman clearly has a high public profile.

A more recent phenomenon is that the power of the Fed to influence markets is not limited to the chairman. It has become relatively commonplace for regional Fed bank presidents to be quoted in news articles and to appear on various market-oriented television and radio programs. For example, in early February 2014, in an interview on Fox Business News, Dallas Federal Reserve president Richard Fisher said he thought the central bank should continue to reduce bond purchases despite falling U.S. stock prices and currency turmoil in overseas economies.[13] The same week Dow Jones reported that Dennis Lockhart, president of the Federal Reserve Bank of Atlanta, said he believed U.S. stocks were in correction mode and doubted that the markets had recently been in a bubble.[14] The high profile of Federal Reserve regional bank presidents is in sharp contrast to the relative anonymity of individuals in those positions generations earlier. Historically, few investors knew who the presidents of the regional Federal Reserve banks were and fewer yet cared about their views on developments in the financial markets.

Why This Book Is Important

The fact that a single statement by a Fed official can create or destroy billions of dollars in wealth highlights the importance for investors to understand how Fed policy affects security markets. Our purpose in writing this book is to provide a general overview of the Fed's role in the financial markets but, more important, to offer investors a road map that can be used in designing an investment portfolio that takes account of Fed policy. In detailing our road map for investors, we offer a rationale for each investment strategy along with empirical evidence supporting the efficacy of the strategy. Most important, the recommended strategies come with clear explanations and easy-to-follow descriptions of the processes needed to execute the strategies. All that is required to implement the recommended strategies is a cursory knowledge of the security markets. We hope you find the book interesting, insightful, and, most important, beneficial in forming and modifying your investment portfolio.

Our research findings, accumulated through close scrutiny of the interaction between Fed policy and security returns over the last 30 years, provide overwhelming evidence that the Fed signals valuable clues that investors can use to greatly enhance portfolio performance. These clues are readily available to investors who know how to interpret and apply the signals. In spite of the overwhelming evidence linking Fed policy and security returns, we find that many financial pundits often misinterpret and/or incorrectly apply the Fed's signals. In this book, we identify common investment traps and show investors how to avoid them. The book begins with a general overview of basic Fed features that are essential for successfully monitoring and applying Fed signals. Subsequent chapters detail the relationship between Fed policy actions and the returns to a broad array of asset classes and security types.

Demystifying the Fed

As the central bank of the United States, the Federal Reserve (Fed) controls the U.S. money supply, assists in the regulation of U.S. depository institutions, and, when needed, assumes the role of lender of last resort. To ensure that monetary policy is conducted independently of political pressures, the Fed is intentionally separate from the federal government. In spite of its independence, political decisions and political pressures play an important role in influencing Fed policy decisions. In 1977, Congress gave formal recognition to the monetary objectives of the Fed by identifying the Fed's "dual mandate." According to the dual mandate, the Fed is to apply its policies to promote the goals of maximum employment and stable prices (essentially, low inflation). The power of the Fed is derived primarily from its authority over these two prominent aspects of the economy.

Although each of the Fed's tasks is important to the financial markets, we focus on the Fed's monetary objectives, which as noted above are to promote maximum employment and maintain price stability (control inflation). The Fed executes these objectives through its power to control the money supply. The basic process involved in executing Fed monetary policy is illustrated in Figure I.1.

Figure I.1   Fed Monetary Policy Process

As formalized by the dual mandate, the Fed's goals are to promote maximum employment and keep inflation low. Having responsibility for these economic indicators may sound like a reasonable assignment; however, executing these two objectives can be fraught with peril. The following discussion offers an explanation of the interaction of the items in the first two boxes in Figure I.1.

How Does the Fed Change the Money Supply?

Essentially all changes in the money supply are initiated through the Fed's most powerful monetary policy tool: its open market operations. The execution of the Fed's open market operations are conducted, appropriately enough, by the Federal Open Market Committee (FOMC). If the Fed believes that the economy would benefit from monetary stimulus—that is, an expansion of the money supply—the Fed directs the FOMC to purchase U.S. government bonds. The purchase of bonds replaces the bond holdings of financial institutions (banks) with cash, which the banks then lend to customers, who put the funds to productive use by expanding business operations. Thus, the FOMC's purchase of bonds results in more money circulating through the economy, which represents an increase in the money supply. As a response to the 2008 financial crisis, the Fed initiated a program referred to as quantitative easing (QE) to shore up the financial markets. QE is essentially nothing new but the Fed's open market bond purchase program on steroids (but lest we confuse Ben Bernanke with Alex Rodriguez, unlike in professional sports, this performance-enhancing activity is perfectly legal).

At the time of the writing of this book, monetary easing has continued to be the dominant Fed policy, but if the Fed believes that inflation is becoming the overriding concern, its policy will likely shift to monetary tightening. To execute this shift, the Fed will direct the FOMC to sell bonds, thus replacing bank cash holdings with bonds. An increase in the bond holdings of banks diminishes the money available to create bank loans. This action will help put the brakes on the economy. Thus, the ultimate result of FOMC bond sales is a reduction in money circulating through the economy.

An acknowledged tenet for policy makers is that financial markets abhor uncertainty. With that in mind, the Fed generally provides a signal—albeit often a bit muddled—of its long-term monetary policy intentions. Alan Greenspan famously was quoted as saying, "What I've learned at the Federal Reserve is a new language which is called 'Fed-speak.' You soon learn to mumble with great incoherence."[15] The instrument of choice for signaling market participants about impending shifts in Fed strategy is the Fed discount rate, which is the rate on loans the Fed extends to banks. The amount of lending that actually results via the discount window (from the Fed to banks) is minimal; however, the discount rate has historically offered a reliable signal of the Fed's long-term policy intentions. An increase in the discount rate signals that the Fed will be more restrictive in its open market operations (a reduction in the amount of future bond purchasing, or perhaps the FOMC will sell bonds). In contrast, a decrease in the discount rate signals that future policy will be "easy" (the FOMC will expand its bond purchase program).

To recap, the Fed executes its monetary policy intentions through the purchase and sale of U.S. government bonds, which is conducted by the FOMC. To avoid creating undue turmoil in the financial markets from an unexpected policy move, the Fed uses the discount rate as a signal of its long-term policy intentions. A rate increase is intended to signal market participants to expect the Fed to initiate a more restrictive policy at some point in the near future. In contrast, a decrease in the Fed discount rate signals market participants to expect an expansive future monetary policy in the coming months.

Why Does the Fed Need Targets?

Every semester, one of the coauthors of this book, Gerry Jensen, asks his students at Northern Illinois University to guess how long it takes between the initiation of action through the FOMC and the appearance of a perceptible response in the Fed's final goals (inflation and/or employment). When he gets no response, he announces, "That is correct; nobody knows how long it takes for Fed actions to work their way through to the final goals." It is for this reason that the Fed needs targets. It would be imprudent for the Fed to meet and finalize its directives to the FOMC and then schedule a follow-up meeting one year afterward to evaluate the impact of its action. By then, the economy may have fallen into a deep recession or inflation may be surging out of control. Essentially, the Fed is like a football field goal kicker, but the goal posts aren't stationary; in fact, they are constantly moving. We are reminded of a quote by President Dwight D. Eisenhower: "In preparing for battle I have always found that plans are useless, but planning is indispensable."[16]

The Fed needs to have a reliable economic variable that it can monitor on a near-term basis to determine whether FOMC actions have had a short-term impact. The Fed uses a number of alternative variables as targets; however, the federal funds rate is the most prominent of these alternatives. The federal funds rate is the rate on loans that banks extend to one another. It is important not to confuse the federal funds rate with the Fed discount rate, which is the rate the Fed charges on loans it extends to banks. Federal funds loans are generally very short term in nature, thus giving rise to their classification as the market for overnight money. Thus, although the Fed does not set the actual level of the federal funds rate, it does set a target or desired level for that rate. The Fed's actions via the FOMC are reflected relatively accurately and quickly by movements in the federal funds rate, and this makes the rate an effective indicator for the Fed and for astute investors.

Thus, relative to other targets, the federal funds rate is recognized for its effectiveness in reflecting near-term developments in the financial markets. Developments in the short-term market for financing usually precede similar developments in the market for long-term financing and ultimately in broad economic activity (e.g., inflation and unemployment). It is the linkage between the market for short-term financing, long-term financing, and economic activity that ultimately determines the reliability of the federal funds rate as a target.

Although changes in the Fed discount rate generally provide a reliable indicator of future policy actions, the Fed has been known to give the financial markets a head fake. For example, on February 19, 2010, the Fed increased the Fed discount rate, thus signaling impending tightening of monetary policy. For the subsequent several months, the federal funds rate gradually but consistently increased in concert with the February 19 signal of tighter money. However, in June 2010, the federal funds rate reversed course and headed back down, suggesting that the Fed was applying an easier policy, not a tighter policy. In the months that followed the February 19, 2010 discount rate increase, the discount rate remained unchanged; however, the federal funds rate fluctuated considerably, mostly moving down but occasionally exhibiting several consecutive months of increase. This episode makes it clear that it is important to monitor the federal funds rate to determine the degree to which the Fed is actually applying the policy signaled by a change in the discount rate.

Indicators of Fed Policy

In our published research papers, we have developed a measure of monetary conditions that combines the two prominent interest rates discussed above: the Fed discount rate and the federal funds rate. As was noted above, the discount rate is interpreted as a signal of the Fed's long-term (or broad) policy objectives. We use the Fed discount rate to classify the Fed's long-term policy intentions, or what we term *stance*. Specifically, an increase in the discount rate signals impending policy tightening and thus initiates a restrictive Fed policy stance. In contrast, a discount rate decrease signals the initiation of a period of easy money, or an expansive policy stance.

We rely on the federal funds rate to provide a gauge of the rigor of the Fed's monetary policy action, or what we term the *stringency* of Fed policy. An increase in the federal funds rate indicates that Fed actions are resulting in a more constrained market for short-term funds. Such changes should generally coincide with a prior increase in the discount rate if the Fed's actions are consistent with its broad policy intentions. A decrease in the federal funds rate indicates that the stringency of Fed policy is subsiding. Assuming consistency between Fed actions and broad policy, such a decrease in the funds rate should coincide with a prior decrease in the Fed discount rate.

Our Classification of Fed Policy

In developing our measure of monetary conditions, we use an approach that is both objective and easy to apply. To ensure the accuracy of the indicator, however, our measure relies on the confluence of two observable components of monetary policy: stance and stringency. Therefore, in the following sections, we explain each of the two components and the process we use in designing a combined measure of monetary conditions that incorporates both components.

Broad Fed Policy Intention (Stance)
- *Expansive*: Initiated by a decrease in the Fed discount rate. Subsequent decreases in the rate only serve to reinforce the Fed's expansive stance. Policy stance remains expansive until the Fed discount rate is increased.
- *Restrictive*: Initiated by an increase in the Fed discount rate. Subsequent increases in the rate only serve to reinforce the Fed's restrictive stance. Policy stance remains restrictive until the discount rate is decreased.

Fed Actions in the Short-Term Market (Stringency)
- *Expansive*: Initiated by a decrease in the federal funds rate. Subsequent decreases in the rate only serve to reinforce that the Fed's actions in the short-term market continue to be expansive. Policy stringency remains expansive until the rate is increased.
- *Restrictive*: Initiated by an increase in the federal funds rate. Subsequent increases in the rate only serve to reinforce that the actions in the short-term market continue to be restrictive. Policy stringency remains restrictive until the rate is decreased.

Combined Measure of Monetary Conditions

- *Expansive*: Both stance and stringency are expansive. The Fed decreased the discount rate and followed it up with actions that resulted in decreases in the federal funds rate. In other words, both components signal that the Fed is following an easy money policy. Since 1966, Fed policy has followed an unconstrained or expansive policy approximately one-third of the time.

- *Restrictive*: Both stance and stringency are restrictive. The Fed increased the discount rate and followed it up with actions that resulted in increases in the federal funds rate. In other words, both components signal that the Fed is following a tight money policy. Since 1966, approximately one-third of months are classified as constrained or restrictive policy months.

- *Indeterminate*: One measure of Fed policy is expansive, and the other is restrictive. The Fed is signaling a broad policy (stance) that is expansive (restrictive); however, its actions suggest that it is pursuing the opposite policy. The indeterminate classification captures the remaining one-third of the time when the Fed's policy intentions cannot be clearly classified.

Table I.1 summarizes the alternative monetary policy classifications that we use throughout our analysis.

Table I.1   Alternative Monetary Policy Classifications

		Broad Fed Policy (Stance)	
		Expansive	*Restrictive*
Rigor of Fed Actions	*Expansive*	Expansive	Indeterminate
(Stringency)	*Restrictive*	Indeterminate	Restrictive

How to Classify Monetary Conditions

Fortunately, the two measures we rely on in classifying monetary conditions—the discount window primary credit rate (more popularly known as the Fed discount rate) and the federal funds rate—are both readily available to investors at the website http://www .federalreserve.gov/releases/h15/data.htm. Formally, the Fed discount rate changed names in January 2003, but for our purposes, the rate continues to serve essentially the same signaling role. A change in the discount rate (primary credit rate) happens relatively infrequently and is widely publicized when it occurs; however, if you happen to miss it, you can find the change posted at the website mentioned here. Unlike the discount rate, the federal funds rate adjusts constantly on the basis of market forces and Fed actions. We rely on the effective monthly federal funds rate, which is an average of the daily rates during the month, to provide an indicator of Fed actions over the month.

Table I.2 reports a portion of the discount rate (primary credit rate) series and the effective federal funds rate series from 2010. We use these two portions to illustrate the application of our monetary-environment classification approach. As indicated by the first series of data, the discount rate was increased from 0.50% to 0.75% on February 19, 2010. This was the first change in the discount rate since the rate was decreased from 1.25% to 0.50% on December 16, 2008. Thus, since the February 19, 2010, change was an increase, it initiated a restrictive Fed policy stance. As of early 2014, the discount rate remained at 0.75%, which is consistent with the traditional stability the rate exhibits. The second series shows that from January 2010 to February 2010, the federal funds rate increased from 0.11% to 0.13%. Since the prior change in the federal funds rate was a decrease, this change in the federal funds rate initiated a Fed policy

Table I.2   Discount Rate Series (2008–2010) and Federal Funds Rate Series (2010)

Discount Rate

Date	Rate, %
March 18, 2008	2.5
April 30, 2008	2.25
October 8, 2008	1.75
October 29, 2008	1.25
December 16, 2008	0.5
February 19, 2010	0.75

Federal Funds Rate

Date	Rate, %
January 2010	0.11
February 2010	0.13
March 2010	0.16
April 2010	0.20
May 2010	0.20
June 2010	0.18

of restrictive stringency. Therefore, we would classify the monetary environment as restrictive since both indicators (stance and stringency) are restrictive.

To make our results practical for investors, we classify monetary environments on the basis of *prior* month changes in the indicator variables. In other words, we make sure the measures would have been available to investors before the return measurement interval.

For example, when applied to the data in Table I.2, the increase in the discount rate in February 2010 creates a restrictive Fed policy stance for March 2010. Likewise, the increase in the federal funds rate from January 2010 to February 2010 creates a restrictive Fed policy for stringency in March. Therefore, since both indicators signal restrictive policy, monetary conditions are classified as restrictive for March 2010. In other words, we lag the monetary environment a month after an initial change in the two rates to give investors time to reallocate their portfolios before we measure the return associated with the existing monetary environment.

Continuing the process to subsequent months, since the discount rate has not changed again since the February 2010 increase, stance has been restrictive from March 2010 through the time of this writing. Remember that the monetary indicator maintains its prior classification until the rate reverses. The federal funds rate increased in March 2010, maintaining restrictive stringency and a restrictive monetary environment for April. May is also classified as restrictive since the federal funds rate increased in April. Also, June is maintained as restrictive since the federal funds rate stayed constant in May. Since the funds rate dropped in June, July initiates a period of expansive Fed stringency. Since stance is restrictive in July and stringency is expansive, July 2010 is classified as indeterminate. This reflects a Federal Reserve head fake as the Fed signaled via the discount rate increase in February 2010 that investors should expect a tight policy for the coming months. The Fed followed through with the signaled policy for only four months before losing its nerve, perhaps because of fears that a tight policy would harm the fragile recovery before it had gotten firmly established.

Although our monetary conditions classification approach can seem a little daunting because of the two separate input measures, it is really fairly simple. Remember that all one has to do to classify the current monetary environment is to look at both series and identify the most recent change in each rate. For example, in classifying the monetary environment as we are writing this section in February 2014, we look at the discount rate and see that it is still 0.75% and that the last change was the increase in February 2010, a full four years earlier. Therefore, the Fed stance is classified as restrictive. We then look at the effective federal funds rate and see that the rate decreased from 0.09% in December 2013 to 0.07% in January 2014, thus making stringency expansive. Since stance is classified as restrictive and stringency is classified as expansive, we would classify the monetary environment in February 2014 as indeterminate. It probably comes as no surprise to most investors that monetary policy has been classified as indeterminate for much of the last four years. There has been a great deal of uncertainty about when and if Fed tightening will begin.

Conclusion

In this Introduction we established the tremendous influence that the Federal Reserve has on the financial markets. This influence is felt through the application of monetary policy, which in turn greatly affects security returns. For investors who know what to look for, we believe the Fed provides reliable signals of the direction of its future policy. We lay out a process that we believe can be used to effectively classify monetary conditions into one of three alternative states: expansive, indeterminate, and restrictive. In financial market parlance, expansive policy is often referred to as easy money and restrictive policy is called tight money. When the Fed is not offering a clear message, we classify the environment as indeterminate.

We use these monetary environment classifications throughout the rest of the book, and so it is important that you remember the basic classification approach. As a simple reminder, when the Fed increases policy rates, it is following a restrictive or tight money policy. The interest rate can be viewed as the rental rate on money; thus, a higher policy rate means a higher rental rate and a greater cost of obtaining money. A reduction in Fed policy rates corresponds with an expansive policy and easier money. With a reduction in policy rates, the Fed is signaling a lower rental rate and increased availability of money.

In subsequent chapters we evaluate these monetary policy classifications relative to returns for a number of different types of securities. Each chapter offers a variety of financial market observations and financial anecdotes, along with our empirical findings. We hope you find the book enjoyable; however, our overriding objective is to demonstrate how investors can use monetary conditions to guide investment decisions and enhance portfolio performance.

Readers who want to better understand why interest rates matter and the connection between interest rates and financial assets should read the Appendix in the back of the book before proceeding to Chapter 1. The Appendix details several ways in which interest rates influence security prices.

CHAPTER **1**

FED MONETARY POLICY AND THE PERFORMANCE OF TRADITIONAL ASSET CLASSES

> In the stock market, as with horse racing,
> money makes the mare go.
> > *Martin Zweig, from* Martin Zweig's
> > Winning on Wall Street

It is widely acknowledged that Fed policy plays an important role in the performance of U.S. security markets. Among investors, however, there is considerable debate about whether investors can actually use monetary policy changes to improve their investment performance. We all know that investors are bottom-line-oriented. For them, the value of any indicator variable, such as Fed policy shifts, depends on whether that variable can be used to their advantage. With that consideration in mind, this chapter is devoted to the evaluation of the historical performance of the traditional broad asset classes (U.S. stocks, U.S. bonds/notes, and U.S. money market securities).

Expansive or Restrictive?

In addition to debates about the practical relevance of Fed policy shifts, market participants' opinions differ over which Fed policy regime (expansive or restrictive) is most advantageous for investors. To help resolve the debate about the appropriate use of Fed policy shifts, this chapter examines security performance across the three monetary policy environments that were defined in the Introduction: expansive, indeterminate, and restrictive. We report historical returns and risks of the traditional security classes during each of the three environments over the period 1966–2013. We choose to start our sample period in the mid-1960s to coincide with the market's increased recognition of the relevance of Fed policy (see Box 1.1 for further discussion). Importantly, as was noted in the Introduction, our findings in this chapter and subsequent chapters rely on lagged measures of the monetary indicator variables; that is, investors could actually monitor and use the variables to guide their decisions. Thus, the returns we report could be easily captured by an investor who casually monitors the monetary indicators.

Box 1.1 The Rise of the Fed

The Introduction referenced the near-rock-star status that Federal Reserve officials maintain; however, such stardom has not always been the case for those officials. The Fed's failure to prevent the financial market's collapse during the Great Depression of the 1930s was viewed as evidence that Fed policy was relatively impotent. Similarly, Fed officials were viewed as overseers of an institution that was largely ineffective. This view was maintained by many until the seminal work of Nobel Prize–winning economist Milton

---

Friedman and Anna J. Schwartz offered an alternative perspective. In their book *A Monetary History of the United States, 1867–1960*, which was published in 1963, Friedman and Schwartz presented an argument that contrasted sharply with the widely held view that Fed policy had relatively little influence on the economy. In essence, Friedman and Schwartz offered a monetarist challenge to the Keynesian view, which contended that the Great Depression resulted from a lack of investment. Friedman and Schwartz argued that the lesson to be learned from the Great Depression wasn't that Fed policy was ineffective but that a poor Fed policy could be disastrous. The two economists convincingly detailed several policy mistakes made by the Fed in the late 1920s and early 1930s. According to those authors, these mistakes resulted in the Fed applying a tight monetary policy that elevated a normal recession into the Great Depression. The Friedman and Schwartz argument regarding the Great Depression was so novel that the authors published the Great Depression chapter from their book as a stand-alone paperback titled *The Great Contraction, 1929–1933*, which appeared in 1965. These works were instrumental in advancing the relevance of monetary policy and the substantial influence of Fed policy on economic conditions.

Fed Watchers

For years, there has been a prominent and devoted segment of investment managers who have closely followed Fed pronouncements. This group is often referred to as Fed watchers. The sentiment of this group is captured by Martin Zweig in the quote at the beginning of this chapter: "In the stock market, as with horse racing, money makes the mare go."[1] Zweig's statement suggests that an expansive (easy money) policy benefits investors, and this is supported by the markets' euphoric response to the announcements of continued quantitative easing that have occurred in the post-2008 period.

The positive sentiment regarding easy money is not universally held, however. In many instances commentators have questioned the rationality of the extreme positive investor responses to news of continued monetary easing. There are even some pundits and investment managers who believe that Fed tightening is good for the market because it signals that the Fed believes the economy is sound. For example, a 2013 *USA Today* article claimed that historical data show that the stock market actually goes up during periods of Fed tightening. The article contends that "the broad U.S. stock market rose in value during 10 of the past 11 cycles in which the Fed was raising interest rates."[2]

Risk Plays a Role

Although investors are keenly focused on returns, that isn't the only thing that matters to them. Investors are also interested in the riskiness of those returns, that is, how certain the returns are. With investments, risk is most often measured as the variability of returns. Although investors prefer higher returns over time (i.e., they like returns), they prefer investments that have a lower variability of returns over time (i.e., they dislike risk).

Obviously, investors would rather own an investment that averages a return of 10% per year than one with an average return of 7% per year. But that tells only half of the story. Investors prefer an investment that earns 10% each and every year for five years to one that returns 20, 10, 0, −20, and 40%, respectively, over five years.[3] The average return of the second investment is 10% annually, but the returns are all over the map. The risk/return trade-off is fundamental to both investment theory and investment practice.

The most common way of describing investment return variability is by using the standard deviation, a statistical measure that indicates how uncertain the average return has been over time. The standard deviation shows how much variation or dispersion from the mean (or average) exists in any data series. A data series with all the observations clustered very close to the mean value will have a very low standard deviation. In contrast, a data series with widely dispersed points will have a high standard deviation. The standard deviation provides the investor with much more information than does the range, which is simply the difference between the highest and lowest values over time. If returns are normally distributed, approximately two-thirds of the returns fall within one standard deviation of the mean (or average) return. Additionally, with a normal distribution, approximately 95% of the returns fall within two standard deviations of the mean.

And the Winner Is . . .

Table 1.1 reports U.S. stock market performance across our three monetary environments over our 48-year sample period. Throughout this chapter and in select future chapters, we define the U.S. stock market to be the returns to the S&P 500. To avoid an overdose of monotony, however, we occasionally introduce a little variation to the proxy we use for the U.S. stock market. Be on the lookout for alternative proxies for the U.S. market later in the book.

Table 1.1   U.S. Stock Market Performance: January 1966–December 2013

	All Monetary Conditions (576 months)	Expansive Monetary Conditions (172 months)	Indeterminate Monetary Conditions (209 months)	Restrictive Monetary Conditions (195 months)
S&P 500 return (annualized)	10.56%	15.18%	11.10%	5.89%
Inflation rate (annualized)	4.16%	2.86%	4.33%	5.13%

Note: We follow the standard approach of annualizing mean monthly returns by multiplying the monthly value by 12. This approach is applied throughout the rest of the book.

As Box 1.2 indicates, you shouldn't let this little bit of variation in market proxy cause you concern. The alternative U.S. market proxies are highly consistent in the long run; however, they can vary over time. Each proxy has its own merits that support its use in particular situations.

Table 1.1 reports U.S. stock market performance by monetary environment and also reports the annualized inflation rate across the three environments. We classify monetary conditions on a monthly basis, and therefore we use monthly return series in deriving our performance (return and risk) measures. We annualize the monthly measures for expositional purposes; it is much easier to interpret and relate to annual values than to monthly values. When have you ever heard a friend report the monthly rate on his or her new mortgage? Throughout the rest of this chapter and the rest of the book, we follow the same process (reporting annual values by converting or annualizing monthly measures).

Box 1.2   What Is the Return on the U.S. Market?

How did the market do? is a question investors ask on a daily basis. To get a sense of the performance of the overall market, we look to the performance of several different market indexes. These indexes vary in their composition: some have as few as 30 securities whereas others have thousands, and some are value-weighted whereas others are price-weighted. Here are five common market indexes:

- *S&P 500*: a market capitalization–weighted index of 500 large companies trading on the New York Stock Exchange (NYSE) or the Nasdaq. The Nasdaq is an American stock exchange that includes stocks not listed on the NYSE.
- *Dow Jones Industrial Average* (DJIA): a price-weighted index of 30 large companies trading on the NYSE or Nasdaq.
- *Nasdaq Composite*: a market capitalization–weighted index of all 3,000-plus stocks that trade on the Nasdaq.
- *Russell 3000*: a market capitalization–weighted index of the largest 3,000 companies that trade on the NYSE, Nasdaq, and the OTC Markets Group. The firms included in the Russell 3000 represent 98% of the total market capitalization of the U.S. stock market. On the basis of this characteristic, the index is frequently identified as a total-market index.
- *Russell 2000*: a market capitalization–weighted index of the smallest 2,000 stocks in the Russell 3000 index.

Despite the dramatic differences in index composition, the correlation among these alternative indexes tends to be quite high. For instance, the S&P 500 has 500 different securities and is

(continued)

---

value-weighted; that is, each of the component returns is weighted by the firm's market capitalization. In contrast, the Dow Jones Industrial Average has only 30 securities and is price-weighted; that is, each of the component returns is weighted by the firm's stock price. Yet the correlation or relationship of changes in one index with respect to the other is extremely high. From 1988 through 2013, the correlation of quarterly returns between the two indexes was 98.8%.[4]

Table 1.2 shows the annual returns for a recent 10-year period for each of the indexes.

Table 1.2   Annual Index Returns in Percent: 2004–2013

Year	S&P 500	Dow Jones Industrial Average	Nasdaq Composite	Russell 3000	Russell 2000
2004	10.88	3.10	9.16	11.90	18.33
2005	4.91	−0.60	2.17	6.12	4.55
2006	15.79	16.30	10.28	15.72	18.37
2007	5.49	6.40	10.55	5.14	−1.57
2008	−37.00	−33.80	−40.03	−37.31	−33.79
2009	26.46	18.80	45.32	28.34	27.17
2010	15.06	11.00	18.02	16.93	26.85
2011	2.11	5.50	−0.83	1.03	−4.18
2012	16.00	7.26	17.45	16.42	16.35
2013	32.39	26.50	40.12	33.55	38.82
Mean	9.21	6.05	11.22	9.79	8.01
Standard deviation	18.80	16.17	23.43	19.36	18.45

Although the correlation among the indexes is on average very high, there are substantial deviations in performance. The DJIA recorded the lowest mean return among the market indexes with a value of only 6.05%, whereas the Nasdaq reported the highest value at 11.22%. As an investor, I would have been much happier earning the market return of 11.22% over the 10-year period instead of the market return of 6.05%. The other market indexes recorded mean returns that were comparable with one another and fell squarely between the two extremes. As expected, the risk of the indexes mirrors their mean returns in all cases, supporting the fundamental risk/return trade-off.

The performance of the indexes on a year-by-year basis shows considerably more disparity than do the summary measures. For instance, in 2009 all the indexes exhibited strong returns; however, the DJIA returned nearly 19%, whereas the Nasdaq Composite returned more than twice that amount at over 45%. Investors in DJIA index funds were probably pleased by the turnaround from 2008, but Nasdaq investors were downright euphoric. In 2007 the Russell 2000 showed a slight negative return whereas the Nasdaq Composite had a double-digit positive return.

Table 1.1 indicates that over our full sample period (576 months) the stock market fared pretty well, providing investors with an average annual return of 10.56%. It is instructive to think of inflation as eating away at investors' returns, and so what is left after deducting inflation is considered an investor's real return. A positive real return means that after accounting for inflation, an investor has more purchasing power than before. For the full sample period, stock investors were able to increase their purchasing power by 6.4% per year (10.56% − 4.16%).

Stock Returns and Monetary Conditions

The final three columns of Table 1.1 separate performance by monetary environment. Incredibly, the data show that stock returns are approximately three times higher when monetary conditions are expansive than are returns earned when conditions are restrictive. Furthermore, the inflation rate is 1.8 times lower during expansive environments relative to restrictive environments; this further shows the superiority of returns during expansive periods. On average, stock investors were able to increase their purchasing power by a phenomenal 12.32% per year (15.18% − 2.86%) during expansive monetary environments. In stark contrast, the dismal performance of stocks during restrictive monetary environments is highlighted by the observation that investors realized less than 1% net of inflation. This is an amazing result considering that restrictive periods constitute a large percentage—33.9% (195/576)—of the entire sample period. Over these nearly 16 years during the sample period, investors advanced their purchasing power by only 0.76% per year. These results indicate that the monetary environment offers a well-defined separation of investment performance into strong and weak categories.

The moderate performance of stocks recorded during periods of indeterminate monetary policy further reinforces the important role that monetary conditions play in the market. During indeterminate periods, investors earned a real return of 6.77% per year (11.10% − 4.33%), not nearly as good as the 12.32% during expansive periods but much better than the 0.76% in restrictive conditions. Since indeterminate periods consist of a blend of both expansive and restrictive environments, the middling performance is expected.

On the basis of Table 1.1, we can clearly chalk one up to Zweig and the rest of the Fed watchers. That euphoric response by the stock market to announcements that the Fed was extending quantitative easing appears to be well justified after all. Similarly, the investor consternation that has accompanied signals of Fed tightening or tapering also appears to have been a rational reaction on the basis of the historical evidence.

But What About Risk?

We next consider the risk (the volatility) in stock market performance across the monetary environments. If all or most of the return pattern identified in Table 1.1 is concentrated in a few periods, we would question the strength of the relationship. Much like the old adage that you can drown in a river with an average depth of six inches, we want to consider the consistency of the return pattern: How deep is this proverbial river? Furthermore, if the superior performance of stocks during expansive monetary conditions coincides with much higher risk, we could say that the superior performance is simply necessary compensation for the greater risk investors assume during these periods. To address these issues, Table 1.3 reports the standard deviation of returns as well as the 10th and 90th percentile values.

On the basis of the data in Table 1.3, we can conclude that the volatility of returns is similar across the three monetary environments but is highest in expansive conditions and lowest in restrictive conditions. This evidence clearly shows that the superior performance in expansive conditions is not merely compensation for greater risk. Although the higher returns during expansive periods do come with somewhat greater risk, the additional risk is minimal, whereas the additional return is substantial.

In Table 1.3 we consider one last risk dynamic: the notion of upside and downside risk as represented by the 10th percentile and 90th percentile values. See Box 1.3 for further discussion of upside and downside risk. The 10th percentile values suggest that the three environments all have comparable levels of downside risk. For each environment, there was a 1 in 10 chance of experiencing a one-month loss of about 4.5%. In contrast, the upside potential was more limited when monetary conditions were restrictive compared with the other environments. The 90th percentile values indicate that there was a 1 in 10 chance of realizing a monthly return exceeding 6% during expansive and indeterminate conditions, whereas during restrictive conditions the 90th percentile value was a full percentage point lower at about 5.2%.

Table 1.3   U.S. Stock Market Risk: January 1966–December 2013

	All Monetary Conditions (576 months)	Expansive Monetary Conditions (172 months)	Indeterminate Monetary Conditions (209 months)	Restrictive Monetary Conditions (195 months)
S&P 500 standard deviation (annualized)	15.26%	16.34%	15.08%	14.40%
S&P 500 90th percentile value (monthly return value)	5.92%	6.31%	6.12%	5.16%
S&P 500 10th percentile value (monthly return value)	−4.56%	−4.68%	−4.55%	−4.34%

Note: We follow the common approach of annualizing standard deviations of monthly observations by multiplying the value by the square root of 12. This approach is applied throughout the rest of the book.

Box 1.3 If It Goes Up, Is It Really Risk?

When investors use standard deviation as a proxy for risk, returns above the mean and returns below the mean are given equal weight. That seems counterintuitive. How many investors complain because the market price of an asset they own is going up too fast or too far? How many investors—and talking heads—complain about volatility when the markets are advancing? Other than those betting on a price decline, who loses sleep because the markets are volatile on the upside?

Financial professionals occasionally refer to semideviation to distinguish between upside volatility and downside volatility. Semideviation is calculated by setting all deviations above the mean to zero, effectively considering only deviations below the mean. The reasoning behind semideviation is obvious: above-average returns do not *increase* risk, as outperformance is beneficial to investors. Although this is not as efficient, upside and downside risk can be roughly gauged by reporting values near the top and bottom of a return distribution (e.g., reporting the 90th percentile and 10th percentile value as we did in Table 1.3).

One of the authors of this book, Bob Johnson, teamed with Professor Ken Washer of Creighton University to explain downside volatility in an article in the *Journal of Financial Planning*.[5] In that article, the authors show that from 1968 through 2011, Warren Buffett's Berkshire Hathaway had an astounding average annual return of 26.7%. Berkshire's best five years had returns of 102.6%, 75.8%, 63.9%, 57.9%, and 53.8%. Berkshire's worst five years had returns of −75.4%, −58.5%, −49.8%, −46.6%, and −31.4%. Thus, the magnitude of the outliers on the upside was dramatically larger than the magnitude of the outliers on the downside. In fact, with further examination, the authors show that downside risk—deviations

(continued)

below the mean—constitute only 39% of total risk. It appears that at least in Berkshire Hathaway's case, standard deviation actually overestimates risk as most investors would define it. The problem with semideviation is that it has never caught on with investors and is usually referred to only in a smattering of academic articles.

What Month Is Best for Stocks?

As a final assessment of the consistency of the stock return pattern that is reported in Table 1.1, Figure 1.1 illustrates average returns across the 12 calendar months. Previous research has identified significant seasonal patterns in stock returns. In particular, the well-known January effect is based on the observation that stock returns, specifically the returns to small firms, have been exceptionally high in the month of January.

The returns plotted in Figure 1.1 help confirm the consistency of the outperformance of stocks during expansive monetary periods and their underperformance during restrictive periods.[6] In 7 of the 12 months, the average return in expansive conditions was the highest, or in one case tied for highest, of the three environments. Similarly, in expansive conditions, the lowest average return occurred for only one month (September). In contrast, restrictive periods witnessed the lowest average monthly return in 6 of the 12 months. Furthermore, the highest return occurred during restrictive periods for only one month (August) with a tie for highest honors in March. Clearly, the evidence indicates that in expansive funding conditions stocks generally performed well whether the time frame was early, middle, or late in the year, whereas in restrictive conditions stocks generally fared poorly throughout the year.

Figure 1.1   Average Returns on S&P 500: January 1966–December 2013

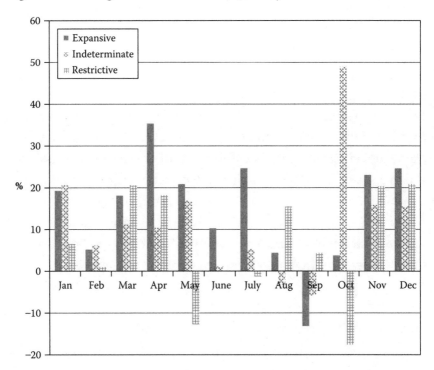

The overall stock return for January offers limited support for the January effect as, contrary to expectations, the average January return is not clearly superior to that of other months, such as April, November, and December. This probably is due to the fact that the returns we report are for the S&P 500, which is an index that consists of the largest market capitalization U.S. stocks. The January effect has long been identified as predominantly a small-firm phenomenon.[7] The evidence, however, clearly indicates that during periods of restrictive monetary policy, January stock returns have been generally dismal. This result is clearly contrary to the implications of the January effect, which highlights January as a favorable period for stock market performance. Overall, it appears that when the Fed is applying a tight money policy, investors should not expect a January market rally.

Fixed Income Tells a Different Story

Following the format of Table 1.1, Table 1.4 reports performance data for the U.S. bond market and the U.S. money market across the three monetary environments. We follow the convention of classifying the two securities in the exhibit as fixed-income because of the fixed contractual payment that both securities promise. We proxy returns to the U.S. bond market with the 10-year Treasury note (T-note) and the U.S. money market with returns for 1-month Treasury bills (T-bills). See Box 1.4 for an explanation of the money market.

Box 1.4   What Is a Money Market Security?

Financial market participants often talk about the money market and capital markets. Securities that trade in the money markets have three distinguishing characteristics: they are all debt instruments that are (1) short term in nature, (2) highly liquid, and (3) relatively low risk and are sold by governments, corporations, and financial institutions to people who temporarily want to invest excess funds. Examples of securities that trade in the money markets are U.S. Treasury bills, negotiable certificates of deposit, commercial paper, repurchase agreements, and banker's acceptances. Money market securities are frequently referred to by investment managers as cash or cash equivalents. Thus, when you hear investment managers discussing their cash holdings, the majority of such holdings most likely consist of money market securities.

In contrast to the money markets, the capital markets are where stocks and longer-term and higher-risk debt instruments (i.e., all instruments outside the money market) trade. There is no magic cutoff point where a low-risk and highly liquid security goes from being considered a money market security to being deemed a capital market security; however, money market securities generally have maturities of one year or less. Some money market securities are extremely short term in nature. For example, some repurchase agreements are overnight repurchase agreements, effectively having a maturity of one day. On the other end of the spectrum, some Treasury bills are issued with an original maturity of one year.

Individual investors generally don't directly purchase individual money market securities but often participate in the money market through money market mutual funds. Virtually all mutual fund organizations include a money market fund in their offerings. This allows a mutual fund investor to keep excess cash balances fully invested at all times.

Investors rarely lose money when investing in money market securities. In fact, unlike stock or bond mutual funds, money market funds are priced at $1 per share. What changes is the rate of interest the fund pays, or the fund's yield. A money market fund is said to "break the buck" when its net asset value falls below $1 per share, meaning that investors have lost money. Until the financial crisis in 2008, the only case of a money market fund breaking the buck occurred in 1994, when the Denver-based Community Bankers U.S. Government Money Market Fund was liquidated at 96 cents on the dollar. In 2008, the New York–based Primary Fund broke the buck when its shares were valued at 97 cents after the write-off of its holdings of Lehman Brothers debt.[8]

The returns for All Monetary Conditions indicate that bond investors were able to beat inflation by over 3% per year on average (7.26% – 4.16%), whereas money market investors advanced their purchasing power by slightly less than 1% per year (5.05% – 4.16%). From the final three columns of Table 1.4, it is readily apparent that monetary conditions influence stocks and fixed-income securities in a very different manner. In particular, the average bond return in expansive periods is very similar to the return during restrictive periods, and the highest average bond return occurs during indeterminate conditions. For T-bills, the average return in expansive periods is nearly 1.5% less than the return earned during restrictive periods (4.26% versus 5.62%). A difference this large in the fixed-income market is substantial. The higher T-bill return reported in restrictive monetary conditions is exactly the opposite of the pattern observed in Table 1.1 for stocks.

Table 1.4   Annualized U.S. Fixed-Income Returns and Risk in Percent: January 1966–December 2013

	All Monetary Conditions, % (576 months)	Expansive Monetary Conditions, % (172 months)	Indeterminate Monetary Conditions, % (209 months)	Restrictive Monetary Conditions, % (195 months)
10-year T-note return	7.26	6.44	8.82	6.30
1-month T-bill return	5.05	4.26	5.17	5.62
Inflation rate	4.16	2.86	4.33	5.13
10-year T-note standard deviation	8.01	8.67	7.84	7.60
1-month T-bill standard deviation	0.91	0.73	0.94	0.98

After deducting inflation, T-notes performed by far the worst during restrictive conditions, offering an average annual real return of only 1.2% versus 3.6% and 4.5% for expansive and indeterminate periods, respectively. T-bills also performed worst during restrictive periods once inflation is deducted, providing an average real return of 0.5% versus 0.8% and 1.4% for indeterminate and expansive periods, respectively. In terms of real returns, the return pattern for fixed-income securities is similar to that for stocks. Thus, the evidence indicates that investors in stocks and fixed-income securities have made the largest gains in purchasing power during periods of expansive monetary policy. For fixed-income securities, the gains can be attributed mostly to the relatively low inflation rate that investors experienced under expansive conditions.

The final rows in Table 1.4 show the risk of the two fixed-income security series. For the 10-year T-note, risk is highest during expansive periods and lowest during restrictive periods. In contrast, T-bills show the opposite pattern, with risk being highest during restrictive periods and lowest during expansive periods. The extremely low risk associated with T-bills supports their common treatment as the risk-free security. See Box 1.5 for a discussion of the risk of Treasury securities. Therefore, in light of the relative certainty in T-bill returns, their superior real return performance during expansive periods becomes even more compelling.

Box 1.5   Are Treasury Securities Really Risk-Free?

Assume you are a very conservative investor and have been told that U.S. Treasury securities are risk-free. You decide to buy a newly issued 30-year U.S. Treasury bond for $1,000 that promises to pay

(*continued*)

---

you 4% annual interest (paid semiannually), and in 30 years you will receive your $1,000 back. One year has passed, and you discover that you need to sell the bond. No worries, right? The bond is risk-free. You call your broker, and he tells you that he can sell the bond for $847.76. What happened? Aren't Treasury securities risk-free?

Treasury securities are free from default risk. That is, holders of the debt of the U.S. Treasury can be assured that they are going to receive their interest and principal payments in full and in a timely manner. The reason for this is that the U.S Treasury "owns the printing press" and will simply print more currency to pay back debtholders.[9]

Why did the bond fall in value? It did so because interest rates in the market have risen since the time the bond was issued, making the bond less attractive than newly issued Treasury debt with otherwise identical features. In fact, in our example, newly issued Treasury bonds are paying 5% interest, making your 4% interest bond look less attractive. U.S. Treasury securities are free from default risk, but they do have price risk. If you do not hold a bond to maturity, you may incur a loss if you are forced to sell after interest rates have risen. For instance, suppose you purchased one of the most popular Treasury exchange-traded funds (ETFs)—Vanguard's Long-Term Treasury ETF (VUSTX)—on July 31, 2012, at a net asset value of $14.00. If you decided to sell it on December 30, 2013, you would have netted $11.02. Despite collecting $0.72 in dividends during the time you owned it, you would have lost $2.26 over that time period. Your return on investment would have been a loss of over 16%. Not exactly risk-free.

Treasury bond prices can rise just as quickly as they fall. If you had purchased VUSTX for $11.20 on October 30, 2008, you could have sold it for a tidy profit at $13.64 on December 30 of the same year. After collecting dividends of $0.18, you would have earned a rate of return of 23.3% on risk-free Treasury bonds.

The two major risks bondholders face are default risk and price risk. Treasury securities are free from default risk but not price risk.

Putting It All Together

As a summary of the performance of the securities, Figure 1.2 illustrates the relationship between the return series for the traditional asset classes and inflation in the three monetary environments.

Figure 1.2 Average Annualized Returns on Traditional Asset Classes: January 1966–December 2013

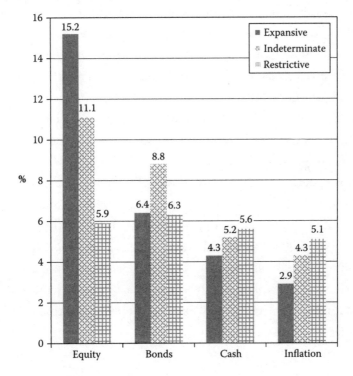

Throughout most of early investment history, investors focused their attention on establishing the appropriate split between equities and bonds, with money market securities (cash) used as a liquid reserve to finance immediate cash needs. See Box 1.6 for additional information on the asset allocation decision. Figure 1.2 indicates that the allocation decision across traditional assets would have benefitted substantially from perusal of Fed monetary policy.

Box 1.6   Strategic Versus Tactical Asset Allocation

Asset allocation refers to an investor's holdings across broad classes of investments. For many years, an allocation of 60% in bonds and 40% in stocks was considered standard fare, and many foundations, pension funds, and endowments had asset allocations that approximated this 60–40 mix. Because stocks are generally considered more risky than bonds, investors with a greater appetite for risk could afford to reach for higher returns by having an allocation that had a larger percentage invested in stocks. In contrast, investors with a lower ability and willingness to accept risk would have a smaller proportion invested in the traditionally less volatile and lower-earning bond category.

The importance of asset allocation (the choice of the relative mix of asset classes held) versus security selection (the choice of specific assets within those asset categories) has been hotly debated for years. In a widely referenced study, investment practitioners Gary Brinson, L. Randolph Hood, and Gilbert Beebower found that asset allocation policy explained more than 90% of performance variation across funds.[10] Subsequent studies have challenged that contention

---

and have determined that although it is important, the asset allocation decision is responsible for substantially less of the performance variation across funds. Many now believe that asset allocation and security selection are equally responsible for investment performance. This is certainly good news for active managers.

Strategic asset allocation refers to the process by which an investor chooses his or her long-term target allocations. These are the weights that the investor wants to maintain over time. To maintain these weights, as one class outperforms the other, investors will periodically rebalance back to the target weights. For instance, if bonds outperform stocks, the investor will need to sell some bond holdings and buy more stock to maintain the desired mix. Rebalancing may be triggered by deviations from the strategic allocation (if, for instance, either category deviates by more than 5% from the target weights) or may be done periodically, say, quarterly or annually. Strategic asset allocation tends to be a somewhat passive approach to investing.

Tactical asset allocation, by contrast, is an active approach to investing in which the investor chooses to adjust the portfolio's asset class weightings on the basis of forecasts or expectations of returns. For instance, if an investor anticipates that stocks will outperform bonds in the short run, that investor will more heavily weight stocks. After this outperformance, the investor will rebalance the portfolio to take advantage of his or her revised expectations of future asset class performance. Sector rotation is simply a form of tactical asset allocation and refers to adjusting the specific mix of stocks within the stock category in the asset allocation context.

Conclusion

Overall, the evidence reported in this chapter supports the superior performance of both stocks and fixed-income securities in expansive monetary conditions. For stocks and fixed-income securities, the real returns are prominent under expansive conditions and negative or negligible during restrictive periods. Thus, historically investors have made substantial gains in purchasing power when the Fed has been in an easy policy mode. In contrast, investor well-being has languished when the Fed has maintained a tight policy. No wonder Fed watchers have cheered announcements of easing and feared announcements of tightening.

In the rest of this book, our objective will be to provide you, the investor, with guidance that is designed to allow you to cheer periods of Fed tightening as well as Fed easing. We will focus our attention on questions such as the following: What actions will allow you to most effectively take advantage of a period of expansive Fed policy when securities in general have fared well? What can you do to modify your portfolio to benefit from a period of Fed tightening or at the very least reduce the negative effects of a restrictive Fed policy?"

CHAPTER 2

MONETARY CONDITIONS AND STYLE INVESTING

Value investing is at its core the marriage of a
contrarian streak and a calculator.

Seth Klarman from a speech at the
CIMA conference, October 2, 2008

It has become standard operating procedure to classify investors in common stock according to their underlying investment philosophies or styles. The investment style followed by an equity investor is determined by the basic features of the securities that theinvestor chooses to include in his or her portfolio. Some investors focus on identifying out-of-favor or underappreciated securities and are classified as *value investors*. Value stocks are typically identified as stocks selling at a low price relative to a fundamental factor such as earnings or sales. Other investors look for prominent, high-flying companies that are expanding faster than the general economy; such investors are labeled as *growth investors*, and the high-fliers they purchase are growth stocks. Growth stocks are generally purchased more on the basis of future expectations than on the basis of past or current results. Although some investors are firmly in one camp or the other, growth and value need not be mutually exclusive strategies. Some investors adopt a hybrid style, incorporating the principles of both the value and the growth schools. The term *growth at a reasonable price* (GARP) describes one such strategy.

Investors also are distinguished by the pond they choose to fish in. Some investors like to buy large, well-known firms such as Coca-Cola and Procter & Gamble; these are the kinds of firms that are in the Dow Jones Industrial Average or the S&P 500 Index. Others prefer to invest in much smaller, relatively unknown firms. These investors want to identify and buy shares in companies before they have hit the big time and become household names. After all, Microsoft and Apple—in fact, all large and successful companies—were small nascent firms at one point in time.

It certainly isn't just individual investors who align themselves with a particular style; institutional investors do the same thing. Mutual funds are typically marketed according to their investment style. Many funds even have the terms *value* and *growth* embedded directly in their names (e.g., the Fidelity Value Fund and the Vanguard U.S. Growth Fund). Other fund names refer to the size of the firms that a fund targets (e.g., the USAA Small Cap Stock Fund and the Nuveen Large Cap Core Fund). Some funds have both elements in their names (e.g., the Vanguard Small Cap Value Fund and the T. Rowe Price Mid-Cap Growth Fund). This allows investors to pinpoint the exact style they wish to pursue and is a way to distinguish funds from one another. These specialized funds tend to stay true to their school, allowing investors to get exposure to a specific sector of the market.

Although the investment world has been inundated by studies reporting performance metrics that refer to the different style strategies, little attention has been paid to the role that Fed policy decisions play in the strategies' success. We believe this omission represents an unfortunate oversight as there is strong reason to believe that Fed policy plays a key role in determining each strategy's success. Just as shoppers adjust their buying habits when their incomes change, we believe that investors should alter their investing behavior when the Fed adjusts the purse strings for the economy. Do you really want to be holding a freezer full of filet mignon when your family income drops substantially? We believe it is imperative that investors monitor Fed policy decisions to structure their portfolios so that they can avoid having a portfolio that is inappropriate for the new monetary environment. In the following sections, we first discuss the features of each aspect of style investing and then establish the role that monetary policy plays in each strategy's success.

Firm Size

One of the most common investment styles is based on the market capitalization, or size, of the firms that an investor favors. Market capitalization, or simply market cap, is the market value of a firm's equity and is calculated by multiplying the number of firm shares outstanding by the firm's current stock price. For example, in the energy sector, a large-cap investor would favor shares in firms such as Exxon Mobil (XOM), which had a market capitalization in early 2014 that exceeded $400 billion. In contrast, a small-cap investor would lean toward firms such as C&J Energy Services (CJES), which had a market capitalization of approximately $1 billion in early 2014. It may seem odd to refer to a firm with a market cap of $1 billion as a small firm, but in the relative scheme of things it is small.[1] Smaller firms in a sector tend to focus their operations on a niche activity within that sector; for example, CJES offers hydraulic fracturing services to oil and gas exploration companies. Finally, mid-cap investors follow a Goldilocks strategy and choose firms that are "just right": those with market capitalizations that are not too high or too low.

Interest in firm size as an investment criterion was spurred by research in the 1970s and early 1980s that showed that an investment in small firms (small-caps) earned much higher returns than did an investment in large firms. But it wasn't just that the returns to small firms exceeded those to large firms. One would certainly expect that result because smaller firms are generally riskier than large firms. In fact, one of the fundamental tenets of investing is that there is a risk/return trade-off and that higher-risk securities in the long run *should* provide higher returns. The research validated that tenet as investments in small firms indeed generated returns that exceeded those from large firms, but the research extended the basic tenet and showed that returns to small firms were superior *even after adjusting for risk.*

The Anomalous Small-Firm Premium

In one of the earliest studies of firm size and returns, Professor Marc Reinganum of the University of Southern California reported evidence that a portfolio composed of the smallest firms (the 10% of firms with the smallest market caps) produced an unexpected or abnormal return of 12% per year.[2] The abnormal return refers to the return over and above what would be expected after taking risk into account. Furthermore, he showed that the unexpected return for the smallest firms exceeded the unexpected return for the largest firms (the 10% of firms with the highest market caps) by the astounding margin of more than 20% per year. Needless to say, these findings got the attention of the investment community. Ultimately, this research was instrumental in establishing the small-firm effect or small-firm anomaly.

In the investing world, an anomaly is a return pattern that is inconsistent with prevailing wisdom about the way returns should behave, something that stumps the profession (see Box 2.1). A common mistake is to equate the small-firm anomaly with the observation that an investment in small firms earns a higher than average return over time. Such an observation is not an anomaly because as was mentioned above, small firms are riskier than average and thus should earn higher returns. The anomaly is that even after we adjust for the higher risk of small firms, the returns are still higher than warranted. In other words, an investment in small-firm stocks has been shown to provide abnormal returns. Figure 2.1 shows mean annual returns for the five size quintiles; "Small" consists of the 20% of firms with the smallest market capitalization and "Big" consists of the 20% of firms with the largest market caps.

Box 2.1   Investment Anomalies

An *investment anomaly* is a return relationship that cannot be explained by experts in the investment profession. Much of this chapter deals with common anomalies such as the size effect and the price-to-sales (P/S) effect. However, a litany of anomalies have been and continue to be investigated and dissected by business school professors and investment practitioners. Many business school professors have earned tenure and been promoted partly as a result of their publication of empirical evidence that is not consistent with the latest and greatest theories of how the investment markets should work. Although there is no standard categorization of anomalies, they most commonly fall into four categories:

1. *Fundamental*: based on some fundamental variable such as price-to-earnings (P/E) ratio or firm size (market cap).

(*continued*)

2. *Technical*: based on past price or volume relationships. The Dogs of the Dow theory is an example. This anomaly posits that the worst performing stocks in the Dow Jones Industrial Average outperform the average over the next year.
3. *Calendar*: return relationships based on time. The turn-of-the-month effect (returns are highest at the end of the month) and the day-of-the-week effect (returns are lowest on Monday) are examples.
4. *Other*: a catchall category that includes everything from firms with heavy insider buying to firms being added to an index.

Although most anomalies have a basis in economic reality, others result from spurious correlation and can be explained by data mining. That is, if you look long and hard enough, you can find two data series that are highly correlated but there is no causal relationship between them. A prime example of spurious correlation is the Super Bowl Theory of the Stock Market. Market analysts have noted that if a premerger NFL team wins the Super Bowl, the market advances, whereas if a premerger AFL team wins, the market declines. Through 2013, the indicator was correct a remarkable 74% of the time. In fact, the highly respected *Financial Analysts Journal* published an article in 1989 titled "Did Joe Montana Save the Stock Market?"[3] The title referred to the fact that in the 1989 Super Bowl, legendary quarterback Joe Montana drove the San Francisco 49ers 92 yards in the final three minutes of the game to score a touchdown and beat the Cincinnati Bengals 20–16, thus rescuing the market from an inevitable decline. The Super Bowl indicator receives a great deal of attention because it combines two of the biggest obsessions of Americans: the largest single sporting event in the United States and investing.

Figure 2.1 illustrates the returns for the five portfolios (quintiles) that are formed on the basis of firms' market capitalization. The portfolios are created by ranking all actively traded U.S. stocks by their market caps and separating them into their respective categories; firms ranked in the highest 20% are included in the "Big" portfolio, and firms ranked in the lowest 20% are placed in the "Small" portfolio. Each year the firms are reranked and assigned to the appropriate portfolio/quintile.

The data show that the average annual return to the quintile that includes the firms with the smallest market capitalization (Small) exceeds the returns to the Big quintile by 3.4% per year. The higher return for Small relative to the average is consistent with the small-firm anomaly; however, the difference is relatively minor compared

Figure 2.1 Average Annual Returns to Size Portfolios: 1966–2013

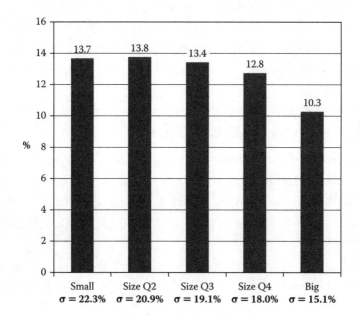

with the differences reported in the original research that discussed the small-firm anomaly.[4] Furthermore, because small firms have greater risk than do large firms, the reported return difference does not offer huge compensation for the higher risk assumed with a small-cap strategy. The risk of each portfolio, as represented by the standard deviation (σ), is reported on the horizontal axis below each of the mean annual return bars. For example, the standard deviation of the Small quintile is 22.3%, versus 15.1% for the Big quintile. Recent evidence suggests that the small-firm effect has diminished considerably over time, particularly since its widespread publication in the 1970s and 1980s. The moderate small-firm premium that we report here is consistent with the diminished small-firm effect. This is not surprising as one would expect investors to pounce on an anomaly once it became widely publicized. If more investors fish in the small-firm pond than did before the discovery of the anomaly, small-firm shares are bid up and their future returns are driven lower.

If investors want to monitor the small-cap segment of the market, they can do so by following a small-cap market index. Two of the more popular indexes—the Russell 2000 and the S&P SmallCap 600—and a sampling of ETFs based on those indexes are explained in Box 2.2.

Box 2.2   Getting Small-Cap Exposure

Now that you see that small-capitalization stocks outperform large-capitalization stocks, you may be wondering how you can get exposure to that segment of the market. There are several small-cap indexes; two of the more popular are the Russell 2000 and the S&P SmallCap 600.

The Russell 2000 is the most popular small-capitalization index and is composed of the smallest 2,000 stocks in the Russell 3000

Index, which includes the largest 3,000 U.S. stocks. Even though it contains two-thirds of the stocks that appear in the Russell 3000, it represents only about 10% of the total market capitalization of that index. To give you some perspective on the size of the firms in the index, the median market capitalization of the Russell 2000 as of April 2014 was $684 million. In contrast, the median market capitalization on the large-cap S&P 500 index was over $17.1 billion. There are numerous exchange-traded funds (ETFs) that are based on the Russell 2000 Index, including the iShares Russell 2000 Index Fund (IWM), the Vanguard Russell 2000 Index (VTWO), and the SPDR Russell 2000 ETF (TWOK).

The S&P SmallCap 600 is designed to measure the performance of 600 small companies in the United States. It represents slightly more than 3% of the total U.S. market capitalization and includes companies with a market cap between $350 million and $1.6 billion. The median market cap is over $1.0 billion, much higher than that of the Russell 2000. As with the Russell 2000 Index, many ETFs are based on the S&P SmallCap 600, including the iShares S&P Small-Cap 600 (IJR), the SPDR S&P Small Cap 600 ETF (SLY), and the Vanguard S&P Small-Cap 600 ETF (VIOO).

Investors desiring exposure to the small-cap segment of the U.S. stock market can get it inexpensively through any of the ETFs that are based on these two indexes.

Value and Growth

Another common investment style is predicated on company price multiples or price relatives. Price multiples consist of ratios that measure a firm's stock price relative to one of its financial characteristics.

The most prominent price multiples are price to earnings (P/E), price to sales (P/S), price to book (P/B), and price to cash flow (P/CF). Each price multiple has the same numerator (stock price per share) but has a different fundamental firm feature in the denominator. For example, P/E is derived from price per share divided by earnings per share (EPS),[5] and P/S equals price per share divided by sales per share. Price multiples have been a prominent aspect of investment analysis since the early years of the U.S. stock market's existence. Benjamin Graham and David Dodd published the first widely acknowledged investment text, the iconic *Security Analysis,* which advocated the use of price multiples in investment analysis (see Box 2.3).

Box 2.3   The Influence of Graham and Dodd's
Security Analysis

Warren Buffett is widely considered the most successful investor of all time. He learned his craft from his mentor, Columbia University professor Benjamin Graham. Graham and his colleague at Columbia David Dodd collaborated to write a text that spawned the field of fundamental investment analysis and has been referred to as the "bible of fundamental analysis." In the foreword to the sixth edition, Buffett credits *Security Analysis* and another book by Graham, *The Intelligent Investor*, with laying out a "roadmap for investing that I have now been following for 57 years."[6] Buffett has such high regard for Graham that he wrote forewords to later editions of each of Graham's seminal works. In fact, Buffett named one of his sons Howard Graham Buffett in honor of his mentor.

The basis of *Security Analysis* is that an investor should determine the "true value" or "intrinsic value" of an investment through

---

an examination of the firm's fundamentals, which include the P/E ratio, dividend history, stability of earnings, and other quantitative factors. Graham believed that you should invest only if there is an adequate margin of safety to protect the investment. His concept of the margin of safety is simply the difference between an asset's price and its intrinsic value. If you can purchase an asset at a substantial discount from its intrinsic value, you have a margin of safety available for absorbing the effect of miscalculations or worse than average luck. Buffett has referred to margin of safety as the "central concept of investing." The establishment of these principles led to Graham's being known as "the father of value investing."

The Anomalous Value Premium

Widespread interest in price multiples was increased among investors by investment research in the 1970s and 1980s that showed a strong association between price multiples and subsequent stock returns. For example, McMaster University professor Sanjoy Basu provided evidence that firms with low P/E ratios (the 20% of firms with the lowest P/E ratios) returned about 4.5% per year more than was implied by their risk, whereas firms with high P/E ratios (the 20% of firms with the highest P/E ratios) earned about 3% less than warranted.[7] Again, these results were seized upon by investors eager to enhance their portfolios' performance. Overall, the research on price multiples led to recognition of the value effect or value anomaly and ultimately to the proliferation of the value and growth investment styles. The value effect is the anomalous observation that investing in the stocks of firms with low price multiples (e.g. price to earnings, price to sales, and price to book value) has historically offered investors abnormal returns. Figure 2.2 shows the returns of the five quintiles of firms ranked by their price-to-sales (P/S) ratios. The formation of the five portfolios follows the same process we used to identify the market-cap portfolios in Figure 2.1 but replaces market cap with P/S ratio.

Figure 2.2 shows that the firms with the lowest P/S ratios (value stocks) offer the highest average annual return, whereas the firms with the highest P/S ratios (growth stocks) offer the lowest average annual return. The difference in returns between low and high P/S portfolios is rather substantial at 5.7% per year. Compounding that large difference in returns over a number of years produces an enormous difference in final results. Furthermore, the return difference is diminished only slightly by the fact that the low P/S portfolio has marginally higher risk, as represented by standard deviation (σ). The standard deviation is reported on the horizontal axis and shows

Figure 2.2 Average Annual Returns on Price to Sales Portfolios: 1966–2013

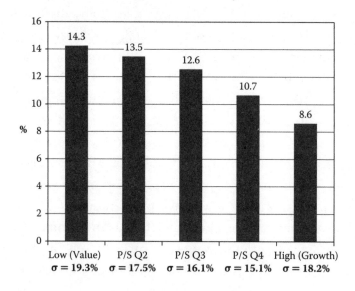

a value of 19.3% for value stocks versus 18.2% for growth stocks. The value anomaly is based on the observation that value stocks offer considerably higher returns while subjecting investors to only slightly more risk. Recognizing this anomalous result before it was widely acknowledged helped make fortunes for Warren Buffett, Bill Ruane, John Neff, Seth Klarman, Wally Weitz, Charles Brandes, and a plethora of other prominent value investors.

The Features of Value and Growth Investors

Investors who follow a value investment style favor firms that have low price multiples. A firm's price multiple can be viewed as the collective assessment by investors of that firm's financial prospects. In general, a low price multiple indicates that investors believe the firm's prospects are limited. Firms with low multiples are frequently identified as out of favor or neglected stocks. Since value investors target firms with low multiples, they can be viewed as bargain hunters. Warren Buffett has been quoted as saying, "Whether we're talking about socks or stocks, I like buying quality merchandise when it is marked down." Value investing is contrarian in nature, involving the purchase of shares of companies that have been beaten down and are out of favor with other investors.

In contrast to value investors, growth investors typically target firms with more robust price multiples. A high price multiple indicates that investors are optimistic about the future prospects for the firm and thus believe the stock warrants a high price relative to its fundamental financial characteristics. Growth firms can be viewed as glamour companies, that is, firms that get the most positive press and tend to be the most admired. Growth investors tend to be attracted to such firms because they believe they hold the most future promise.

Finally, there are investors who prefer to form portfolios that have middling price multiples. This can be done by targeting firms with moderate price multiples or forming a portfolio with a mixture of stocks, some with high price multiples and others with low multiples. For obvious reasons, this investment strategy is frequently referenced as a blend, mixed, or core strategy.

At the time of the writing of this book, Amazon represents a classic growth firm (glamour company) in the technology sector. In early 2014, Amazon sold at a P/E ratio of 1,475, which means investors were willing to pay an incredible $1,475 for every $1 of Amazon earnings. In contrast, at that time, Hewlett-Packard (HP) was widely considered a value company in the technology space. In early 2014, HP sold at a P/E of 11, indicating a willingness on the part of investors to pay only $11 per dollar of earnings generated by HP. Value investors are more likely to be attracted to HP, whereas growth investors are likely to prefer Amazon. Investors applying a blend approach may include both stocks in their portfolios.

It should be noted that the relative price multiples of firms tend to change over time. Today's growth stock may be tomorrow's value stock. In fact, one classification of value stocks is as fallen angels, which are firms that were once high-flying, glamour firms but have fallen on hard times and are currently out of favor with investors. In early 2014, JCPenney was a company that could be considered a fallen angel. In early 1994, JCPenney sold with a P/S ratio of 0.62. Twenty years later, its P/S ratio was 0.17, less than one-third of its 1994 value. There are numerous additional examples of firms that have transitioned from growth to value status, and some stocks have even transitioned from growth to extinct status. For example, everyone is familiar with the rise and fall of firms such as Value America, Borders, Netscape, Gateway, and Blockbuster, each of which experienced the wild ride from glamour to neglected to extinct over their relatively short existence.

Monetary Conditions and Style Investing

Many successful investors tactically alter their investment style at times in an attempt to take advantage of changes in market conditions. Such investors rely on a variety of indicators to offer guidance on when to transition from one investment style to another. In the following sections, we present evidence that can be used to evaluate the benefits of using monetary conditions as a guide in altering one's investment style. We start by evaluating the relationship between monetary conditions and market cap and then progress to examining monetary conditions and price multiples; finally, we investigate the relation between monetary conditions and strategies that combine both market cap and price multiples.

Monetary Conditions and Firm Size

Figure 2.3 presents the returns to the five size quintiles for each of the three monetary environments. The return differences across the three monetary environments are astounding. The evidence in the figure clearly indicates that to effectively apply a market-cap strategy, an investor should carefully monitor the monetary environment.

Consistent with the evidence reported in Chapter 1, Figure 2.3 shows that stocks in general prosper during periods of expansive monetary policy; however, small stocks perform incredibly well during expansive periods. In marked contrast, small stocks perform remarkably poorly during periods of restrictive policy. An investor applying a small-cap strategy during expansive periods would have earned over 28% per year, whereas the same strategy would have earned the investor only 5.8% when monetary conditions were restrictive. Remember from Chapter 1 that the inflation rate was considerably higher during restrictive monetary periods (5.1%) than

Figure 2.3 Annual Returns on Size Portfolios by Monetary Environment: 1966–2013

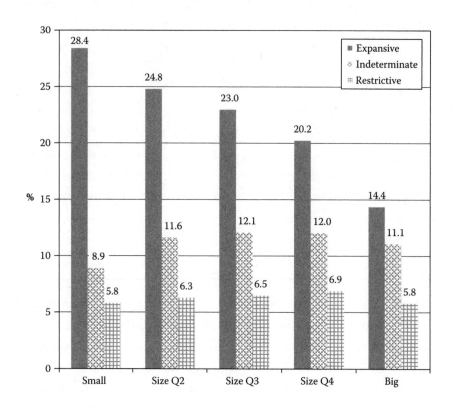

during expansive monetary periods (2.9%). Thus, during expansive periods, the superior performance of small stocks becomes even more impressive as the real (or inflation-adjusted) return is enormous. In contrast, during restrictive periods, the dismal performance of small stocks is highlighted by the observation that they barely eked out a return exceeding the average inflation rate.

Interestingly, during indeterminate and restrictive monetary periods, the returns reported in Figure 2.3 show virtually no evidence of a material small-firm effect. Instead, during these two monetary environments, it is the three middle quintiles (portfolios) that show the best performance. Thus, it would appear that the small-firm effect is really a small-firm-in-expansive-monetary-conditions effect.

Risk, Monetary Conditions, and the Small-Firm Effect

To get a comprehensive picture of the performance of the market-cap strategies, we next consider the risk of the strategies across the three monetary environments. Following the format of Figure 2.3, Figure 2.4 plots the standard deviation for each of the five market-cap strategies.

In general, the expected relationship between firm size and risk is confirmed in Figure 2.4: smaller firms have above-average risk. However, a more important observation is that risk is relatively invariant across monetary conditions within each market cap quintile. Incredibly, the return data reported in Figure 2.3 show that one of the lowest returns is recorded for small firms during restrictive monetary conditions (5.8%), whereas Figure 2.4 shows that during restrictive periods this portfolio incurs the highest risk level (23.7%). Contrary to the proclamations of professional gamblers, a very low average return accompanied by very high risk is not an appealing long-term strategy. Clearly, applying a small-cap strategy under restrictive monetary conditions has been a disaster. In contrast, applying a small-cap strategy during expansive periods has had amazing results. For example, during expansive periods a small-cap strategy relative to a large-cap strategy yielded a huge return benefit (28.4% versus 14.4%) with only a minor increase in risk (22.2% versus 16.2%). We suspect most investors would jump at the opportunity to add 14.0% per year to their returns if it cost them only an additional 6.0% in risk.

On the basis of the returns reported in Figure 2.3 and the risk reported in Figure 2.4, we can determine the return earned per unit

Figure 2.4   Annual Risk of Size Portfolios by Monetary Environment: 1966–2013

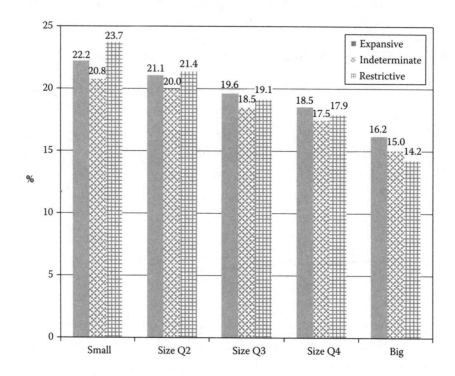

of risk or, more directly, the return-to-risk ratio. During expansive monetary periods, the return-to-risk ratio for the small-cap portfolio is 1.27 (28.4/22.2), whereas the return-to-risk ratio for the same portfolio under restrictive conditions is only 0.24 (5.8/23.7). Earning a portfolio return that exceeds portfolio risk—that is, earning a return-to-risk ratio greater than 1—is a remarkable feat in the stock market. Incredibly, during expansive monetary periods, each of the four smallest portfolios achieved this remarkable feat. In contrast, during restrictive periods, none of the portfolios produced a return-to-risk ratio above 0.41.

Value-Weighting Versus Equal-Weighting the Stocks in a Portfolio

Now that you have seen our basic approach for evaluating the performance of a portfolio or strategy, it is important that we clarify our procedure for creating portfolios. We follow the same procedure throughout the book. The standard procedure for creating portfolios and the one we rely on is value-weighting the individual firms that are included in each portfolio. Value-weighting means that each firm's impact on the portfolio's or index's return is commensurate with the firm's market cap (size). For example, a value-weighted technology index would give much greater weight (over 260 times more) to Apple, which had a market cap of $523 billion in May 2014, than it would to Synaptics, which had a market cap of $2 billion in early 2014. In contrast, an equal-weighted index, as the name implies, would apply an equal weight to each firm.

Value-weighting firms in an index (or portfolio) has two distinct advantages. First, value-weighting reflects the actual status that a firm has in the economy. Who could realistically argue that Synaptics has as much influence on the stock market or aggregate investor wealth as Apple? Second, as firm values grow, a value-weighted index automatically adjusts for the influence of each firm on the index because the applied weight is the firm value. In contrast, an equal-weighted index requires periodically rebalancing the firms included in the index to readjust them to equal weights. For example, the weight for stocks that appreciated would be adjusted downward, whereas the weight of firms whose stock prices had depreciated would be adjusted upward. See Box 2.4 for a discussion of the merits of value-weighted versus equal-weighted indexes.

Box 2.4 Which Is Better, a Value-Weighted or an Equal-Weighted Index?

You may have thought that once you made a decision to purchase a particular group of stocks, your financial fate was sealed. Not so fast; it turns out that the way you decide to weight the stocks in your portfolio also has the potential to substantially alter your financial outcome. For example, Table 2.1 shows the performance of an equal-weighted investment and a value-weighted investment in the U.S. stock market over the period 1966–2013. Both indexes include exactly the same set of stocks but weight the stocks differently.

The difference in performance reported in Table 2.1 is attributed entirely to the difference in weighting approach. In an equal-weighted index, small firms are given equal weight relative to big firms. In contrast, a value-weighted index gives small firms less weight. From our previous discussion of the small-firm effect, we know that small firms have generated considerably higher returns than big firms have; thus, it is logical that the equal-weighted index would produce a higher return. In addition, we know that small

Table 2.1 Performance of Equal-Weighted versus Value-Weighted U.S. Stock Indexes: 1966–2013

U.S. Stock Portfolio	Mean Annual Return	Standard Deviation	Return-to-Risk Ratio
Equal-weighted index	14.08%	20.03%	0.70
Value-weighted index	10.64%	15.81%	0.67

Note: The U.S. stock indexes reported in the table are from the Center for Research in Security Prices at the University of Chicago and include all U.S. stocks that are actively traded.

firms have more risk than large firms, and so the higher standard deviation for the equal-weighted index is expected.

Many investors are firm believers in equal-weighting the stocks in their portfolios, probably at least partially, as a result of the evidence shown in Table 2.1. As you probably could have predicted, some investment companies have created products that cater to these preferences. For example, whereas the S&P 500 index is a value-weighted index, Guggenheim offers a product that applies equal weights to the 500 stocks in the S&P 500. As we noted previously, equal-weighting the stocks in an index is not as easy as value-weighting them because any appreciation or depreciation in price creates unequal weights. Therefore, the index/portfolio components have to be periodically rebalanced to an equal weight by selling the stocks that have appreciated and purchasing more of the depreciated stocks. For example, Guggenheim rebalances its equal-weighted S&P 500 fund on a quarterly basis to reestablish equal weights. All this rebalancing does not come without costs: Guggenheim charges 0.40% annually for its equal-weighted S&P 500 fund, whereas Vanguard charges 0.05% annually for its traditional value-weighted S&P 500 version.

What have we learned? On the plus side, equal-weighted indexes have generally produced higher gross returns. On the minus side, the higher returns have been accompanied by higher risk and higher fees. Thus, it appears there is no clear-cut winner. Investors who like equal-weighting their portfolio components have evidence to support their preference, as do investors who prefer value-weighting.

Before we leave this issue, we cannot resist throwing in one more consideration: What impact do monetary conditions have on the

(continued)

decision? Table 2.2 reports the performance of the equal-weighted and value-weighted versions of the U.S. market index (same indexes as above) across monetary environments.

The evidence in Table 2.2 suggests that the equal-weighted versus value-weighted debate becomes even more complicated when one considers monetary conditions. It appears that equal-weighting is far more beneficial when monetary conditions are expansive; the difference in returns is over 12% per year, with an increase in risk of less than 5%. During expansive periods, the equal-weighted index produces a return-to-risk ratio of 1.35, whereas the same ratio for the value-weighted index is only 0.96. In contrast, during both indeterminate and restrictive periods, an investor would have been much better off with the value-weighted index; not only would the investor have achieved higher returns, he or she would have taken significantly less risk and paid lower transactions costs.

Table 2.2 Equal-Weighted versus Value-Weighted Performance by Monetary Environment: 1966–2013

	Mean Annual Return (Standard Deviation) and [Return-to-Risk Ratio] by Monetary Environment		
U.S. stock portfolio	Expansive Period	Indeterminate Period	Restrictive Period
Equal-weighted index	28.92% (21.37%) [1.35]	10.47% (19.07%) [0.55]	4.87% (19.28%) [0.25]
Value-weighted index	16.19% (16.78%) [0.96]	10.85% (15.42%) [0.70]	5.51% (15.27%) [0.36]

Thus, for investors who plan to select an approach and stick with it, there is a justification for either value-weighting or equal-weighting. Investors with a lower risk appetite would prefer value-weighting, whereas those more focused on returns would prefer equal-weighting. However, it is crystal clear that the best approach is to use monetary conditions to guide the selected weighting procedure. This is of course the approach we advocate.

Monetary Conditions and Price Multiples

Figure 2.5 plots returns for portfolios formed on the basis of price multiples relative to the three alternative monetary conditions.

We choose to focus on the P/S ratio because unlike other multiples (earnings and cash flow in particular), the P/S ratio can never be negative—stock price and firm revenue are never negative—and so we don't have to worry about negative multiples, which become nonapplicable observations. Furthermore, the price multiples all give very similar results, and so whether we use price to earnings (P/E), price to book (P/B), or price to cash flow (P/CF), our results will not differ materially from what we report using the P/S ratio.

Monetary Conditions and the Value Premium

The returns plotted in Figure 2.5 identify a strong association between monetary conditions and the P/S ratio portfolios. Despite the fact that price multiples and firm size are unique firm characteristics, the return patterns are remarkably consistent across Figure 2.3 and Figure 2.5. Once again, during indeterminate and restrictive monetary periods, the return pattern across P/S ratios is relatively diminished, with the best performance accruing to the

Figure 2.5   Annual Returns on Price to Sales Portfolios by Monetary Environment: 1966–2013

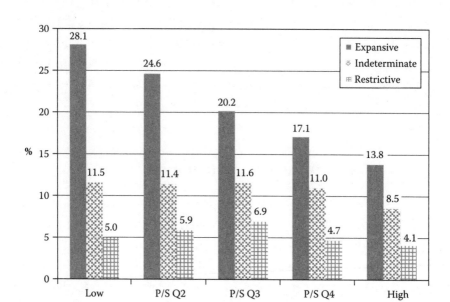

Q3 portfolio. In stark contrast, during expansive monetary periods, there is a prominent pattern in returns across the portfolios. Specifically, under expansive conditions, the low P/S stocks (value stocks) produce a return of 28.1%, which is over twice the 13.8% return provided by high P/S stocks (growth stocks).

Although the returns plotted in Figure 2.5 show a definite pattern, the standard deviations plotted in Figure 2.6 indicate no discernible pattern in risk.

Combining the data from the two figures, it is clear that the 28.1% return earned by value stocks during expansive monetary periods versus the 13.8% return for growth stocks does not represent compensation for greater risk as the standard deviations for both

Figure 2.6   Annual Risk of Price to Sales Portfolios by Monetary Environment: 1966–2013

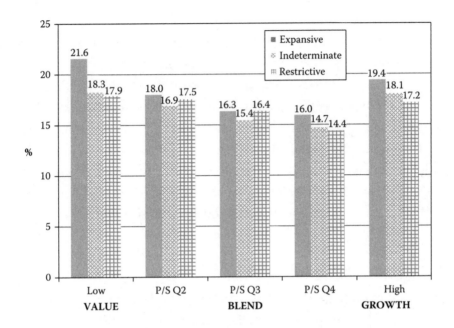

portfolios are very similar at 21.6% and 19.4%, respectively. Thus, during expansive periods, the return per unit of risk for value stocks was 1.30 (28.1/21.6), whereas growth stocks offered a return-to-risk ratio of only 0.71 (13.8/19.4). Furthermore, the performance of growth stocks during periods of indeterminate and restrictive monetary policy has been putrid. These strategies record the lowest return with some of the highest risk measures, producing pitiful return-to-risk ratios of only 0.47 and 0.24.

In light of the similarity in risk across the various portfolios, the returns reported in Figure 2.5 can be directly compared across portfolios. Any significant difference in returns that is observed in Figure 2.5 cannot be attributed to compensation for greater risk as the standard deviations are generally quite comparable across all the portfolios.

Overall, it is apparent from Figures 2.5 and 2.6 that a strategy that targeted value firms during expansive monetary periods paid off handsomely whereas targeting value firms during indeterminate and restrictive periods was an awful approach. During indeterminate and restrictive periods, the best strategy would have been to target moderate price-to-sales firms (a blend strategy). The relatively strong performance of value stocks in expansive conditions is reinforced when we consider that inflation was also substantially higher during restrictive relative to expansive monetary conditions (see Chapter 1). That is, inflation ate away much less of an investor's return in periods with expansive monetary conditions.

Combining Size and Price Multiples

Our discussion of style investing to this point has separately considered the style components: market cap and price multiples. In practice, however, investors frequently combine the two components when developing an investment strategy. For example, common strategies that combine the two include the following nine portfolios: small-cap value, small-cap blend, small-cap growth, mid-cap value, mid-cap blend, mid-cap growth, large-cap value, large-cap blend, and large-cap growth. The traditional investment style grid is composed of these nine portfolios. Many different characterizations of style are utilized by different investment firms.

Classifying Firms by Style

Relative to the healthcare sector, we offer the following examples from early 2014 to illustrate the classification of firms into particular boxes within the style grid. An investor following a small-cap growth strategy would probably target a firm such as Opko Health (OPK). Opko is a pharmaceutical and diagnostics company that focuses on the discovery, development, and commercialization of novel and proprietary medical treatments. Opko has a market capitalization of $3 billion and a P/S ratio of 36.0. At the other corner of the investment style grid, an investor following a large-cap value strategy would probably target a well-known company such as Pfizer, which has a market capitalization of $197 billion and a P/S ratio of 3.4. Like Opko, Pfizer focuses on the discovery, development, and commercialization of medical treatments, but on a much larger scale and scope.

The Returns to Style

Figure 2.7 reports returns for the four corner portfolios from the style grid: small-value, small-growth, large-value, and large-growth. In forming the portfolios in the grid, we separate firms across three size dimensions as follows: the largest 20% of firms are big, the smallest 20% of firms are small, and the middle 60% are mid-size. We follow the same process in classifying the firms by their P/S ratios as growth, value, and blend. The nine portfolios are then identified by the intersection of the two independent sorts, ultimately creating the nine unique combinations. For exposition purposes, we choose to report only the four extreme portfolios, that is, the four corner portfolios of the style grid. Below each return bar in Figure 2.7 we report the standard deviation (σ) of that portfolio.

Once again, we observe the general stair-step pattern in returns as we progress from large firms to small firms and from growth firms to value firms. As was noted previously, this result is not new as investors have long recognized the return benefits associated with investing in small firms and value firms. With an annual return

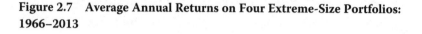

Figure 2.7   Average Annual Returns on Four Extreme-Size Portfolios: 1966–2013

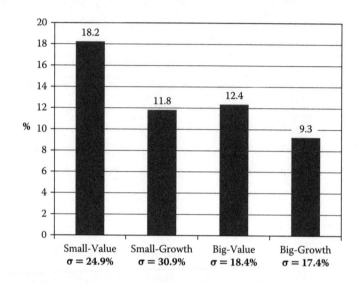

of 18.2%, the small-value portfolio dominated the return produced by the other portfolios. Surprisingly, however, the small-growth portfolio, with a standard deviation of 30.9%, exhibited by far the highest volatility of the four portfolios. The portfolios' return-to-risk ratios from left to right are 0.73, 0.38, 0.67, and 0.53, which supports the superiority of the small-value strategy from a reward-to-risk standpoint.

Monetary Conditions and Style Points

Figure 2.8 reports the performance of the four corner portfolios across the three alternative monetary environments. Although the small-firm effect and the value effect are widely recognized in the investment management industry, what is less recognized is the tremendous influence that monetary conditions have on these return anomalies.

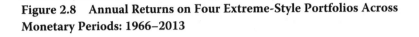

Figure 2.8   Annual Returns on Four Extreme-Style Portfolios Across Monetary Periods: 1966–2013

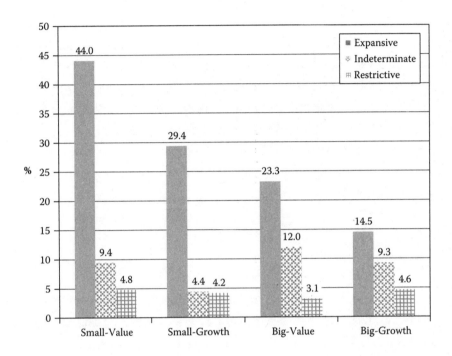

The returns in Figure 2.8 confirm that the small-firm effect and the value effect are both prominent phenomena in expansive monetary conditions. In contrast, neither effect stands out under indeterminate or restrictive monetary conditions. This figure makes it clear that one should carefully monitor the monetary environment before selecting any of the alternative investment strategies.

The 44.0% average annual return reported for the small-value portfolio during expansive monetary conditions is not a misprint. The portfolio composed of small firms with low price-to-sales multiples did indeed generate an annual return that averaged 44.0% in expansive monetary conditions. Amazingly, this return is over three times the return generated by the big-growth portfolio during expansive conditions, which was a healthy but much more modest 14.5%. During indeterminate monetary conditions, the clear winner was the big-value portfolio, which returned a respectable 12.0%; however, during restrictive conditions, the big-value portfolio was the biggest loser, generating a return of only 3.1%. The portfolio returns clearly indicate that monetary conditions dictate which of the style strategies is superior and which is inferior. In light of the amazing return patterns in Figure 2.8, we wouldn't be surprised if many of you are going back to the Introduction to confirm that you know how to apply the monetary conditions classification approach.

A Rationale for the Returns

In evaluating any investment strategy (or apparent anomaly), it is always wise to consider the rationale underlying the strategy. Everyone is familiar with anecdotes that connect stock market performance with sunspots, the length of hemlines on skirts, coal production in the United Kingdom, or the winner of the Super Bowl. In contrast to such random observations (does anyone really believe that sunspots or the winner of a sporting event has anything to do with stock market performance?), there are strong reasons to believe that the monetary policy of the Federal Reserve influences the general performance of the stock market. When funds are more readily available or are expected to be more readily available, the general market prospers because of greater economic activity and easier access to financial capital; a rising tide raises all boats. More particularly, however, we believe that certain types of firms are bound to be more greatly influenced by monetary conditions. Specifically, we believe that small firms are more sensitive to monetary conditions because they generally have less access to sources of capital. In tighter monetary conditions, smaller firms have more trouble acquiring funds through bank loans and issuing bonds than do large firms. In addition, out of favor or neglected firms (value stocks) are likely to have heightened sensitivity to monetary conditions. For these firms, the prospect for increased fund availability is of much greater importance. Although the blue chip glamour companies also welcome increased fund availability, they are not nearly as reliant on the availability of those funds for survival.

Implementing a Style-Based Investment Strategy

Establishing an investment style can be as easy as making a single purchase in a mutual fund or exchange-traded fund (ETF). For more on the similarities and differences between mutual funds and ETFs, see Box 2.5. For example, an investor wishing to follow a small-cap strategy could purchase shares in Vanguard's Strategic Small Cap Equity Fund (VSTCX) or BlackRock's iShares Core S&P Small-Cap ETF (IJR). Investment firms also offer products for investors who are enamored with the more sophisticated style-based strategies. For example, Fidelity offers a Small Cap Value Fund (FCPVX) as well as a Large Cap Growth Enhanced Index Fund (FLGEX). There are even funds that focus on the most extreme portfolios [the PowerShares Zacks Micro Cap Portfolio (PZI) and the First Trust Dow Jones Select MicroCap Index Fund (FDM)].

Box 2.5   Mutual Funds Versus ETFs

Mutual funds and ETFs are very similar investment structures in many respects.[8] In fact, many investors treat them as if they were interchangeable. Both are pooled investment vehicles—this means all shareholders get the same treatment—that give investors access to a diversified portfolio with a relatively modest initial investment. Although most mutual funds are actively managed and most ETFs are passive investment vehicles, there are passively managed mutual funds and actively managed ETFs.

The three main differences between mutual funds and ETFs concern liquidity, services offered, and taxes. ETFs are more liquid than mutual funds. An ETF trades like a stock, and the price remains fluid throughout the trading day. Mutual funds, by contrast, are priced once a day—at the end of the trading day—and trade at a mutual fund's net asset value. The trades for investors who place orders to buy or sell shares of a mutual fund on a specific day all occur at the mutual fund's net asset value, which is computed at the end of the trading day. Thus, investors can day-trade ETFs but not mutual funds.

Mutual funds generally provide investors with more services than are offered to ETF investors. For example, mutual fund investors can establish automatic investment plans and can make costless transfers from one fund in a fund family to another. In addition, mutual funds allow for the automatic reinvestment of dividends in shares, or partial shares, of the fund; no such reinvestment plans exist in ETFs.

Finally, ETFs tend to be more tax efficient than mutual funds. Typically, an investor who holds an ETF in a taxable investment account will generate a lower tax liability than will be the case with a similar mutual fund in the same account. It is beyond the scope of this book, but the rationale is that in the eyes of the IRS there are fewer taxable events in an ETF than in a mutual fund.

For investors who wish to be a little more ambitious, building a portfolio from individual stocks can be both rewarding and a lot of fun. The market cap and price multiple data needed to get started are readily available from virtually any website that reports financial data. A couple of our favorite websites are Yahoo Finance (http://finance.yahoo.com) and Google Finance (https://www.google.com/finance).

Conclusion

As was noted in this chapter, investors are now routinely separated into camps on the basis of the investment strategies or styles that they choose to apply. The most prominent strategies are based on firm price multiples and firm size. Value investors are frequently labeled as bargain hunters; they look for attractively valued stocks that others have rejected. In contrast, growth investors tend to target high-profile firms that have experienced recent success. Investor strategy also varies with preferences regarding firm size. Large-cap investors prefer dominant, widely recognized firms, whereas small-cap investors target less recognized firms with less dominant market positions. What we have shown in this chapter is that regardless of your selected investment strategy, it is wise to make the monetary environment a prominent consideration. We have shown that the success of each investment strategy is dependent on Fed policy moves.

CHAPTER 3

STYLE INVESTING EXTENSIONS

> I can calculate the movement of stars, but
> not the madness of men.
>
> *Sir Isaac Newton*

A re investors rational? This is a question that has been hotly debated by financial market participants for many years, but considering all the financial bubbles that have occurred throughout history—from Tulipmania and the South Sea Bubble in the seventeenth and eighteenth centuries, respectively, to the dot-com and real estate bubbles in more recent times—the verdict seems abundantly clear. Sir Isaac Newton uttered the above quote after losing his fortune investing in shares of the South Sea Company in the early eighteenth century. The South Sea Company was formed after the War of the Spanish Succession and was granted monopoly trading rights with Spanish colonies in South America and the West Indies. The company was the ultimate speculative endeavor, as it had no real assets or even any tangible prospects. The most curious part about Newton's involvement was that he invested early on in the South Sea Company, watched his shares rise, and cashed out with a handsome profit. However, he was lured back into the investment after he watched the share prices continue to rise. If Newton had understood a little about behavioral finance, he might have been able to avoid financial ruin.

The Debate Between Market Efficiency and Behavioral Finance

The intellectual discussion of the rationality of investors and the investment markets pits advocates of behavioral finance against efficient market adherents. Behavioral finance represents a sort of merger of the disciplines of finance and psychology. The basic idea behind this school of thought is that cognitive, emotional, and social biases affect individuals' and institutions' investment decisions, resulting in irrational decision making that has the potential to create recurring patterns in stock returns.

In contrast, finance academicians have largely adopted the efficient markets theory (EMT), and it continues to be widely taught in business schools throughout the world. In 2013, Professor Eugene Fama of the University of Chicago was awarded a Nobel Prize in economics largely for his work in the late 1960s and early 1970s establishing the EMT. The EMT is based on the premise that investors always make rational decisions and that asset prices reflect those rational actions. Advocates of the EMT posit that at any time security prices reflect all relevant information and that any new information is quickly taken into account by market participants. The efficiency of markets makes it impossible for investors to consistently beat the market and earn abnormal returns for any given risk level. Thus, EMT zealots would have us believe that investors should not attempt to beat the market.

The EMT was and continues to be controversial in both the academic and the practitioner communities. One of the staunch opponents of EMT is Warren Buffett, who has shown his disdain for much of academic finance and advised in his 2008 letter that shareholders "beware of geeks bearing formulas."[1] In a famous debate between Buffett and the advocates of market efficiency in 1984, Professor Michael Jensen of the University of Rochester, speaking on behalf of EMT advocates, claimed that Buffett's record was something of a statistical fluke and that in any study of market performance there would be some individuals who dramatically beat the market and were simply statistical outliers.[2] Buffett cited his own record along with the record of other followers of the value investing school advanced by Columbia professor Ben Graham as evidence that markets are not as efficient as EMT proponents proclaim. Buffett's sidekick at Berkshire Hathaway, Charles Munger, had a wonderful take on EMT:

> Efficient market theory [is] a wonderful economic doctrine that had a long vogue in spite of the experience of Berkshire Hathaway. In fact one of the economists who won—he shared—a Nobel Prize and as he looked at Berkshire Hathaway year after year, which people would throw in his face as saying maybe the market isn't quite as efficient as you think, he said, "Well, it's a two-sigma event." And then he said we were a three-sigma event. And then he said we were a four-sigma event. And he finally got up to six sigmas—better to add a sigma than change a theory, just because the evidence comes in differently.[3]

In recent years, the field of behavioral finance has dramatically increased in popularity as evidence has mounted suggesting that investor rationality may not always prevail and that markets may not be as efficient as EMT advocates would have us believe. In fact, there are now several scholarly journals devoted entirely to the field of behavioral finance. The creation of journals such as the *Journal of Behavioral Finance*, the *Review of Behavioral Finance*, and the *Journal of Behavioral and Experimental Finance* and the establishment of the Driehaus Center for Behavioral Finance at DePaul University offer proof that many in the academy are embracing the tenets of this rapidly growing field.

We contend that the investment implications of the efficient markets theory and behavioral finance are strongly influenced by Fed policy decisions. Therefore, we argue that regardless of which theory you believe more accurately describes security performance, you should be cognizant of changes in Fed monetary policy. Whether the decisions of market participants are driven more directly by rational or irrational factors, there is no question in our minds that the expected availability of money is a key consideration for decision makers. For example, if you were in a situation in which you were going to commit a considerable sum of money to an investment, would your decision be influenced by your expectations about the future availability of money? We certainly hope so. We believe, and we hope you agree, that an individual's or firm's appetite for risk is directly related to the expected availability of money. With money expected to be more readily available, investment in risky ventures (such as a stock investment or a capital investment by a firm) becomes more palatable because a mistake becomes less critical. As we discuss the various investor behavioral biases in the sections that follow, keep in mind the relevance that Fed policy, along with the general level of money, will have on the bias. Toward the end of this chapter, we will examine how Fed policy relates to the return patterns that researchers have attributed to investors' behavioral biases. Our findings clearly link the return patterns to changes in

Fed policy, once again establishing the importance of monitoring the Fed before making any investment decision.

Some Popular Behavioral Finance Biases

One reason the academic finance profession was slow to accept the field of behavioral finance as a legitimate discipline is that it revolves around stories or anecdotes and is difficult to empirically test in a rigorous fashion. Academic finance has historically focused on concepts and theories that can be tested by professors who need to publish in academic journals to earn tenure and promotion. A small sampling of some of the more popular behavioral finance biases is provided below. Be honest: How many of these behaviors do you exhibit?

Confirmation Bias

Confirmation bias is the tendency to place too much weight on evidence that confirms our views and too little weight on evidence that runs counter to our views. In other words, we choose to believe what we want to believe. Investors are inundated with information and can find positive and negative information concerning the overall market, sectors, or individual companies. One need only tune in to 24-hour business news channels and hear so-called experts arguing that markets will soon take off or collapse.[4] When we hear someone touting a stock that we own, we perk up our ears and take that message to heart. In contrast, when someone is advancing a message counter to our beliefs, we tend to dismiss the messenger as a crackpot and tune him or her out.

Confirmation bias is certainly not limited to the investing front. It is quite prevalent in many other walks of life, particularly the political arena. Many media outlets recognize this and cater to one side or the other of the political spectrum. Whole networks have been built and continue to thrive on the basis of confirmation bias. We are reminded of the quote from Will Ferrell playing newsman Ron Burgundy in the movie *Anchorman 2:* "Why do we have to tell the people what they need to hear? Why don't we tell them what they want to hear?"

Loss Aversion Bias or Disposition Bias

A widely recognized behavioral bias is the tendency of investors to sell high-performing stocks (winners) too early while holding on to losers too long. By selling a winner, an investor is able to report a large gain and bask in the glory of his or her investment prowess. In contrast, investors may hold losers for extended periods, using the rationale that until a loser is sold, the loss is only a paper loss. Investors often plot a strategy of planning to sell a losing investment when the price gets back to the purchase price. This is colloquially referred to as get-evenitis. Some technical trading strategies are built around this bias. When this is taken to the extreme, an investor following this strategy is left holding a portfolio of losers.

The interesting aspect concerning loss aversion bias is that it flies directly in the face of rationality with respect to the U.S. tax code. Investors must pay capital gains taxes on investments sold at a profit, whereas realized investment losses can be used to off-set investment gains in computing personal income taxes. All else equal, a rational investor should realize losses and let gains ride. Selling an investment at a loss forces an investor to recognize his mistake. Conversely, selling an investment at a profit allows the investor to pat herself on the back and feel a tremendous sense of pride in a job well done.

Hindsight Bias

How many people do you know who claim they foresaw the financial crisis that began in 2008? To hear experts and nonexperts talk, you would think that nearly everyone saw it before it took place. We freely admit we didn't. The fact is that the vast majority of market participants, including most experts, were blindsided. Hindsight bias is the phenomenon in which people see past events as having been predictable and reasonable to expect. After the fact, people see their own predictive abilities in a much more favorable light than they warrant.

Much of the controversial field of technical analysis is built on hindsight bias. Market technicians study past price and volume relationships to predict future price movements. Often referred to as chartists, they examine stock price charts and believe that certain patterns with exotic names such as head and shoulders, diamond tops, ascending triangles, and double tops consistently repeat themselves. After the fact, market technicians can point to obvious patterns. Identifying those patterns before the fact is slightly more difficult, to say the least. Let's just say that for every pattern that works there are quite a few false positives.

Overconfidence Bias

It perhaps comes as a surprise to no one that investors are overly confident in their beliefs and abilities. Although investors espouse a wide variety of opinions, the one thing they all agree on is that each of them has above-average investment ability. In our conversations with friends and colleagues, we have been unable to identify any investor who admits to having underperformed the market.[5] Worse yet, studies consistently show that those who are the most confident in their predictions generally are the most inaccurate. Remember this observation when you hear that blowhard on TV or at your next party offering definitive stock advice. It turns out that the skills required to be a proficient forecaster overlap substantially with the skills necessary to accurately assess one's forecasting limitations. With this evidence in mind, you may want to alter your thinking from "he is so confident in his opinion, he must be correct" to "he is so confident in his opinion, he must be 'full of incorrectness.'"

Even the experts exhibit overconfidence in their forecasts. In his book *The Signal and the Noise*, Nate Silver cites the results of the Philadelphia Federal Reserve's survey of professional forecasters. The forecasters are asked to place a 90% confidence band—that is, a band such that they are 90% certain their prediction will fall within the band—around the growth of the U.S. economy. Since 1968, the economy's growth has been outside the band nearly half the time.

The bad investing habits induced by overconfidence include assuming more risk than is warranted, failing to diversify, concentrating investment in a few familiar securities, and trading too often. A real-world example that perhaps best exemplifies overconfidence is the behavior of many individuals during the tech bubble of the 1990s. During that period, individuals with no investment experience placed huge investments in technology stocks that had virtually no record of financial performance. Even for the most experienced investor, these securities were a speculative undertaking. To make matters worse, many novice investors upped the ante by borrowing a large percentage of the money they invested.[6] Borrowing money to purchase stock is referred to as buying on margin, and the strategy effectively magnifies the risk of the investment. The last thing individuals should have done when investing in tech stocks was to magnify the risk, but their confidence in the future success of the tech firms blinded them to reality. Ultimately, the popping of the tech bubble in the early 2000s subjected most of the novice investors to a major dose of reality.

Overreaction Bias

Traditional style investing strategies have mostly revolved around market capitalization and price multiples; however, more recently investors have focused considerable attention on a stock's past performance. In particular, Werner DeBondt, a finance professor at the University of Wisconsin, and Richard Thaler, a finance professor at Cornell, identified a consistent pattern in stock returns over time. In a widely cited paper published in 1985, DeBondt and Thaler showed that the stocks that performed the worst over the past several years (Losers) outperformed the stocks that had performed the best (Winners) by more than 30% over the subsequent five years.[7] This observation ultimately became recognized as the long-run reversal in stock returns. DeBondt and Thaler argued that the observation could be attributed to behavioral biases ingrained in investor trading. Specifically, their contention is that investors overreact to good news and bad news, which drives prices beyond their intrinsic or true value. In other words, investors become too optimistic about stocks that are performing well and too pessimistic about stocks that are doing poorly. According to this overreaction theory, investors eventually recognize their error and adjust their prices, and stock prices reverse to their true value. Thus, overreaction to a firm's unusually good or bad financial situation ultimately leads to a reversal in stock prices in the long run.

Our View on Efficient Markets Theory Versus Behavioral Finance

We believe that both theories have considerable merit, but as indicated above, we believe that both would benefit from an infusion of Fed policy considerations. In our opinion, the EMT serves as the best explanation for how markets typically function. Consistent with EMT, we believe that the vast majority of investors generally make investment decisions that are rational and economically sound. However, we believe it would be irrational to dismiss the overwhelming evidence showing that investors often exhibit behavioral biases in their trading. Clearly, investors do not always behave in a way that could be described as rational and economically sound. Although it may seem that proponents and opponents of EMT have diametrically opposed views, this is not necessarily the case. Ironically, market efficiency is a necessary ingredient for investment managers to make a profit. For example, an investment manager purchases a stock that is selling below its true or intrinsic value, planning to profit on the appreciation when the price returns to its "correct" or "efficient" value. However, if markets are inefficient, there is no reason to expect the price to return to its correct value. With respect to market efficiency and the merits of active investing, we share the viewpoint of the late economist Peter Bernstein, who claimed: "Active management is extraordinarily difficult, because there are so many knowledgeable investors and information does move so fast. The market is hard to beat. There are a lot of smart people trying to do the same thing. Nobody's saying that it's easy. But possible? Yes."[8]

In the remainder of this chapter we consider the relationship between monetary conditions and the long-run reversal pattern, which is generally attributed to investors' behavioral biases. As we have argued in this book, we believe that Fed policy decisions have the potential to alter investors' opinions and investment decisions and thus affect the structure of the long-run reversal pattern that numerous researchers have documented.

The Evidence on Long-Run Reversals

We begin our empirical analysis by taking an updated look at the return pattern identified by DeBondt and Thaler more than 25 years ago. Figure 3.1 reports average annual returns for the five quintiles (portfolios) ranked on the basis of a firm's stock performance over the last five years. The Loser portfolio includes stocks that ranked in the lowest performance quintile over the prior five years, and the Winner portfolio consists of stocks that performed the best over the prior five years. Consistent with our previous approach, we value-weight the return for each stock in each of the five quintiles.

Figure 3.1 Average Annual Returns on Reversal Portfolios: 1966–2013

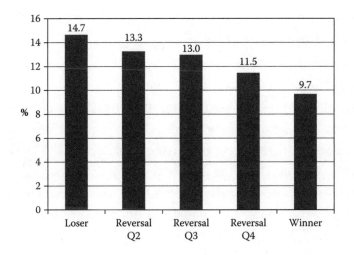

The returns plotted in Figure 3.1 confirm the superiority of the Loser portfolio relative to the Winner portfolio and thus confirm the long-run reversal phenomenon. Over the sample period, the Loser portfolio generated a return of 14.7%, which exceeded the return generated by the Winner portfolio (9.7%) by 5.0% per year. In light of this dramatic difference in performance, it is no wonder that researchers tried so hard to find an explanation for the substantial premium offered by poorly performing stocks (Losers). As you may expect, investors quickly went to work developing strategies to exploit the anomaly; after all, there was money to be made. The long-run reversal anomaly offers credence to the idea that investors should buy on weakness and sell on strength. Warren Buffett advocates a similar philosophy in arguing that an investor should "be fearful when others are greedy and greedy when others are fearful." Once again, the Oracle of Omaha seems to have been on top of the long-run reversal effect. A practical investment strategy purported to outperform the market that relies on the reversal phenomenon is the Dogs of the Dow investment strategy explained in Box 3.1.

Box 3.1 Dogs of the Dow

One of the oldest and most frequently cited trading strategies said to outperform the market is the Dogs of the Dow theory. This strategy simply involves purchasing, in equal dollar amounts, the 10 highest dividend-yielding stocks (those with the highest ratio of dividends to stock price) out of the 30 stocks in the Dow Jones Industrial Average (DJIA) at the beginning of the year. The investor holds those 10 stocks for the full calendar year before rebalancing at year-end and establishing equal positions in the 10 new highest dividend-yielding stocks at the beginning of the next calendar year. This is one of the many contrarian investment strategies that rely on purchasing out-of-favor issues. You may be wondering why the 10 highest dividend-yielding stocks are considered dogs. The reason is that firms seldom drop their dividends, and so high dividend-yielding stocks are generally created when a firm's stock price falls, that is, when the firm goes out of favor. The assumption behind the trading strategy is that once the market recognizes the value in these companies, the stock prices will rise (and dividend yields on these issues will fall); investors will reap the rewards, take the proceeds, and reinvest in the current group of DJIA stocks that are the most unpopular and undervalued. In effect, the investor will always be invested in the most undervalued stocks in the DJIA.

How has the theory performed? Table 3.1 summarizes the performance of the Dogs of the Dow strategy over the 20-year period 1992–2011.

Table 3.1 Performance Comparison in Percent of the Dogs of the Dow Strategy Versus DJIA (all returns are annualized and are before taxes and transactions costs)

Period	Dogs of the Dow	DJIA	Outperformance
2011	16.3	8.4	7.9
Three years (2009–2011)	17.9	15.0	2.9
Five years (2007–2011)	3.4	4.4	−1.0
Ten years (2002–2011)	6.7	6.1	0.6
Twenty years (1992–2011)	10.8	10.8	0.0

Data are from http://www.dogsofthedow.com.

(*continued*)

As is indicated in Table 3.1, the strategy basically treaded water from 1992 through 2011. Note that these returns are before taxes, transactions costs, and fees that would be incurred by investors following this strategy. After deducting these expenses, the strategy would significantly underperform the DJIA benchmark. It appears that the Dogs of the Dow theory has been a bit of a dog with respect to performance.

Obviously, the next step is to look at the long-run reversal effect relative to monetary conditions. Figure 3.2 does just that as it presents the performance of the five past-performance portfolios across the three alternative monetary environments.

Once again, the stair-step pattern across the portfolios is prevalent during expansive monetary periods but absent during indeterminate and restrictive monetary periods. The 30.2% average annual return generated by the Loser portfolio during expansive monetary periods is truly astounding, but even the 17.1% average return earned by the Winner portfolio during those periods is nothing to scoff at. There is clearly a substantial drop-off in performance from the Loser portfolio to the Q2 portfolio; in fact, the return falls by over 8%, which far exceeds the total drop over the next four portfolios.

In Chapter 2, we showed that small firms and value firms prosper during expansive monetary periods, and now we see that out-of-favor stocks (Losers) also excel when conditions are expansive. Just as we combined the small-firm effect and value-firm effect in Chapter 2, a similar approach could be applied here. Imagine the possible returns one could generate if one targeted small, value, and losers during expansive monetary periods. We are going to leave that combination to your imagination, but believe us, the results are

Figure 3.2   Average Annual Returns on Reversal Portfolios: 1966–2013

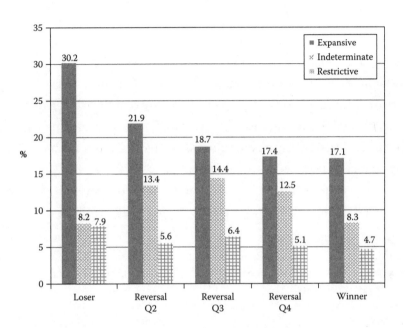

pretty spectacular. We have a lot of ground to cover, and we cannot split and splice every conceivable firm characteristic if we are going to get through it all. However, that doesn't prevent you from trying the strategy on your own.

Moving away from the returns in expansive periods, the patterns in Figure 3.2 during indeterminate and restrictive periods are pretty interesting. The Loser portfolio does about equally well (poorly) during indeterminate and restrictive periods (8.2% versus 7.9%). The 8.2% return for the Loser portfolio during indeterminate periods is the lowest among all the portfolios. The best performing portfolio during indeterminate periods is the Q3 portfolio, producing a pretty strong 14.4% annual return. It is ironic that the portfolio with middling past performance performs best when monetary conditions are middling.

We next evaluate the risk of each of the five portfolios across the three monetary environments. Figure 3.3 shows evidence consistent with expectations as the Loser portfolio has the highest risk level. That is logical in that the Loser portfolio contains firms that have performed very poorly over the previous five years. The Winner portfolio has the second highest risk, which is also consistent with expectations as these firms have shown exceptional performance over an extended period. Exceptionally poor performance and strong performance are generally associated with stocks that experience substantial price moves over time.

It is worth pointing out a couple of comparisons between Figures 3.2 and 3.3. First, note that during indeterminate monetary

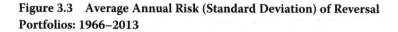

Figure 3.3   Average Annual Risk (Standard Deviation) of Reversal Portfolios: 1966–2013

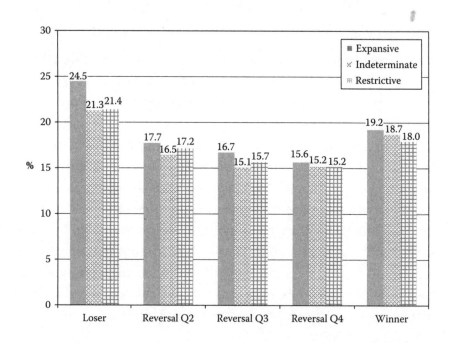

conditions the Q3 portfolio shows the lowest standard deviation (15.1%). In Figure 3.2, the same portfolio reported the highest return under indeterminate monetary conditions (14.4%). Thus, this middling portfolio really did excel when conditions were indeterminate. In stark contrast, in expansive and restrictive conditions the Winner portfolio produced the lowest return (and the second lowest under indeterminate conditions), but this portfolio had the second highest risk level across all three environments. Therefore, we can clearly declare that the Winner portfolio is the biggest loser. In general, it appears that investors would be wise to steer clear of Winners no matter what monetary conditions prevail.

At this point we should talk a bit about what really constitutes risk to an investor. The risk measure we report here is consistent with the conventional definition of risk, which is volatility or variability in returns. But if the Loser portfolio has higher volatility because the stocks are trending up in value, which on average they are, is that really risk? How many investors lament stock market volatility when their stocks or the market rose in value? Likewise, the volatility of the Winner portfolio is particularly troubling. It is larger than the volatility of any other portfolio except the Loser portfolio. But in this case, since the average returns of the winner portfolio are lower, the higher volatility is associated with subpar return performance.

Conclusion

In this chapter, we showed that a strategy of targeting out-of-favor stocks (Losers) has paid off handsomely over the long run. More important, however, we show that the success of the strategy is largely dependent on the monetary environment. During expansive monetary conditions, targeting out-of-favor stocks has been a phenomenal strategy as the excess returns earned by the strategy have swamped the strategy's higher risk. In contrast, the strategy gets a rating of mediocre at best when monetary conditions are indeterminate or restrictive.

To this point in the book, our cumulative evidence indicates that the success of the most prominent investment strategies is dependent on monetary conditions. In particular, during expansive monetary conditions, it appears that all the major investment strategies are successful to some extent. However, we identify several strategies that have been outstanding under expansive conditions and others that have been only adequate. We have not yet identified any strategy that excels when monetary conditions are indeterminate or restrictive. But don't despair; we are only at Chapter 3, and there is plenty of time to find that illusive strategy which prospers when Fed policy is constrained.

CHAPTER 4

MONETARY CONDITIONS AND ALTERNATIVE ASSETS

> Commodities tend to zig when the equity markets zag.
> *Jim Rogers, "Breakfast of Champions,"*
> *July 3, 2002.*

Alternative assets are defined as securities that one would not expect to find in a standard investment portfolio. This definition begs the question, What is a standard investment portfolio? and further, Whose expectations are serving as the standard or benchmark? For our purposes, we have identified commodities and real estate as the alternative asset classes to focus on in this chapter. You may say that real estate shouldn't be considered an alternative asset, as according to Gallup, 62% of Americans say they own their primary residence whereas only 52% own stock outright or as part of a mutual fund or self-directed investment account.[1] Likewise, in a 2011 Gallup poll, an astonishing 34% of Americans thought that gold was the best long-term investment, more than any other investment category, including real estate and mutual funds.[2] We accept the fact that real estate and commodities are popular investments and appear in many investors' portfolios, and numerous investors consider them staples of any standard investment portfolio; thus, we proceed with the acknowledgment that these two investment types are not universally recognized as alternative assets.

The popularity of alternative assets generally hinges on the view that they offer investors some financial protection from events that tend to be harmful to the traditional asset classes: stocks and bonds. The mantra of Investing 101 is to diversify by not putting all one's eggs in one basket, and alternative assets are generally considered to be outside the traditional basket of stocks and bonds. The general idea is that investors want to reduce the negative impact that a dramatic drop in the broad stock or bond markets will have on their portfolios. During the decade of the 2000s, investors witnessed two dramatic drops in the stock market, the first occurring with the popping of the tech bubble in the early 2000s and the second with the unprecedented global financial crisis that began in 2008. The wealth destruction that resulted from those two episodes traumatized investors and intensified the focus on alternative investments as hedging instruments or a sort of portfolio insurance against such cataclysmic declines. Although investors may have jokingly referred to their 401(k)s becoming 201(k)s as a result of those events, they found no humor in the realization that the events were requiring them to delay retirement for several years.

Alternative Assets as Inflation Hedges

One of the most damaging yet recurring forces affecting an investor's portfolio is inflation. Inflation can be viewed as eating away at an investor's return. Thus, a double-digit inflation rate, as investors faced during the late 1970s and early 1980s, can be devastating for investors' real wealth accumulation. The two alternative asset classes we consider in this chapter—real estate and commodities—are commonly advocated as inflation hedges because their values are directly tied to the price of real assets. That is, when real asset prices rise, inflation increases and so do commodity and real estate prices while stock and bond prices generally suffer. Although we agree that real estate and commodities hedge inflation risk, we believe that investors have routinely erred in how they have applied the hedge.

Financial commentators and pundits frequently associate an easy Fed monetary policy with the stoking of inflationary forces, and thus they propose that investors should increase their allocation to commodities and real estate during periods of easy money. These financial experts contend that when the Fed is following a tight money policy, inflation hedges should be a minimal part of an investor's portfolio. We believe the financial experts have it completely backward. We argue that investors should use the Fed indicators that we discussed in the Introduction as signals of the Fed's views on inflation. After all, who knows more about inflation than the Fed (the monetary authority)? When the Fed signals an easy money policy, it is because the Fed believes inflationary pressures are minuscule. Thus, we believe this warrants a minimal allocation to inflation-hedging assets, not a heavy allocation as the experts propose. When the Fed initiates a tight money policy, it is signaling that inflation is a prominent and immediate concern. This is when we would advocate an increased allocation to inflation-hedging assets. Thus, our proposed strategy runs exactly counter to the conventional views of financial commentators and pundits. Furthermore, we believe that not all commodities and real estate are created equal in their ability to hedge inflation, and so it is necessary to choose wisely in selecting an inflation hedge.

In the following sections, we first discuss the general properties of both of these two asset classes. We follow that discussion with an examination of their performance relative to Fed policy signals. By the time you finish this chapter, you will have evidence that will help you formulate a dynamic investment strategy that is guided by Fed policy, a strategy that reflects the appropriate composition for the alternative asset portion of your portfolio.

Real Estate Investment

Real estate represents a prominent portfolio component for most investors because of the relatively large proportion of wealth that is tied up in the typical investor's home. However, there is some debate about whether a person's personal residence should be considered an investment. In this chapter, we focus on real estate as an investment rather than on the real estate that represents the equity in an investor's residence. We believe that investors should recognize the unique nature of home equity and that although it should certainly be considered part of one's life balance sheet, it should be classified differently from purely financial assets such as stock and bond investments. There are two basic types of real estate investment: direct and indirect. Investors who engage in direct real estate investment generally do so with the intention of being somewhat actively involved in the management process. In contrast, an indirect investment in real estate is a passive investment and is generally accomplished through a real estate investment trust (REIT): an investment fund that specializes in real estate. To illustrate these two investment approaches, assume an investor wishes to take an ownership stake in the apartment rental business. The investor could make a direct investment by purchasing an apartment complex, but that takes a substantial capital outlay, requiring a financial commitment that the vast majority of investors could not make. Alternatively, the investor could gain an indirect exposure by purchasing shares in a REIT that specializes in owning and renting apartments. In most cases, investors who make a direct investment are actively involved in the management of the apartment building in some way, such as collecting rent payments from tenants, performing routine maintenance, or remodeling apartment units. REIT investors, in contrast, are like any other stock investor: they participate on a passive basis and earn a profit from the dividends received from the stock and the stock's price appreciation. In light of the fact that active participation generally accompanies a direct real estate investment, in this chapter we focus on indirect real estate investment in the form of REITs.

Real Estate Investment Trusts

Contrary to what many investors believe, not all REITs are created equal. Similar to mutual funds, REITs can differ dramatically from one offering to the next. Every REIT invests in real estate–based assets, and as a result of regulations, REITs have a high required dividend payout. To maintain its status as a REIT, any REIT is obligated to distribute a minimum of 90% of annual income as dividends. However, beyond these common characteristics, the differences among REITs far exceed their similarities. REITs range from very risky speculative ventures to relatively low-risk steady income-producing interests.

REIT Types: Separating the Trees from the Forest

What differentiates one REIT from another is the type of underlying real estate that the REIT holds. For example, Annaly Capital Management is one of the largest mortgage REITs. The company owns and manages a portfolio of securities that represent claims on mortgage loans. Equity Residential, in contrast, is a very large REIT that owns and manages apartment complexes. In light of the tremendous diversity in REITs, an investor who is optimistic about the prospects for a particular type of real estate is generally able to identify a REIT that matches his or her specific interest in or expectations about the real estate market in any sector or geographic location.

What About REIT Performance?

Table 4.1 reports the performance for three alternative REIT indexes over the period 1972–2013. REITs can be broadly classified into two categories, which are represented by the equity and mortgage REIT indexes in Table 4.1. The composite REIT represents the combination of the two indexes. Table 4.1 also includes the performance of the U.S. stock and bond market to allow for a direct comparison of real estate performance with the corresponding performance of the traditional capital market securities. We start measuring returns in 1972 because that is the first year in which data for the broad REIT indexes is available.[3] The final column of the table presents a return-to-risk

Table 4.1   Performance for Real Estate Investment Trusts: 1972–2013

Security Index	Mean Annual Return, %	Standard Deviation of Return, %	Return-to-Risk Ratio
Equity REIT	12.82	17.24	0.74
Mortgage REIT	6.96	20.43	0.34
Composite REIT	10.77	17.85	0.60
U.S. stocks: S&P 500	11.21	15.42	0.73
U.S. bonds	7.69	7.90	0.97

ratio, which is calculated as the mean annualized return divided by the annualized standard deviation of return. It provides investors with a measure of how much return they are getting per unit of risk. Of course, the higher the return-to-risk ratio, the better.

The performance of the composite REIT is very similar to the performance of the S&P 500 over the 1972–2013 period. This similarity in performance has caused some investors to question whether the returns to REITs align more closely with stocks or with real estate (see Box 4.1). Although the composite REIT performed comparably with the stock market, the two REIT components experienced considerably different performance during the period. Equity REITs showed a slightly superior performance to stocks during the period as their return-to-risk ratio was 0.74 versus 0.73 for stocks. In contrast, mortgage REITs performed very poorly during the period as they offered a return-to-risk ratio that was less than half the ratio earned by equity REITs and stocks. On the basis of their poor showing in Table 4.1, one might be tempted to dismiss mortgage REITs as a potential investment vehicle; however, before one makes such a hasty decision, we believe further analysis is required.

Box 4.1   Are REITs More Like Stocks or Real Estate?

There is considerable debate in both the investment management industry and among academicians about the classification of REITs. Specifically, are they more stock-like or real estate–like? One of the biggest benefits of REITs is that they are liquid; that is, investors can buy and sell REIT shares the same way they buy and sell shares of General Motors stock. We all know that buying and selling direct real estate involves considerable time and expense. Thus, REIT

(continued)

---

shares turn over at a much higher rate than is the case in direct ownership of real estate. With direct real estate, no one provides the owner with a buy or sell quote on a daily basis; thus, it is impossible to determine the price volatility of direct real estate.

We also know that by their very nature most REITs are diversified, representing ownership in many different real estate properties, not one specific property. Thus, the returns to REITs tend to be more stable than the returns to individual properties, which are subject to more idiosyncratic factors.

Monetary Conditions and REIT Performance

We next evaluate the performance of the broad REIT indexes across the three monetary environments. Once again, for comparison purposes, we also report the returns to U.S. stocks and bonds for the three monetary environments. Table 4.2 shows that like stocks, REITs perform unusually well when monetary conditions are expansive and unusually poorly when monetary conditions are restrictive. Specifically, the composite REIT returns 16.72% when monetary conditions are expansive, which is similar to the corresponding S&P 500 return of 14.68%. The composite REIT returns only 5.09% when conditions are restrictive, which corresponds with an S&P 500 return of 8.47%.

From an investment prospective, the most fascinating, and potentially the most profitable, finding in Table 4.2 is the dramatic difference in performance between mortgage REITs and equity REITs across the various monetary environments. The reason that such differences excite investors is that they portend a potential rotation strategy: moving from one asset class to another depending on

Table 4.2 Monetary Conditions and REIT Performance: Annual Mean Returns and (Standard Deviations): 1972–2013

Security Index	Expansive, %	Indeterminate, %	Restrictive, %
Equity REIT	16.44	12.37	9.77
	(21.69)	(14.10)	(15.47)
Mortgage REIT	19.42	5.80	−4.05
	(23.20)	(18.39)	(19.20)
Composite REIT	16.72	10.59	5.09
	(22.17)	(14.07)	(16.79)
U.S. stocks: S&P 500	14.68	10.61	8.47
	(16.57)	(15.13)	(14.59)
U.S. bonds	6.89	9.89	6.00
	(8.64)	(7.58)	(7.47)

economic circumstances. On average, mortgage REITs have been miserable investments during periods of restrictive monetary policy, earning a negative return (−4.05%) with a high level of volatility (19.20%), a really bad combination. Furthermore, mortgage REITs are only marginally better investments when monetary conditions are indeterminate (earning a 5.80% return with an 18.39% standard deviation). In stark contrast to mortgage REITs, equity REITs perform admirably during both restrictive and indeterminate periods, offering returns that exceed 9.7% in both cases and subjecting investors to only moderate amounts of risk. These results make it clear that an investor who followed a rotation strategy that overallocated portfolio weight to mortgage REITs and stocks under expansive monetary conditions while minimizing the allocation to those securities under restrictive conditions would have substantially enhanced portfolio performance during the 1972–2013 period. Therefore, in spite of their dismal overall performance, it would appear that mortgage REITs do have a role to play in a diversified investment portfolio; however, the evidence in Table 4.2 indicates that their role is very much dependent on the existing monetary environment.

We are all familiar with the old adage that hindsight is 20/20. Obviously, after the fact anyone can identify securities that excelled during certain periods but languished during others. As the talking heads on CNBC prove day after day, in hindsight a plausible reason for that performance can be posited. However, the relevant question is whether there is any reason to suspect that the return patterns will continue into the future. We believe there is a strong economic rationale for our findings that suggests they are indeed relevant for future periods. In particular, mortgage REITs are known to be extremely sensitive to shifting interest rate environments. When inflation expectations shift, there is a corresponding shift in interest rates and individuals holding mortgages significantly alter their prepayment behavior, which changes the cash flows to holders of mortgage-backed securities. Specifically, when interest rates (inflation rates) fall, mortgage holders often prepay their existing mortgages and refinance at lower rates. Conversely, when interest/ inflation rates rise, fewer homeowners prepay mortgages; instead, the less attractive mortgage rates encourage homeowners to stay put in their current homes and avoid changing residences. Furthermore, mortgage REITs are generally very heavily levered (i.e., they borrow large amounts to finance their purchases of mortgage-based securities). Therefore, an increase in interest rates results in an immediate increase in their expenses, and since mortgage payments are generally fixed, there is no offsetting increase in income.

Because monetary policy is based on the Fed's projections for inflation and economic activity—both items that are closely associated with interest rates—the pattern in returns has a very strong economic basis. When the Fed signals an easy-money policy period, mortgage REITs prosper much as traditional stocks do because the greater availability of money, diminished inflationary concerns, and the lower interest rates are relatively beneficial for these rate-sensitive securities. In contrast, a tight money period portends greater inflationary concerns, which tends to be relatively favorable for assets that are less sensitive to shifting interest rates, such as equity REITs. Rental rates on apartments, warehouses, and office buildings tend to adjust with shifts in inflation, and this reduces the sensitivity of equity REITs to inflationary pressures and makes these securities relatively attractive investments during tight policy periods.

A World of REITs to Choose From

Although the discussion of broad REIT indexes above offers a general overview of the performance of REITs, most REIT investors prefer to narrow their real estate ownership to a more refined set of real estate investments. Fortunately, there are numerous REITs that target specific types of real estate investment, and so investors can easily identify a firm that offers a specific real estate exposure. The exposures are not limited to sectors of the real estate market, as many REITs also specialize in geographic regions. In early 2012, there were 166 REITs registered with the Securities and Exchange Commission in the United States. These REITs trade on one of the major stock exchanges—the majority on the New York Stock Exchange—and they had a combined equity market capitalization of $579 billion.[4] Table 4.3 reports several alternative types of REITs and includes examples of two firms in each category.[5]

Before we leave the topic of REITS, it should be noted that even though Will Rogers is rumored to have said, "Put your money in

---

Table 4.3   A Sample of Real Estate Investment Trusts (REITs) by Type

Type of REIT	Real Estate Held	Firm (Ticker Symbol)
Mortgage	Mortgage loans	American Capital Agency Corp (AGNC), Annaly Capital Management (NLY)
Industrial	Warehouses, office buildings	First Industrial Realty Trust (FR), Prologis Inc. (PLD)
Apartment	Apartment buildings	Equity Residential (EQR), Apartment Investment and Management Company (AIV)
Single family	Single-family homes	Silver Bay Realty Trust (SBY), American Residential Properties (ARPI)
Lodging	Hotels and motels	Host Hotels and Resorts (HST), LaSalle Hotel Properties (LHO)
Office	Office buildings	Boston Properties (BXP), Brookfield Property Partners (BPY)
Healthcare	Healthcare properties	HCP Inc. (HCP), Ventas (VTR)
Storage	Self-storage units	Extra Space Storage (EXR), Public Storage (PSA)
Retail	Enclosed shopping centers	Simon Property Group (SPG), Kimco Realty Corp (KIM)

---

land, because they aren't making any more of it," investing in real estate is not without substantial risk. There have certainly been well-documented boom and bust periods in the real estate markets, most recently in the period around the global financial crisis. If you carefully monitor Fed policy, you won't be able to eliminate the risk associated with an investment in REITs; however, our evidence indicates that you will be able to mitigate that risk. The roller coaster ride that some REIT investors have experienced is exemplified by the story of General Growth Properties in Box 4.2.

Box 4.2   General Growth Properties

General Growth Properties (GGP) is one of the largest shopping mall operators in the United States, owning many iconic properties, including Ala Moana Center (Honolulu), Tysons Galleria (Washington, D.C.), and Water Tower Place (Chicago), to name a few. Consistent with most REITs, the firm makes extensive use of leverage (i.e., it borrows heavily to finance its real estate acquisitions). General Growth Properties was growing rapidly during the economic expansion during the early to mid-2000s. The onset of the global financial crisis, however, hit GGP hard. In late November 2008, the company missed a deadline to repay $900 million in loans backed by two of its Las Vegas retail properties. The price of its shares fell 97% in a six-month period. In April 2009, the company filed for Chapter 11 bankruptcy as it simply could not refinance its debt because of the market gridlock that followed the failure of Lehman Brothers Holdings and the credit freeze that paralyzed the financial markets.

However, the story of General Growth Properties does not end in failure: it emerged from bankruptcy in November 2010 and offered new shares to the public. Unlike most Chapter 11 bankruptcies, existing shareholders weren't completely wiped out. In fact, each holder of a General Growth share received one share of new General Growth stock and a fractional share of a spin-off: Howard Hughes Corporation common stock. The investors who stuck with the firm through its darkest hours were handsomely rewarded. Since the emergence from bankruptcy, the shares are up over 100%, outpacing both the S&P 500 index and the composite REIT Index.

Commodity Investment

The popularity of investing in commodities has grown tremendously since the 1970s as a result of two primary developments. First, investors have become increasingly concerned about the damage that a catastrophic event or a period of high inflation can have on their portfolios. Investors have witnessed the devastation inflicted on portfolios by events as diverse as terrorist attacks, hyperinflation, and financial crises. Second, a plethora of commodity-based investment vehicles have been created in the last several years, and this has made it much easier to gain an ownership interest (exposure) in commodities. Traditionally, achieving a direct exposure to a commodity could be a relatively costly and difficult task. Hence, many investors resorted to taking indirect exposures to commodities. For example, an investor wanting to own a position in oil could gain an indirect exposure by purchasing stock in a large oil company such as Chevron or Exxon Mobil. Unfortunately, empirical evidence indicates that investments in stocks that operate in commodity-based businesses are much more closely tied to the performance of the stock market than they are to changes in the price of the underlying commodity.[6] Alternatively, an investor could open a futures-trading account and trade futures contracts on commodities; however, most investors have little desire or the expertise necessary to engage in this activity.

Commodity Investing Made Easier

The creation of commodity-based exchange-traded funds (ETFs) and exchange-traded notes (ETNs) made it dramatically easier for investors to get exposure to commodities. ETFs and ETNs (see Box 4.3) trade just like stocks yet offer unique exposures that would otherwise be difficult for investors to achieve. These securities offer investors the opportunity to match commodity price moves as the securities are designed to track the performance of a particular commodity, a commodity group, or even a broad basket of commodities. For example, SPDR Gold Shares (GLD) is an ETF that represents a claim to an individual commodity; specifically, GLD seeks to replicate the performance of the price of gold bullion. Rather than purchasing physical gold bullion and having to worry about insurance and storage costs, an investor can simply purchase shares of GLD. As an example of a broad commodity ETF, iShares S&P GSCI Commodity-Indexed Trust (GSG) is an ETF designed to track the performance of the S&P GSCI Commodity Index, which is currently composed of 24 different commodities from five broad commodity sectors: energy products, industrial metals, agricultural products, livestock products, and precious metals. Because of the variety of commodities included in the GSG, an investor who purchases shares of this ETF effectively obtains a diversified exposure to a broad array of commodities.

Box 4.3   What Is the Difference Between an ETF and an ETN?

Many investors view ETFs and ETNs as identical products since they have the same primary objective. For example, OIL is an ETN designed to reflect the returns from West Texas Intermediate crude oil, and USO is an ETF that is also designed to reflect the returns from West Texas Intermediate crude oil. There is, however, a fundamental difference between the two securities of which investors should be aware. With an ETF, an investor is purchasing a claim on

(continued)

an underlying asset, whereas an ETN simply represents a promissory note (a promise to pay). Therefore, when an investor purchases an ETF, that investor becomes a claimholder on an actual pool of assets. In contrast, when an investor owns an ETN, that investor becomes a claimholder on the ETN issuer and the creditworthiness of that ETN issuer becomes paramount. To illustrate the difference, an investment company that wants to create a security to track the price of gold could create an ETF by purchasing gold bullion and selling claims to the bullion. The company also could create an ETN by issuing notes that promise to pay a return commensurate with the return earned by gold bullion. Since the value of an ETN is contractually tied to the value of the underlying asset via the promissory note, in many cases ETNs track the underlying asset more closely than an ETF does. Proponents of ETNs commonly cite this as an advantage of ETNs over ETFs. One must remember, however, that this feature comes at the cost of potential credit risk. Investors should always remember that any ETN is only as good as the creditworthiness of its issuer.

A Cornucopia of ETFs and ETNs

We all know that investment bankers are an extremely creative lot; sometimes they may be a little too creative. If there is sufficient demand for exposure to a particular asset class, they will create securities that mimic that exposure. There has been an explosion in the number and scope of commodity ETFs and ETNs since they were introduced in 1993 and 2006, respectively. As of late 2013, there were over 100 commodity ETFs trading in the United States.[7] Table 4.4 presents a number of prominent commodity-based ETFs and ETNs and indicates the particular commodity or

Table 4.4   Prominent ETFs and ETNs

Category	Name	Ticker	Type	Commodity Exposure
Diversified	iShares S&P GSCI Commodity-Indexed Trust	GSG	ETF	A basket of commodities
Diversified	iPath Pure Beta Broad Commodity	BCM	ETN	A basket of commodities
Diversified	PowerShares DB Commodity Index Tracking	DBC	ETF	A basket of commodities
Diversified	Jefferies TR/J CRB Global Commodity Equity Index	CRBQ	ETF	A basket of commodities
Diversified	UBS E-TRACS DJ-UBS Commodity Index	DJCI	ETN	A basket of commodities
Energy	United States Oil	USO	ETF	Crude oil
Energy	Market Vectors Coal	KOL	ETF	Coal
Energy	PowerShares WilderHill Clean Energy	PBW	ETF	Clean energy
Energy	Guggenheim Solar	TAN	ETF	Solar energy
Energy	Market Vectors Uranium+Nuclear Energy	NLR	ETF	Nuclear energy
Energy	First Trust ISE Global Wind Energy	FAN	ETF	Wind energy
Energy	United States Natural Gas	UNG	ETF	Natural gas
Precious metals	iShares Silver Trust	SLV	ETF	Silver
Precious metals	SPDR Gold Shares	GLD	ETF	Gold

(continued)

Table 4.4   Prominent ETFs and ETNs (*continued*)

Category	Name	Ticker	Type	Commodity Exposure
Precious metals	ETFS Physical Platinum Shares	PPLT	ETF	Platinum
Precious metals	ETFS Precious Metals Basket Trust	GLTR	ETF	Gold, silver, platinum, and palladium.
Agricultural	Teucrium Corn	CORN	ETF	Corn
Agricultural	iPath Pure Beta Coffee	CAFÉ	ETN	Coffee
Agricultural	iPath DJ-UBS Livestock Sub TR	COW	ETN	Livestock (lean hogs and live cattle)
Agricultural	iPath Pure Beta Agriculture	DIRT	ETF	A basket of agricultural products
Agricultural	iPath Pure Beta Grains	WEET	ETN	Grains and oilseeds
Agricultural	iShares Global Timber & Forestry	WOOD	ETF	Timber
Industrial metals	PowerShares DB Base Metals	DBB	ETF	A basket of base metals: aluminum, zinc, copper
Industrial metals	iPath Pure Beta Nickel	NINI	ETN	Nickel
Industrial metals	United States Copper Index	CPER	ETF	Copper
Industrial metals	iPath Pure Beta Aluminum	FOIL	ETN	Aluminum

basket of commodities each security tracks. There are also ETFs available for investors who are bearish on commodities (i.e., they expect a commodity's price to fall) in general or for a particular commodity. These are known as inverse ETFs and move in the opposite direction to the fundamental commodity. For instance, the Invesco PowerShares DB Gold Short ETF (DGZ) is designed to provide the holder with a return similar to that of an investor who has "shorted" gold. If gold rises by 1%, the value of the inverse ETF will fall by approximately 1%. In contrast, if gold falls by 1%, the value of DGZ will rise by approximately 1%. Finally, for those who want more variation in their commodity exposure, there are actively managed commodity ETFs. Investors in these securities are banking on the ability of the ETF managers to use their talents to buy and sell commodity instruments and outperform an indexing strategy.

Commodity Performance and the Importance of Diversification

Although investors have held precious metals as portfolio investments for many years, historically, the majority of investors would have never dreamed of holding an ownership interest in commodities such as crude oil, coffee, natural gas, aluminum, and livestock as part of their investment portfolios. The development of commodity futures contracts was intended to assist businesses in hedging adverse price movements of their inputs and outputs, not to assist investors. For instance, airlines buy oil and farmers sell wheat in the futures market. However, once investors discovered that these contracts could be used to hedge adverse price movements of stocks and bonds, trading in commodity-based securities exploded. Investors found that commodity prices generally have little relationship with the price movements of stocks and bonds; that is, commodity prices have a low correlation with stock and bond prices. Therefore, allocating a portion of a portfolio to commodities provides some protection, serving almost like portfolio insurance against adverse movements in stock and bond prices.

The enormous growth in the popularity of commodity investments is due largely to past empirical evidence that shows that commodities offer comparable returns to traditional assets but, more important, have very low correlations with the traditional assets (stocks and bonds). We believe this evidence vastly understates the potential benefits of commodities. In particular, past empirical evidence is based on a static allocation strategy that simply establishes a fixed portion of an investor's portfolio that is dedicated to commodities, thus requiring no action from or insight by the investor. We demonstrate that the benefits of commodities can be dramatically enhanced by casually monitoring Fed policy decisions. In the next section, we report the evidence that has been used by past researchers to promote the benefits of a static allocation to commodities. In the subsequent section, we show that this performance can be dramatically improved by using a dynamic allocation approach that is guided by Fed monetary policy.

Table 4.5 shows the performance (risk and return) of the major commodity groupings as well as presenting their all-important correlations with U.S. stocks and bonds. We report the performance of gold separately because of its unique popularity with the investing public. It should be noted that the statistics reported in Table 4.5 are derived from total returns (see Box 4.4 for an explanation of how the returns to commodities are calculated).

Table 4.5   Commodity Performance and Correlations (various periods)

Security Index	Mean Annual Return, %	Standard Deviation, %	Correlation with Stocks	Correlation with Bonds
GSCI Composite	10.80	19.84	0.09	−0.10
Precious metals	9.21	23.03	0.05	−0.01
Gold	7.12	19.71	0.02	0.04
Energy	12.57	31.09	0.07	−0.10
Industrial metals	9.95	24.17	0.28	−0.13
Agriculture	6.21	20.77	0.09	−0.05
Livestock	8.45	17.64	0.07	−0.04
U.S. stocks: S&P 500	10.74	15.44	1.00	0.15
U.S. bonds	7.70	8.10	0.15	1.00

Note: Data availability for the commodity indexes varied considerably, as shown by the following start dates: GSCI Composite, 1970; precious metals, 1973; gold, 1978; energy, 1983; industrial metals, 1977; agriculture, 1970; and livestock, 1970. Therefore, the performance data are derived from the start date through 2013; we use a start date of 1970 for U.S. stocks and bonds.

Box 4.4   How Commodity Returns Are Calculated

Whereas an investment in stocks or bonds requires a dollar commitment, an investment in a futures contract requires only a commitment of collateral. Therefore, to make an investment in futures contracts comparable to a traditional investment, it is assumed that a like amount of money is invested in U.S. Treasury bills (T-bills). For example, to equate an investment in futures with a traditional purchase of stocks, a $10,000 investment would require paying $10,000 to purchase shares, whereas a $10,000 futures position

(continued)

requires only that the investor agree to take a future action worth $10,000. You can't make a valid comparison of the benefits from the two alternatives because they don't have the same up-front cost. To make the comparison fair, it is customary to assume that when an investor enters a futures position, an accompanying purchase (in this example, $10,000) of T-bills is made. This is the convention followed consistently in the investment management industry and in academic studies. Fortunately, with the advent of ETFs and ETNs, the underlying transactions are made for you.

The performance data in Table 4.5 indicate that commodities have generally performed quite well over the entire period; however, there is considerable variation in that performance. The performance of the GSCI Composite compares favorably with the returns reported for the S&P 500, as the return for the composite is slightly higher and the risk is only moderately higher. The most advantageous feature of commodities, however, is reflected in the correlations of commodities with traditional assets. As a reminder, a correlation of 0 indicates no relationship in returns, a correlation of +1 means returns mirror each other exactly, and a correlation of −1 indicates that returns run exactly counter to each other. To provide some perspective, based on the CBOE S&P 500 Implied Correlation Index, the average correlation between individual stocks in the S&P 500 has generally been between 0.40 and 0.60, but it was considerably higher during the financial crisis, when, it seems, all stocks were moving down in unison.[8] The correlations between commodities and stocks or bonds, in contrast, have been consistently quite small. Correlations that are close to zero imply exceptional diversification potential and the potential to substantially reduce portfolio risk. Hence, the very low correlations in Table 4.5 imply that commodities offer considerable potential for hedging adverse moves in the returns of portfolios composed of traditional securities.

In general, the statistics in Table 4.5 indicate that the risk and return characteristics of the more specialized commodity indexes are less attractive than those of the composite index as the risk is generally considerably higher and the returns are on average somewhat lower. The correlations of the traditional securities with some of the specialized indexes, however, suggest that the specialized commodities may offer superior hedging protection when they are included in a portfolio. In particular, gold with a correlation of 0.02 has the lowest correlation with the stock market of any of the commodities. This observation perhaps supports the popularity of gold as a component of a portfolio that is heavily weighted toward equities. In contrast, industrial metals show a relatively strong correlation of 0.28 with stocks. This is perhaps not surprising in light of the close association one would expect between the performance of the economy and the price of industrial metals. In favorable economic conditions one would expect increased use of metals and a resulting increase in the price of industrial metals and stocks, whereas weak economic conditions are likely to harm both.

Interestingly, the commodity type that offers the most diversification potential for stocks offers the least diversification potential for bonds, and the opposite situation also holds. Specifically, among the specialized commodities, gold exhibits the lowest correlation with stocks and the highest correlation with bonds; however, even then the correlation is extremely low at 0.04. Industrial metals have the highest correlation with stocks and the lowest correlation with bonds. The negative correlation between commodities and bonds indicates that from a diversification prospective, commodities are generally an even more beneficial supplement to a bond portfolio than they are to an equity portfolio.

The data in Table 4.5 confirm the favorable features advanced by the proponents of commodities. In particular, commodities offer fairly attractive returns while providing substantial diversification potential. In the next section, we consider the degree to which Fed policy signals can be used to enhance the benefits associated with a commodity investment.

Monetary Conditions and Commodity Performance

Remember from Chapter 1 that our evidence shows that traditional asset classes tend to perform exceptionally well during expansive monetary periods and perform very poorly during restrictive periods. In light of the unique nature of commodities, we now consider their performance across the three monetary environments to see if their uniqueness carries through to their performance across those environments. Table 4.6 reports the returns across monetary environments for each of the indexes reported in Table 4.5.

In light of the pattern we observed across the traditional asset classes, the returns reported in Table 4.6 are not only surprising but also very refreshing. As was noted previously, diversity in return patterns is an investor's delight because it gives the investor the opportunity to hedge adverse price movements and smooth out portfolio returns. Interestingly, the return patterns for commodities run exactly counter to the patterns exhibited by stocks and bonds, offering investors ample diversification opportunities. Commodities perform poorly when stocks perform well, that is, when monetary conditions are expansive, and commodities prosper when stocks languish, that is, when monetary conditions are restrictive. The contradictory nature of the return patterns strongly motivates

Table 4.6   Commodity Performance and Monetary Conditions (various time periods)

Security Index	Expansive Return, %	Indeterminate Return, %	Restrictive Return, %
GSCI Composite	−0.19	14.28	17.66
Precious metals	7.19	13.49	6.58
Gold	7.85	8.61	4.86
Energy	1.00	19.76	16.89
Industrial metals	−1.96	7.75	23.66
Agriculture	−8.81	10.12	16.53
Livestock	7.46	9.50	8.22
U.S. stocks: S&P 500	16.17	9.76	6.73
U.S. bonds	7.14	9.41	6.30

Note: Data availability for the commodity indexes varied considerably as shown by the following start dates: GSCI Composite, 1970; precious metals, 1973; gold, 1978; energy, 1983; industrial metals, 1977; agriculture, 1970; and livestock, 1970. Therefore, the performance data are derived from the start date through 2013; we use a start date of 1970 for U.S. stocks and bonds.

consideration of a rotation strategy that overweighs stocks under expansive conditions and overweighs commodities when monetary conditions are constrained to any degree (when Fed policy is restrictive or indeterminate).

In general, commodities show similar consistency in performance to what was observed across the various classifications of stock investment styles; however, the patterns are exactly counter. In particular, most commodities prosper (languish) when monetary conditions are restrictive (expansive), whereas the opposite patterns prevailed consistently across the various equity types (see the performance results by style box strategy that were reported in

Chapter 2). The attraction of precious metals as a hedging instrument is apparent as precious metals (including gold) show tremendous consistency in performance across all three monetary environments. For investors not interested in applying a rotation strategy, precious metals offer stability in performance without the need to apply an active investment strategy. Although livestock is a less recognized investment alternative, it also shows remarkable consistency in cross-environment performance. As Box 4.5 shows, not everyone agrees that commodities represent an attractive addition to a portfolio.

Box 4.5 Warren Buffett: The Ultimate Gold Bear

Not everyone is enamored with the hedging potential of gold and other commodities. In fact, Warren Buffett isn't even a fan of diversification in general. He has been quoted as saying, "Diversification is protection against ignorance. It makes little sense if you know what you are doing."[9] For us mere mortals, diversification is not only prudent but necessary.

With respect to gold, Buffett contends that it is simply a speculative investment. "If you put your money into gold or other non-income-producing assets that are dependent on what someone else values that in the future, you're in speculation."[10] Unlike most stocks and bonds, gold (or any other commodity, for that matter) does not generate any cash flows to the holder other than the prospect that it could be sold in the future at a higher price. In other words, Buffett would argue that gold investors subscribe to the greater fool theory. The price of gold is not determined by its intrinsic value but simply by its expected selling price to someone in the future. In a meeting

---

with students at the CFA Institute Research Challenge in March 2011, Buffett explained his rationale concerning gold as an investment as follows: The world's gold stock is about 170,000 metric tons, which if all melded together could create a cube of about 68 feet per side; the cube would be worth about $9.6 trillion. For that much money, one could buy all the cropland in the United States, purchase 16 Exxon Mobils, and have about $1 trillion of walking-around money left over. He asked the students which one they would rather have. He also noted, "You can fondle the cube, but it will not respond."

Tables 4.5 and 4.6 show that precious metals (including gold) exhibit relatively strong performance for the overall period. In addition, the returns have low correlation with the stock and bond market and are relatively invariant to the monetary environment. These characteristics promote the view that precious metals have somewhat unique features compared with the other commodities and are a strong candidate for a strategic or long-term static allocation in an investment portfolio that consists of traditional securities. Maintaining a constant exposure to precious metals is consistent with their recognized role as a safeguard against a wide range of catastrophic events. The flight to precious metals during periods of extreme adversity is a well-documented phenomenon. Thus, our findings suggest that investors may want to maintain a fixed or static allocation to precious metals while using Fed policy changes to adjust their exposure to other commodities.

Finally, although we share Buffett's viewpoint on the limited intrinsic value of gold, we believe it is important to note that there is considerable disparity in the intrinsic values of the alternative precious metals. Whereas gold is used to a very limited degree in industrial applications, silver, platinum, and palladium are used to a much greater extent. Thus, gold serves as a store of value largely because investors have confidence that it will continue to maintain its value. In contrast, the other precious metals retain value to a greater extent on the basis of their role as an input in the manufacturing process.

A Simple Rotation Strategy with Great Potential

A passive investment in precious metals appears to offer considerable benefits as a portfolio component. For investors who wish to pursue a more active approach, however, the performance of the other commodities appears promising. To offer a preliminary indication of the potential benefits of a rotation strategy guided by Fed policy, Table 4.7 reports the performance of three alternative

Table 4.7   Performance of Alternative Strategies: 1970–2013

	Average Annual Return and (Standard Deviation) by Monetary Environment			
Strategy	Full Period, %	Expansive, %	Indeterminate, %	Restrictive, %
Stocks only (S&P 500)	11.17 (15.48)	16.17 (16.48)	9.67 (15.26)	7.95 (14.69)
Commodities only (S&P GSCI Index)	10.80 (19.84)	−0.19 (20.33)	14.28 (17.54)	17.66 (21.51)
Rotation (stocks and commodities)	15.95 (18.56)	16.17 (16.48)	14.28 (17.54)	17.66 (21.51)

strategies: stocks only, commodities only, and a simple rotation strategy with the two asset classes. The simple rotation strategy applied over the period 1970–2013 involves the investor holding an S&P 500 index fund during expansive monetary periods and holding a broad commodity index (S&P GSCI) during indeterminate and restrictive periods.

Table 4.7 reports the performance of each strategy for the full period and in each of the monetary environments. The rotation strategy would have earned average annual returns of 16.17%, 14.28%, and 17.66%, respectively, over the three monetary environments. Furthermore, investors who used such a strategy would have maintained a fairly consistent level of risk (a standard deviation of approximately 19%) over that period. However, because of its lack of diversification—we aren't as confident in our abilities as Buffett is in his—across asset classes, we would not advocate such a strategy. We offer the strategy merely as an indication of the potential that exists in alternative allocation approaches. We encourage investors to use the evidence as a guide in determining which asset classes to over- or underweight when the Fed shifts its policy.

Consistent with our previous advice, we encourage both novice and professional investors to be skeptical of return patterns that are identified in any security market. We have seen our share of head-and-shoulders patterns and Hindenburg Omens and have been enticed by the allure of riding an Elliot wave to the stock market's pinnacle. Further, we have been told that the conference affiliation of the winner of the Super Bowl accurately predicts the direction of the stock market for the subsequent year. We believe it is always wise to ask: Is there an economic or underlying rationale to explain the return pattern? or in other words, Why would one expect the pattern that has been identified to continue in the future? We have seldom been convinced by the responses we have received to our queries. However, in this case, we believe we have a strong reply to such questions, and our response relies on the close association between Fed policy and inflationary pressures.

You may recall that one of the components of the Fed's dual mandate is inflation. Changes in Fed policy are routinely motivated by concern, or lack of concern, about inflationary pressures. The Fed generally initiates a restrictive policy to ward off what it sees as the potential for inflation rising above acceptable levels. Similarly, the Fed initiates an expansive policy when the economy is struggling and inflationary concerns are minimal. Thus, Fed policy and inflationary pressures are closely linked, as are commodity prices and inflationary pressures. After all, inflation represents an increase in prices of underlying goods and services, which would include commodity prices. For example, we all know that a substantial increase in gasoline prices will correspond with an increase in inflation.

Conclusion

In the earlier chapters we showed that a strong pattern exists between monetary conditions and the performance of the U.S. stock market; stocks prosper when monetary conditions are expansive and languish when conditions are restrictive. This pattern is shown to be both prominent and prevalent. Although the strength and consistency in the pattern are fascinating, the pattern is not particularly useful from an investment perspective. Knowing the conditions when stocks tend to excel versus when they generally fade is very interesting, but this knowledge is useful only if one is aware of an investment that follows a different pattern. The evidence presented in the earlier chapters left investors with a lingering question: What do I do with my portfolio when monetary conditions are constrained by the Fed? The evidence we report in this chapter indicates that alternative assets offer investors some nice alternatives. We confirm the widely acknowledged attraction of commodities; they offer reasonable returns yet have very low correlations with traditional securities. Commodities do indeed zig when the market zags. More important, however, we find that commodities have a unique relationship with monetary conditions: they prosper when monetary conditions are constrained and languish when conditions are expansive. Thus, commodities (and to a lesser extent equity REITs) offer a nice reprieve from the dismal performance of the majority of stocks in restrictive monetary conditions. Our evidence points toward a strategy that allocates greater weight to commodities and equity REITs when monetary conditions are constrained while maintaining a heavier allocation to stocks when conditions are expansive.

On the basis of our evidence, an optimal investment strategy would maintain a fixed allocation to precious metals over time while adjusting (based on Fed policy changes) the relative proportion of the portfolio directed toward equities, real estate, and commodities. When Fed policy is expansive, overweighting equities and mortgage REITs is prudent, whereas periods of restrictive or indeterminate policy promote a strategy that overweighs equity REITs and commodities.

In the following chapters we continue our search for securities that deviate from the typical relationship between monetary conditions and stocks. Our quest is to offer guidance that investors will find useful in implementing their portfolio strategies. We will report additional evidence regarding the question, What are the optimal investments to hold when Fed policy is expansive, restrictive, or indeterminate? Chapter 9 presents two broad investment strategies that rely on a number of different investment alternatives, each of which was investigated in an earlier chapter.

CHAPTER 5

SECTOR ROTATION AND MONETARY CONDITIONS

I skate to where the puck is going to be, not to where it has been.

Wayne Gretzky

One of the most popular trading strategies employed by active equity managers is a sector or industry rotation strategy. As the name implies, an investment manager implements a sector rotation strategy by shifting portfolio weights, that is, periodically rotating into some sectors while rotating out of others. The impetus behind sector rotation is the realization that not all sectors perform well at the same time. Implementing a rotation strategy involves moving into the best performing sectors and out of the worst performers; the tricky part, of course, is to make the move *before* a sector becomes the best or worst performer. When we question individuals about why they purchased a particular fund, the most common response we get is, "Because the fund has been doing so well recently." This response is consistent with representativeness bias, which notes that individuals believe recent experience will continue. Representativeness bias motivates investors to purchase or sell a stock on the basis of that stock's recent performance, which in many cases is the worst time to trade the stock. Consistent with representativeness bias, James O'Shaughnessy in *What Works on Wall Street* advocates a sector rotation strategy that is based on near-term past performance. O'Shaughnessy claims that investors are rewarded for buying the strongest and avoiding the weakest stocks because the strong tend to get stronger and the weak to get weaker.

Wall Street Journal columnist and financial guru Jason Zweig believes that performance chasing is what leads investors to underperform. Zweig says, "It is well-known that investors chase past performance, buying whatever has just made the most money for other people." He goes on to say that "to buy more of what has gone up, precisely because it has gone up, is to fall for the belief that stocks become safer as their prices rise. That is the same fallacy that led investors straight into disaster in 1929, 1972, 1999, 2007, and during every other market bubble in history."[1] The evidence is consistent with Zweig's contention that chasing performance is a losing strategy. Numerous researchers have documented that time-weighted mutual fund performance is better than dollar-weighted performance by approximately 1.5 percentage points of return per year.[2] Essentially this means that investors tend to commit money to mutual funds just before returns decline and withdraw funds just before the market rebounds. This is the antithesis of the time-tested motto "buy low and sell high."

We believe the key to applying a successful sector rotation strategy is to identify an indicator that signals a portfolio shift *before* the unusual stock performance. Basing one's stock trading strategy on past price moves is akin to the proverbial closing the barn door after the horse has bolted. Our purpose in this chapter is to determine whether shifts in Fed monetary policy serve as an indicator that can be used to identify rotation points before price moves and thus whether monetary indicators will allow one to skate to where the puck is going to be. More practically, we are interested in evaluating the success of a sector rotation strategy predicated on Fed monetary policy shifts. For more on sector rotation, see Box 5.1.

Box 5.1   Sector Rotation

Sector rotation is most often related to the business cycle and the observation (and belief) that some sectors of the economy systematically outperform other segments during certain portions of the business cycle. Fund managers attempt to align their sector allocations on the basis of the rate at which the economy is expanding (or contracting).

According to Sam Stovall, chief equity strategist of S&P Capital IQ's Equity Research Group and author of *Standard & Poor's Guide to Sector Investing*,[3] equity return correlations differ in relation to changes in the business cycle and certain sectors outperform during different phases of the business cycle. Early in an expansion the technology and transportation sectors outperform, and late in an expansion consumer staples and energy tend to do very well. Stovall found that in the early stage of a recession utilities generally perform well whereas late in a recession consumer cyclicals and financials tend to prosper.

Investors don't have to practice sector rotation on their own, as there are mutual funds with sector rotation as their objective. Two examples are the Sector Rotation Fund (NAVFX) and the Virtus AlphaSector Rotation Fund (PWBAX). Returns from these funds and the S&P 500 Index are provided in Table 5.1.

Returns to each of these funds were lower than the S&P 500 return in each of the four years from 2010 through 2013. Sector

(continued)

Table 5.1   **Annual Returns to Sector Funds and the S&P 500 Index in Percent**

	2010	*2011*	*2012*	*2013*
Sector Rotation Fund (NAVFX)	11.70	−1.64	9.69	16.11
Virtus Alpha Sector Rotation Fund (PWBAX)	13.85	1.58	12.61	31.84
S&P 500	15.06	2.11	16.00	32.39

rotation may sound like an easy procedure to implement, but making it pay off can be quite difficult. One of the primary reasons for the subpar performance of these actively managed funds is that they have both high turnover and high expense fees. Further, we would contend that fund managers tend to rely on business cycle variables as indicators, and these strategies have been shown to underperform strategies that are based on Fed policy shifts. In earlier research, Gerald R. Jensen and Jeffrey Mercer evaluated the merits of asset allocation based on the business cycle versus allocation based on monetary indicators as defined by Fed policy shifts. They found evidence supporting the superiority of using monetary indicators to guide asset allocation decisions.[4]

Our Sector Rotation Strategy

As we have noted, there is a strong economic basis that establishes a relationship between monetary conditions and stock market performance. After all, the Fed controls the money supply and money is the lifeblood of the economy. There are reasons to believe, however, that some sectors are more sensitive to changes in monetary conditions than others. Drawing an analogy to your own situation, assume that you are informed that you will have significantly more money to use next year; for example, you are told you are getting a significant pay raise. On the basis of this news, what are you likely to do with your forthcoming financial windfall? Are you likely to buy a new auto, a new wardrobe, a new house, a new computer, luxury gifts for friends and family members? We believe it is instructive to think of a Fed policy shift in a similar manner, that is, as a signal of the aggregate amount of money that market participants likely will have at their disposal.

In light of the Fed's control of the economy's purse strings, what sectors are likely to benefit most when the Fed relaxes those purse strings? Equivalently, when the Fed signals its intentions to decrease the availability of money, what sectors are likely to be harmed the most? We believe that sectors that are most reliant on discretionary spending have the most to gain from the Fed loosening the purse strings and the most to lose if the Fed chooses to tighten the purse strings. In particular, we would expect that retail firms and firms producing durable products, autos, and business equipment would be most affected by a shift in the monetary environment. In contrast, firms offering necessities such as energy, utilities, food, and healthcare will likely be affected to a lesser extent by changes in monetary conditions.

What Is the Historical Performance of the Different Economic Sectors?

To assess our theory, we evaluate the performance of 16 sector portfolios over the period 1966–2013. The return data for the sectors was obtained from Dartmouth College professor Kenneth French's website.[5] The 16 sectors are consumer goods, food, energy, retail, construction, apparel, mining, financials, transportation, business equipment, fabricated products, chemicals, autos, utilities, durable goods, and steel products. We begin by assessing the overall performance for the 16 sectors without reference to monetary conditions. The overall performance for the sectors, sorted by mean annual return from highest to lowest, is reported in Table 5.2.

Table 5.2   Sector Performance (Annualized Return and Standard Deviation): 1966–2013

Sector	Mean Return, %	Standard Deviation, %	Return-to-Risk Ratio
Consumer goods	13.19	16.79	0.79
Food	13.15	15.30	0.86
Energy	13.11	19.07	0.69
Retail	12.41	18.86	0.66
Construction	12.33	21.31	0.58
Apparel	12.27	21.91	0.56
Mining	12.18	26.11	0.47
Financials	12.07	19.43	0.62
Transportation	11.76	20.20	0.58
Business equipment	11.62	22.91	0.51
Fabricated products	11.57	18.85	0.61
Chemicals	11.38	19.87	0.57
Autos	10.43	22.32	0.47
Utilities	10.06	14.30	0.70
Durable goods	8.98	19.73	0.46
Steel products	8.97	26.15	0.34

The performance results reported in Table 5.2 indicate that for the 48-year period consumer goods offered both the highest annual return and one of the better return-to-risk ratios for investors. The three sectors with return-to-risk ratios of 0.70 or higher were consumer goods, food, and utilities. Consumer goods and food firms are commonly identified as consumer staples firms. These sectors include companies that produce basic products that are widely consumed on a regular basis. Popular consumer goods and food companies include firms such as Procter & Gamble, Clorox, Coca-Cola, and Campbell's Soup. Although these companies are not flashy, over the long run they have provided the highest returns while presenting the second and third lowest risk of all the sectors. In contrast, the auto, durable goods, and business equipment sectors reported rather poor return-to-risk ratios of 0.47, 0.46, and 0.51, respectively. These three sectors reported meager returns with relatively high risk levels. Some companies in these sectors are Ford, General Electric, La-Z-Boy, Apple, Microsoft, and Intel. Although mining offered an annualized return that was quite attractive at 12.18%, the sector had a higher than average standard deviation of returns, resulting in an unattractive return-to-risk ratio of 0.47. Clearly, the sector performance data in Table 5.2 indicate that investing in boring firms has been a winning strategy in the long run. See Box 5.2 for an explanation of why boring pays off.

Box 5.2　Boring Pays Off

We can look to behavioral finance for an explanation of why a strategy of investing in boring companies is a winning one. Dr. Terrance Odean, a finance professor at the University of California at Berkeley,

(continued)

---

explained in a *Wall Street Journal* article that he believes this phenomenon "has to do with the natural tendency to be drawn to what is most exciting."[6] Odean contends that investors are not systematic in the way they determine which stocks to purchase. Essentially, investors buy stocks that capture their imagination and have some sort of sexy story behind them. These types of firms are generally the ones that are profiled in the media, not the kinds of firms that produce soup and dishwashing detergent.

Warren Buffett has made a fortune largely by investing in simple companies that produce or sell relatively mundane products. He stays away from companies that the person on the street doesn't understand. Two examples of boring companies that have been extremely profitable for Buffett are Coca-Cola and Gillette. He has referred to Coca-Cola as the best brand in the world, citing the fact that there are actually Coca-Cola stores that sell branded merchandise—in effect, people are willing to pay to advertise the brand. With Gillette, a company that was acquired by Procter & Gamble, he has summed up his investment by saying, "It's pleasant to go to bed every night knowing there are 2.5 billion males in the world who have to shave in the morning."[7]

Buffett has famously stayed clear of technology companies and "new economy" stocks. In the 1990s, the Oracle of Omaha's aversion to trendy investments was routinely ridiculed by some pundits, so much so that less than two months before the dot-com crash in March 2000, *Barron's* ran a cover story that chastised Buffett for not adapting his investment style to the times.[8] Betting against Buffett may be the ultimate losing investment proposition. His investment style has earned his investors billions of dollars, and that is anything but boring.

Monetary Conditions and Sector Performance

Before we dismiss the poor performance sectors reported in Table 5.2 as unworthy of investment, it is important to remember that even poorly performing securities offer a portfolio benefit if they have unique performance patterns. As we noted previously, there are strong reasons to believe that some sectors will respond to changes in the monetary environment with more or less vigor than others. Specifically, sectors that rely more directly on discretionary spending (e.g., durable goods, autos, retail, and apparel) are likely to be more strongly influenced than are sectors such as food, utilities, consumer goods, and energy. To investigate this premise, Table 5.3 reports the performance of the 16 sectors relative to the three monetary environments.

The returns reported in Table 5.3 show considerable diversity across the three monetary environments.[9] Retail, apparel, and autos show performance that is far superior to that of the other sectors during expansive monetary environments; however, these three sectors report some of the lowest returns in restrictive environments. Thus, these three sectors would have been great portfolio components during expansive monetary periods but would have made dreadful portfolio additions when conditions were restrictive. For example, in December 2002, the Fed shifted from applying a restrictive monetary policy to applying an expansive policy. Over the subsequent 12 months, an investor who purchased the retail index at the time of the policy shift would have earned a return of 26.90%. In contrast, in July 2004, the Fed shifted its monetary policy from an expansive policy to a restrictive policy; over the next 12 months an investor holding the retail index would have lost 17.99%

Since the retail, apparel, and autos sectors have a very strong reliance on the level of discretionary spending, the observed strong

Table 5.3   Sector Performance (Annualized Returns) and Monetary Conditions: 1966–2013

	Mean Annual Return Across Monetary Environment, %		
Sector	Expansive	Indeterminate	Restrictive
Consumer goods	16.52	14.95	8.36
Food	18.61	14.39	7.00
Energy	12.22	15.35	11.47
Retail	27.03	10.39	1.68
Construction	22.63	10.22	5.50
Apparel	28.45	8.26	2.31
Mining	21.76	13.62	2.19
Financials	14.95	14.55	6.88
Transportation	22.38	7.56	6.89
Business equipment	19.14	10.71	5.96
Fabricated products	20.99	8.42	6.65
Chemicals	19.43	12.39	3.19
Autos	25.42	9.03	−1.28
Utilities	9.36	12.76	7.77
Durable goods	20.87	7.58	−0.02
Steel products	14.65	6.18	6.93

return patterns are consistent with our previously explained economic reasoning. According to our reasoning, a shift in Fed policy that signals a future change in fund availability affects firms in these sectors because discretionary funds are expected to become more or less accessible. A signal of tighter future funding forces individuals to reduce spending on nonessential goods and services, whereas a signal of easier money motivates individuals to spend more on discretionary items. The strong return patterns for retail, autos, durable goods, and apparel offer support for the view that the return patterns are systematic rather than merely a random observation.

The sectors with the most consistent performance across the monetary environments are energy, utilities, food, financials, and consumer goods. Since these five sectors are frequently identified as being composed of firms that provide necessities, this result also fits nicely with our economic rationale. The majority of spending for the products and services offered by firms in these sectors is generally considered nondiscretionary. Fed policy shifts that signal changes in fund availability are likely to have a relatively muted impact on the firms in these sectors because of the nondiscretionary nature of their receipts.

Cyclical and Defensive Sectors

The 16 sectors can also be grouped into two broader classifications: cyclical and defensive firms. *Cyclical firms* are defined as firms whose profits are strongly correlated with the strength of the overall economy. These firms tend to perform well when the economy is thriving. Sectors such as autos, construction, manufacturing, and technology are considered cyclical in nature. When the economy is thriving, consumers purchase more new cars, build more houses, and purchase more computers than they do when the economy is sputtering. In contrast, *defensive firms* are firms whose performance is largely independent of the business cycle. Food and beverages, household and personal care products, healthcare, and utilities are noncyclical or defensive in nature. People need to eat, brush their teeth, go to the doctor, and heat their homes whether the economy is strong or weak. That doesn't mean individuals won't change their spending behavior. It is common for people to alter spending patterns within a sector; for instance, with a weaker economy they may shift from steak to hamburger or from shopping at Macy's to shopping at Walmart. Consequently, not all firms that produce or sell nondiscretionary products would be considered defensive to the same extent.

What Is Beta?

To arrange the sectors on a continuum from cyclical to defensive, we calculate each sector's sensitivity to market conditions (i.e., the beta for each sector). Beta is a statistical measure of risk; it is the appropriate risk measure when one is considering a security in the context of the market as a whole. Intuitively, beta measures an asset's risk relative to that of a broad market index, such as the S&P 500. A beta of 1 indicates that the security moves roughly the same amount and in the same direction as the market. That is, if the market moves up 1%, stocks with a beta of 1 will on average advance by 1%. An instructive way to view beta is as a magnification factor relative to the market. On average, securities with betas greater than 1 experience price moves that are magnified relative to the market; they move up more when the market advances and down more when the market declines. In contrast, securities with betas less than 1 experience relative price moves that are magnified by a factor less than 1 compared with the market. That is, on average, their price moves are dampened relative to the market's swings. Betas are commonly computed for portfolios and sectors as well as for individual securities. For more on beta, see Box 5.3.

Box 5.3 Beta as a Measure of Risk

Stanford University professor Dr. William F. Sharpe developed the capital asset pricing model (CAPM) in the early 1960s, and it revolutionized financial theory and practice. The key insight in the model is that the proper way to measure the risk of an individual security is not by the volatility of its returns but by how much risk it adds to an already diversified portfolio. This makes sense because most individuals hold at least somewhat diversified portfolios. The model formalizes the risk and return trade-off that is central to investment theory. Specifically, it posits that over the long run, on average, higher-risk securities (as measured by beta) should earn higher returns. The model has been used throughout the investment management industry for years and is considered standard fare in undergraduate and graduate business schools around the world. For his work, Sharpe was awarded a Nobel Prize in economics in 1990.

The good news is that investors don't need to calculate security betas. Many financial websites compute betas for you, and you can simply look them up. Some of the most popular websites with beta calculations are Yahoo Finance (http://finance.yahoo.com/), Google Finance (https://www.google.com/finance), Reuters (http://www.reuters.com/finance/stocks), and MSN Money (http://money.msn.com/stocks/). The betas reported by different services may vary somewhat, as they are calculated over different time periods and against different market indexes.

The following is a listing of betas for 10 of the largest capitalization stocks:

Berkshire Hathaway	0.53
Boeing	1.28

(continued)

Exxon Mobil	0.71
General Electric	1.75
IBM	0.62
Intel	1.89
Microsoft	0.90
3M	1.16
Walmart	0.31
Walt Disney	1.31

Source: MSN Finance as of February 25, 2014.

How Does Beta Relate to Cyclical and Defensive Firms?

Sectors with relatively high betas are generally classified as cyclical sectors; the price moves for these sectors have historically been magnified relative to the market's moves. In contrast, sectors with relatively low betas generally experience price moves that are dampened relative to the market's moves; such sectors are classified as defensive. The betas for the 16 sectors are illustrated in Figure 5.1.

The information in Figure 5.1 illustrates the relative sensitivities of the 16 sectors to the general stock market. The betas range from a low of 0.56 for the utility sector to a high of 1.30 for the steel products sector. With relatively low betas, defensive sectors display below-average reactions in response to market moves. Utilities, for example, on average move only about half as much as the average stock in response to a market move. Thus, whether the market experiences a strong upward or downward move, the reaction by the utility sector is generally in the same direction as the market move but is significantly smaller.

Figure 5.1 Betas for 16 Sectors

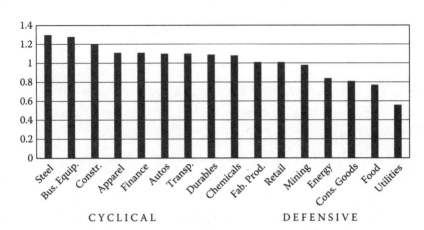

The highest betas of the cyclical sectors are 1.30 for the steel products sector and 1.28 for the business equipment sector. For the cyclical sectors each sector's price reaction to a market move is magnified to some degree. For example, on average, the steel products and business equipment sectors display price moves that are consistent with the general market move but about 1.3 times as pronounced.

Applying a Simple Sector Rotation Strategy

To explain the relevance of our discussion of discretionary spending, beta, and defensive versus cyclical sectors, we provide a simple trading rule. An investor could apply a simple rotation strategy by using the return patterns identified in Table 5.3 to rotate across sectors. For example, a logical and simple application would be to hold the top-performing sectors during each of the respective monetary environments. To illustrate this simple rotation strategy, we report the performance for five alternative rotation strategies that are based on allocating across the top five through top nine performing sectors. We don't consider rotation strategies with fewer than five sectors because of the somewhat limited diversification such strategies would entail. Investors who want to be relatively aggressive will choose fewer sectors, and those who want to be more conservative will choose more sectors. For example, relatively aggressive investors would choose the top five performing sectors in each monetary environment (from Table 5.3) and allocate 20% to each of those sectors.

In general, each rotation strategy is heavily weighted toward cyclical stocks during expansive periods and toward defensive stocks when monetary conditions are restrictive. For example, during expansive periods, the top five sector rotation holds equal weights of apparel, autos, retail, construction, and transportation. This portfolio has a beta of 1.1, which is the average of the betas of the five sectors. In contrast, during restrictive periods, the top five sector portfolio consists of equal weights of energy, consumer goods, utilities, food, and steel products and has a beta of 0.86. Finally, as you might expect, the portfolio's composition during indeterminate periods shows more diversity across defensive and cyclical categories as it holds energy, food, mining, consumer goods, and financials and has a beta of 0.90.

An alternative rotation strategy can be built around beta. In particular, the strategy would hold sectors with the highest betas (most cyclical sectors) during expansive periods and hold sectors with the lowest betas (most defensive sectors) during restrictive periods. The strategy would hold sectors with moderate betas during indeterminate monetary conditions. This approach would produce comparable results; however, evidence produced by the authors indicates that they would be somewhat inferior.[10] The crucial factor for determining sector performance is based on the level of discretionary spending. For example, the two sectors that perform best during expansive conditions are apparel and retail. Although these sectors are not the most cyclical (they don't have the highest betas), they are extremely reliant on discretionary spending. The relatively weak performance of the steel products and financials sectors during expansive environments further supports this view. These two sectors are strongly cyclical (they have high betas), yet their relatively weak performance during expansive conditions is consistent with their relative lack of reliance on discretionary spending.

Sector Rotation or Buy and Hold?

The performance for the five alternative rotation strategies is reported in Table 5.4. For comparison purposes, Table 5.4 also shows the performance of a buy-and-hold approach, which is frequently labeled as a "do nothing" strategy. We assume that the buy-and-hold strategy holds equal weights of the 16 sectors across the entire time span 1966–2013.

The performance reported in Table 5.4 indicates that each of the rotation strategies produced a higher return than did the

Table 5.4 Performance of Rotation Strategy Versus Buy and Hold

Strategy	Annualized Return, %	Standard Deviation, %	Return-to-Risk Ratio
Rotation (top 5)	15.62	16.50	0.95
Rotation (top 6)	15.26	16.20	0.94
Rotation (top 7)	14.95	16.27	0.92
Rotation (top 8)	14.63	16.45	0.89
Rotation (top 9)	14.29	16.41	0.87
Buy and hold	11.59	16.36	0.71

buy-and-hold approach, with the best performance produced by the top five sector rotation strategy. This strategy produced an average annual return that was over 4% higher than the buy-and-hold strategy, yet added only 0.14% in risk.

At this point, two major caveats should be noted about the data used in our sector performance investigation. First, the sector returns obtained from the Kenneth French website are derived by value-weighting the firms within each sector. As we noted in Chapter 2, value-weighting diminishes the role of small firms relative to large firms. Our earlier evidence indicates that relative to large firms, small firms have substantially stronger patterns across the monetary environments. Therefore, the sector performance results reported in this chapter understate what could have been obtained by an investor who tilted his or her portfolio toward smaller stocks when applying the rotation strategy. To illustrate the potential gain from relying on equal-weighted returns rather than value-weighted returns, we recalculate the rotation strategy performance. Using the top five rotation strategy as our example, equal-weighting the firms within each sector increases the portfolio return from 15.62% to 17.49%, a gain of nearly 2% per year.

Second, the simple rotation strategy ignores some obvious unexploited opportunities that may be available for more adventurous investors who wish to target individual stocks. For example, the strategy calls for overweighting stocks that are more sensitive to discretionary spending when monetary conditions are expansive, and this means an investor following the strategy would overweight the retail sector. The retail sector, however, includes firms as diverse as Walmart, Nordstrom, and Zale Corporation. In May 2014, Yahoo Finance reported the betas for these three at 0.38, 1.04, and 2.33, respectively, which would categorize Walmart as defensive, Zale as cyclical, and Nordstrom as a cyclical lean. Furthermore, one would clearly identify Zale's and Nordstrom's performances as being more sensitive to the level of discretionary spending than Walmart's.

With these caveats noted, Figure 5.2 shows the wealth effect associated with the simple rotation strategy versus the buy-and-hold strategy. We use the top five rotation for illustrative purposes. Although the return difference between the rotation and benchmark strategies (as reported in Table 5.4) is fairly spectacular at 4.03%, the difference in wealth accumulation is truly astounding. An investor's wealth would have grown from $10,000 to $1.33 million if the investor had followed the passive benchmark strategy of holding all 16 sectors over the 1966–2013 period. In stark contrast, an

Figure 5.2 Growth of $10,000 in Rotation Strategy vs. Buy and Hold Strategy: 1966–2013

Note: The figure applies a logarithmic scale to the vertical axis.

investor's $10,000 investment in the simple rotation strategy would have grown to a remarkable $9.04 million. The return difference of 4.03% (15.62% – 11.59%) produced a difference in accumulated wealth of $7.71 million. Remarkably, the rotation strategy produced 5.8 times the wealth of the buy-and-hold approach. This incredible wealth difference makes it apparent why investment managers scratch and claw for every bit of investment return they can produce. See Box 5.4 for further discussion of the amazing properties of wealth growth.

Box 5.4   Compound Interest: The Eighth Wonder of the World

The iconic physicist Albert Einstein is claimed to have once identified the power of compound interest as "the most powerful force in the universe." Numerous books espouse the practical implications that this most powerful force has for wealth building. Princeton University professor Burton Malkiel in *The Random Walk Guide to Investing* notes, "The amount of capital you start with is not nearly as important as getting started early." Malkiel argues, "Procrastination is the natural assassin of opportunity. Every year you put off investing makes your ultimate retirement goals more difficult to achieve."[11]

Over the last 70 years, the S&P 500 has averaged a geometric monthly return of 0.9054% and U.S. Treasury bonds have averaged a geometric monthly return of 0.4471%.[12] We used these average returns in compiling the figures reported in Table 5.5, which shows wealth accumulation at age 60 for an investor who starts investing at various ages. We assume an investment of $100 per month in stocks (or bonds) from the starting age to age 60.

Table 5.5 Growth of $100 per Month Security Investments

	Accumulated Wealth at Age 60 from	
Starting Age	Stock Investment	Bond Investment
20	$824,703	$167,982
30	$272,320	$89,079
40	$85,032	$42,882
50	$21,530	$15,835

As you can see, it pays to start investing early. If an investor starts putting money to work in the stock market at age 20 instead of age 30, she will accumulate over $552,000 more. Remarkably, the additional $552,000 is created by investing only $12,000 (120 × $100) more in the market. The extra 10 years of investing—and more important the compounding of returns—nets the investor terminal wealth that is more than three times what is achieved by starting 10 years later. This illustrates the investment truism "Time in the market is more important than timing the market." As Morgan Housel, investment columnist for the Motley Fool, has said, "How long you stay invested for will likely be the single most important factor determining how well you do at investing."

It is also interesting to note that the power of compounding magnifies the difference in monthly returns between bonds and stocks. The monthly stock return is almost exactly double the monthly bond return. Yet for an investor who starts at age 20, the terminal wealth compiled from a stock investment is nearly five times the amount realized from an investment in bonds.

The Performance of Precious Metal Mining Stocks

As we noted in Chapter 4, a 2011 Gallup poll found that 34% of Americans viewed gold as the best long-term investment. Because of the widely documented infatuation with gold, in this section we present a thorough evaluation of the performance of gold miners relative to other precious metal mining firms. You may remember that in the material on alternative assets (Chapter 4) we evaluated the performance of gold and precious metals relative to monetary conditions, and so you may be wondering why we are repeating that analysis. The findings in Chapter 4 were based on the performance of precious metals futures contracts, whereas we now explore the performance of a precious metals position using the stocks of both gold mining and precious metal mining companies. The findings in Chapter 4 showed that using Fed policy shifts to design a fluctuating/dynamic allocation to precious metals offered comparable performance to a fixed/static investment in precious metal futures. We now investigate whether this conclusion extends to an investment in precious metal mining firms.

There is a potential major advantage of investing in the stock of a precious metal mining company versus investing in a precious metal futures contract. In particular, a futures contract investment is profitable only if the price of the underlying precious metal appreciates. In contrast, an investor in the stock of a precious metal mining company can gain even without a rise in precious metal prices. Mining companies pay dividends from the profits they generate from their mining operations. Therefore, even if precious metal prices do not appreciate, an investment in a precious metal miner may pay off for an investor. Over the years, precious metal mining companies have become extremely efficient in extracting their desired ore, and thus they have paid significant dividends to their shareholders even during periods when precious metal prices languished.

Table 5.6 reports performance data for four alternative precious metal indexes. The first two indexes (common stock indexes) are composed of the common stocks of precious metal mining companies. In light of the stature that gold has in the investment arena, the first index (gold miners index) includes stocks of firms that focus on gold extraction. The second index (precious metal miners) is more diversified and includes precious metal miners of all varieties (gold, silver, platinum, and palladium). It should be noted that precious metal mining firms frequently focus on particular precious metals; however, in their mining operations they extract a variety of different metals. For comparison purposes, we also include two indexes that are composed of futures contracts on precious metals. The performance of the two commodity futures indexes is repeated from Table 4.5.

The performance data in Table 5.6 clearly illustrate that there are vast differences in the return characteristics of the stock-based versus futures-based indexes. Relative to the futures-based indexes,

Table 5.6 Performance of Precious Metal Investments

Precious Metal Index	Mean Annual Return, %	Standard Deviation, %	Correlation with Stocks	Bonds
Common stock indexes				
Gold miners	13.48	33.29	0.23	0.06
Precious metal miners	17.79	37.50	0.38	−0.03
Commodity futures				
Gold futures	7.12	19.71	0.02	0.04
Precious metal futures	9.21	23.03	0.05	−0.01

Note: Data availability dictated that we measure returns from 1973 through 2013 for the two common stock indexes and the precious metal futures index. Return data for the gold futures index started in 1978.

the stock-based indexes produced much higher returns, which is consistent with the value creation associated with metal mining. As we noted above, taking an ownership interest in a mining company (buying common stock) allows an investor to capture gains from two fundamental sources: increases in precious metal prices and mining profits. In contrast, gains in futures contracts are based only on the price appreciation component. The difference in returns is astounding as the stock-based indexes return approximately 1.9 times more than the futures-based indexes.

Although the difference in returns favors the stock-based indexes, the futures-based indexes have the upper hand with respect to risk. The stock-based indexes are extremely volatile as indicated by their standard deviations of 33.3% and 37.5% versus their futures-based counterparts, which have standard deviations of 19.7% and 23.0%. As they say, there are no free lunches in the financial markets. To gain the higher returns of the stock-based precious metal position, an investor would have had to accept the higher risk.

The correlation measures provide additional support in favor of the futures-based exposure. In particular, the much lower correlation that the futures-based indexes have with stocks implies that they offer superior diversification potential. Remember that our discussion in Chapter 4 indicated that one of the primary attractions of precious metals is their ability to serve as portfolio insurance. With a correlation near zero, a poor outcome in the stock market has a 50% chance of being offset by a good outcome in precious metal prices (i.e., those prices potentially provide a "silver" lining). These odds are diminished considerably for investors who achieve precious metal exposure by purchasing common stock of precious metal miners. The difference in correlations supports the claim that a futures-based exposure offers a more direct exposure to precious metal prices. In contrast, a stock-based investment offers more direct exposure to the general stock market and tracks overall stock returns more closely. Box 5.5 provides more practical information about the alternative approaches to an exposure to precious metals.

Box 5.5   Are You a Metal Fan?

When referring to metal here, we aren't talking about heavy metal bands such as Metallica, Black Sabbath, and Iron Maiden but about precious metals such as gold, silver, platinum, and palladium. There are three fundamentally different approaches that investors can use to attain an exposure in precious metals: a direct, an indirect, and an artificial direct approach. We use gold as the metal of choice in delineating the three approaches:

- *Direct exposure* by purchasing gold bullion. This is the worst choice for most investors, as purchasing gold bullion often involves hidden transactions costs as well as additional storage and insurance costs.
- *Artificial direct exposure* by entering a futures position in gold with T-bills posted as collateral. This allows investors to control large positions in gold with small initial commitments of capital, that is, high leverage. However, leverage is a double-edged sword and can lead to significant gains as well as losses over relatively short periods. This is not a good choice for most individual investors, as it requires active management and continuous monitoring of futures contracts with different maturities.
- *Indirect exposure* by purchasing stock in a gold mining firm [e.g., Barrick Gold Corporation (ABX)]. This is not a pure play

(*continued*)

---

on the metal as it exposes the investor to the operating risks of the company. Specifically, poor management decisions may lead to a decline in the price of the gold mining firm even during periods of rising gold prices. This method requires specific expertise in analyzing mining companies.

Investors who want to take a position in gold should not despair. There are exchange-traded funds that provide a means to attain a diversified position in any of the three methods delineated above:

- Gold ETFs backed by physical gold include SPDR Gold Shares (GLD) and iShares COMEX Gold Trust (IAU). The investor gets direct exposure to physical gold but doesn't have to worry about taking delivery of the physical gold, storing it, and insuring it.
- ETFs backed by gold futures contracts include PowerShares DB Gold Fund (DGL) and UBS E-TRACS CMCI Gold Total Return (UBG). The investor obtains an artificial direct exposure to gold but doesn't have to concern himself or herself with actively buying and selling individual gold futures contracts because professional managers perform that function.
- ETFs of gold mining companies include Market Vectors Gold Miners ETF (GDX) and Global X Pure Gold Miners ETF (GGGG). This allows investors to obtain diversified positions across many gold mining companies, lowering the risk that an idiosyncratic event will befall a particular gold mining stock.

The performance of these three different categories of ETFs can vary dramatically, as the annual returns reported in Table 5.7 indicate.

Table 5.7   Annual Returns to Alternative Gold Exposures: 2010–2013

	2010, %	2011, %	2012, %	2013, %
Physical gold (New York spot price)	29.68	10.19	6.95	−28.04
Physical gold ETFs				
SPDR Gold Shares (GLD)	29.27	9.57	6.60	−28.33
iShares COMEX Gold Trust (IAU)	29.46	9.57	6.89	−28.25
ETFs backed by gold futures				
PowerShares DB Gold Fund (DGL)	27.89	8.55	5.33	−29.63
UBS E-TRACS CMCI Gold Total Return (UBG)	28.05	9.23	6.13	−29.09
ETFs of gold mining companies				
Market Vectors Gold Miners (GDX)	33.91	−16.10	−8.88	−54.02
Global X Pure Gold Miners (GGGG)	NA	NA	−14.41	−52.45

Note: GGGG started trading in March 2011.

In general, investors know that their success with stock investing depends on the particular stocks they choose; after all, stocks are a heterogeneous asset class. However, if you invest in a standardized asset such as gold, how much difference can the structure of the investment make? The returns reported in Table 5.7 provide the answer to this question: a tremendous difference.

The ETFs backed by physical gold and gold futures tracked the spot price of gold pretty closely. There was relatively little difference within or between these two types of ETFs; however, the physical gold ETFs consistently outperformed the futures-based ETFs. In contrast, there was a greater dispersion of returns between the two gold mining ETFs, and more surprisingly, the gold mining ETFs

(continued)

performed dramatically differently than did the other two types of investments.

It should be noted that the returns to all six of these ETFs outperformed the S&P 500 in 2010 and 2011, when the S&P 500 returned 15.1% and 2.1%, respectively. However, this relationship reversed in 2012 and 2013, when the S&P 500 posted gains of 16% and 32.4%, respectively. In 2013, gold investors experienced a particularly negative result as they lost more than 28% and under-performed the market by more than 60%. Who said gold is a great store of value?

Precious Metal Mining Stocks and Monetary Conditions

Table 5.8 reports the average annual returns and standard deviations for the four precious metal indexes for each of the three monetary environments.

The data in Table 5.8 indicate that gold mining firms exhibited return patterns that were closely aligned with the general stock market. Specifically, the gold miner index advanced dramatically when monetary conditions were expansive (return = 21.8%) but languished when conditions were restrictive (return = 2.1%). In contrast, the precious metal miners index produced a very strong return that was relatively invariant to monetary conditions.

Relative to the gold miner index, the two futures-based indexes displayed less variation across monetary conditions and also far less volatility within each environment. However, the mean return for the futures-based indexes was far lower than that of the precious metal

Table 5.8 Precious Metal Investment Performance by Monetary Environment: 1993–2013

	Mean Annual Return (Standard Deviation)		
	by Monetary Environment, %		
Precious Metals Indexes	*Expansive*	*Indeterminate*	*Restrictive*
Common stock indexes			
Gold miners	21.80	16.55	2.14
	(35.71)	(33.65)	(30.29)
Precious metal miners	19.83	20.43	13.00
	(42.27)	(35.65)	(34.59)
Commodity futures			
Gold futures	7.85	8.61	4.86
	(18.98)	(17.62)	(22.43)
Precious metal futures	7.19	13.49	6.58
	(19.41)	(23.52)	(25.66)

Note: Data availability dictated that we measure returns from 1973 through 2013 for the two common stock indexes and the precious metal futures index. Return data for the gold futures index started in 1978.

miner index in each of the three environments. Overall, the evidence indicates that each of the indexes has its advantages and disadvantages. However, for the record, we are inclined to achieve our precious metal exposure by investing in precious metal miners. Even though precious metal miners entail more volatility, the vastly higher returns and their consistency of performance across monetary periods are very appealing. As in our earlier discussions, we are not advocating precious metals or for that matter any asset class as a stand-alone investment. Rather, we advocate adding a precious metal exposure to a well-diversified portfolio of assets. Furthermore, it would appear that maintaining a consistent and significant precious metal exposure across all monetary environments is the most appropriate allocation approach.

I'm sure you have seen ads advocating the tremendous advantage associated with adding a precious metals exposure to your portfolio.

One ad even touts the advantage of gold by noting that the price of gold has never gone to zero (Is that really something to broadcast?). In any case, if you are going to assume a position in gold, this discussion should give you cause to think about the form of your position.

Implementing a Sector Rotation Strategy

Historically, it would have been extremely costly for an investor to construct portfolios to match the performance of different sectors. Fortunately, the creation of sector mutual funds and sector ETFs has made it easy for investors to replicate the performance of specific industry sectors. In addition, these funds have greatly facilitated the application of sector rotation strategies. What was once a strategy that was strictly the purview of large institutions and high-net-worth investors is now available to investors with portfolios of more modest size. Table 5.9 reports a sampling of the sector mutual funds and ETFs that are now readily available to investors.

Table 5.9   Sector Mutual Funds and ETFs

Sector	Mutual Fund	Exchange-Traded Fund
Autos	Fidelity Select Automotive Portfolio (FSAVX)	First Trust NASDAQ Global Auto (CARZ)
Construction	Fidelity Select Construction & Housing (FSHOX)	PowerShares Dynamic Build & Construction (PKB)
Consumer cyclicals and retail	Alpine Global Consumer Growth (AWCGX)	SPDR S&P Retail (XRT)
Consumer staples	Vanguard Consumer Staples (VCSAX)	Consumer Staples Select Sector SPDR (XLP)

Sector	Mutual Fund	Exchange-Traded Fund
Energy	Waddell & Reed Advisor Energy (WEGAX)	Energy Select Sector SPDR (XLE)
Financials	John Hancock Financial Industries (FIDAX)	PowerShares Financial Preferred (PGF)
Healthcare	T. Rowe Price Health Sciences (PRHSX)	Vanguard Health Care (VHT)
Natural resources	Thrivent Natural Resources (TREFX)	iShares Global Materials (MXI)
Industrials	Putnam Global Industrial (PGIAX)	Vanguard Industrials (VIS)
Technology	Dreyfus Technology Growth (DTGRX)	iShares US Technology (IYW)
Telecom services	Fidelity Select Telecommunications (FSTCX)	Vanguard Telecommunication Services (VOX)
Transportation	Fidelity Select Transportation (FSRFX)	iShares Transportation Average (IYT)
Utilities	Franklin Utilities (FKUTX)	Utilities Select Sector SPDR (XLU)
Gold (mining stocks)	Fidelity Select Gold (FSAGX)	Market Vectors Gold Miners (GDX)
Precious metal (mining stocks)	Vanguard Precious Metals and Mining (VGPMX)	PowerShares DB Precious Metals (DBP)

On the basis of the performance data reported in Table 5.3, an investor could easily design a rotation strategy by utilizing the mutual funds and ETFs reported in Table 5.9. Specifically, the performance data suggest that a prudent strategy would be to over-weight autos, construction, consumer cyclicals, industrials, technology, and transportation when monetary conditions are expansive.

In other words, when the Fed shifts to an easy policy (decreases policy rates), investors would be wise to increase their allocation to these six sectors, which tend to be very reliant on the level of discretionary spending. In contrast, when conditions are restrictive, the strategy overweights consumer staples, energy, healthcare, natural resources, telecom services, utilities, and precious metal mining companies. That is, when the Fed shifts to a restrictive policy (increases policy rates) investors should increase their allocation to these seven sectors, which tend to be relatively invariant to the level of discretionary spending. This type of rotation strategy offers considerable diversification across sectors in each monetary environment. Furthermore, since mutual funds and ETFs hold numerous firms within each sector, investors are also provided good diversification within sectors.

Conclusion

In this chapter we evaluated the performance of various economic sectors relative to the three monetary environments. Our findings show that sectors that rely most heavily on discretionary spending (e.g., autos, durables, business equipment, retail, and construction) prosper when monetary conditions are expansive and languish when monetary conditions are restrictive. In contrast, we show that sectors that are less sensitive to disposable income levels (e.g., consumer goods, food, utilities, and energy) perform fairly well whether monetary conditions are expansive, indeterminate, or restrictive. To provide a preliminary perspective on the ramifications of these return patterns, we offered a look at a simple rotation strategy that is guided by shifts in Fed policy.

Our very simple rotation strategy produced returns that exceeded the benchmark by over 4% per year while keeping risk very comparable to that of the benchmark. You may feel the 4% return premium does not represent huge compensation for the extra hassle and the higher transactions costs associated with using monetary conditions to execute a rotation strategy. We are sympathetic to that opinion, but we want to advise you that this was only our preliminary investment strategy offering. There is much more to follow, and it gets even better. Thus, the 4% annual gain should be viewed as simply an appetizer for the main course, which is yet to come.

CHAPTER 6

INTERNATIONAL STOCKS

> The tallest building in the world is now in Dubai,
> the biggest factory in the world is in China, the largest
> oil refinery is in India, the largest investment fund in
> the world is in Abu Dhabi, the largest Ferris wheel
> in the world is in Singapore.
>
> *Fareed Zakaria,*
> *journalist and author*

Although most investors recognize the benefits of global diversification, they concentrate their holdings in their domestic markets. This tendency is known as home country bias. A 2013 Franklin
Templeton Global Investor Sentiment Survey showed that although
65% of the world's investments (as measured by market capitalization) are outside the United States, 39% of U.S. investors had all their
assets in the United States. A 2013 Fidelity study showed that U.S.
investors keep about 72% of their investments in their home market. However, as the economy has become more globalized, investors have increasingly looked beyond their countries' borders when
searching for stock investments.

Consistent with the emphasis of these statistics, the most common question posed about foreign investing is: How much should I invest in foreign markets? However, we believe the most important questions is: When should I increase my allocation to foreign markets, and which foreign markets should I target? As we have shown in the earlier chapters, there is a relative shortage of securities that perform well when Fed policy is restrictive. Therefore, a tempting strategy is to adopt a policy of rotating out of U.S. stocks and into foreign stocks whenever the Fed adopts a restrictive monetary policy. However, as we will show in this chapter, such a simple approach would be a disaster. Instead, by monitoring Fed policy decisions you can gain valuable information that will allow you to effectively address which markets to target and when.

In the next section we start by presenting information that will allow you to assess the benefits of a static exposure to foreign equities. We follow that presentation with information about the degree to which you can enhance your foreign market exposure by monitoring Fed monetary policy and using Fed shifts to implement a dynamic allocation strategy.

International Markets: Developed, Emerging, and Frontier

When performing a global examination of stocks, investment analysts routinely separate markets into three broad categories: developed, emerging, and frontier. Developed markets consist of countries that have the largest and most advanced economies and also tend to have the most sophisticated financial systems. In general, emerging markets have less developed economies and financial systems than do developed markets. Emerging markets are followed in level of development by frontier markets, which generally have even smaller markets with less sophistication. Frontier markets are commonly considered a subcategory of emerging markets. Table 6.1 reports the countries included in each of the three broad classifications according to MSCI as of November 2013.

In 1969, the MSCI World Index was created, and it contained 16 countries. Today, the MSCI World Index is composed of the 23 developed markets identified in Table 6.1. A popular variation of the developed market index is the MSCI EAFE Index, which excludes the two North American developed markets (Canada and the United States). EAFE is an acronym for Europe, Australasia, and the Far East. The EAFE Index is commonly used by U.S. investors as a proxy for the foreign developed market.

The first four countries listed under "Emerging Markets" are frequently identified by their acronym, BRIC. The BRIC countries are considered by many investors to be the most prominent emerging

Table 6.1 Developed, Emerging, and Frontier Markets

Developed Markets	Emerging Markets	Frontier Markets
Australia, Austria, Belgium, Canada, Denmark, Finland, France, Germany, Hong Kong, Ireland, Israel, Italy, Japan, Netherlands, New Zealand, Norway, Portugal, Singapore, Spain, Sweden, Switzerland, United Kingdom, United States	*Brazil, Russia, India, China, Egypt, Indonesia, Mexico, Philippines, Poland, South Africa, South Korea, Turkey,* Chile, Colombia, Czech Republic, Greece, Hungary, Malaysia, Peru, Taiwan, Thailand	Argentina, Bahrain, Bangladesh, Bulgaria, Croatia, Estonia, Jordan, Kazakhstan, Kenya, Kuwait, Lebanon, Lithuania, Mauritius, Morocco, Nigeria, Oman, Pakistan, Romania, Serbia, Slovenia, Sri Lanka, Trinidad and Tobago, Tunisia, Ukraine, Vietnam

market countries. The United Nations Development Programme projects that by 2020, the combined economic output of the BRIC nations will surpass the aggregate output of Canada, France, Germany, Italy, the United Kingdom, and the United States. Brazil and Russia are touted as the emerging market participants that are likely to attain dominant positions as suppliers of natural resources, and India and China are projected to establish dominance as producers of finished goods. Growth in the BRIC countries is closely tracked as an indicator of global economic growth.

Another common subgroup of emerging markets is the Big Emerging Market (BEM) economies. The BEM economies include the first 12 countries listed under "Emerging Markets." Those countries are in italics in Table 6.1. Several of the BEM countries are expected to transition to developed market status in the coming years.

The emerging markets are commonly further segmented by classifying the less developed emerging markets as frontier markets. As of April 2014, the MSCI Frontier Market Index included the 25 countries listed in Table 6.1; however, several markets are currently being considered as additions to the index. Some of the potential additions are Saudi Arabia, Bosnia and Herzegovina, Botswana, Ghana, Jamaica, Palestine, and Zimbabwe. Currently, the frontier market is the most populated category and is likely to expand on its lead in the next few years.

Investing in International Equity Markets in Practice

Investors are generally aware of at least one investment vehicle they can use to gain exposure to the developed markets. Many investment companies offer mutual funds that track the stock performance of one or more of the developed markets. For example, Vanguard's 500 Index Fund tracks the S&P 500 and is one of the largest mutual funds in the world, with an astounding total asset value of over $160 billion as of March 2014. Obviously, numerous investors are aware that the 500 Fund exists. DWS Investments offers investors the EAFE Equity Index Fund, which tracks the EAFE Index. The two funds mentioned above are passively managed; however, there are numerous geographically focused funds that are actively managed and attempt to outperform their respective benchmarks. Table 6.2 reports several geographically focused investment vehicles, some of which provide access to less recognized regions of the globe.

Why Should You Invest Internationally?

Investors are increasingly recognizing the benefits associated with allocating a portion of their portfolios to international equities. As a result of the greater growth possibilities of foreign country economies, international equities have the potential to provide investors with greater returns. This is particularly true for the equities of emerging market countries. Security values in many emerging markets are growing rapidly because of their populations' increasing disposable income, which accompanies those countries' economic growth. Perhaps the more certain benefit associated with investment in foreign equities is the potential these markets offer for providing diversification. Since each country is affected by economic factors that are somewhat unique, foreign investments can offer relief from negative economic events that primarily afflict an investor's home country. The data in Table 6.3 show the returns, standard deviations, and correlations for two developed market equity indexes.

The performance of the two developed market indexes was incredibly similar over the 44-year sample period. Both the returns and the risk for the developed market indexes were quite comparable, and this resulted in return-to-risk ratios that differed only slightly; the low

Table 6.2   Global Equity Investment Vehicles

Market	Geographic Region	Security (Ticker Symbol)
Developed	Developed markets outside of the United States	Russell International Developed Markets Fund (RINYX)
	Developed markets in Europe, Australia, Asia, and the Far East	iShares MSCI EAFE Index Fund (EFA)
	Canadian small cap	IQ Canada Small Cap ETF (CNDA)
	Developed markets in Europe, Asia, and Australia	Vanguard Developed Markets Index Fund Investor Shares (VDMIX)
	Small-cap developed market equities outside the United States	iShares Developed Small-Cap ex North America ETF (IFSM)
Emerging	Diversified emerging markets	Oppenheimer Developing Markets Fund (ODMAX)
	Brazil	iShares MSCI Brazil Index ETF (EWZ)
	Russia	ING Russia Fund (LETRX)
	India	DMS India MidCap Index Fund (DAIMX)
	Hong Kong, China, Taiwan	Fidelity China Region Fund (FHKCX)
	Chile, Colombia, Peru	FTSE Andean 40 ETF (AND)
	Southeast Asia	Fidelity Emerging Asia Fund (FSEAX)
Frontier	Diversified frontier markets	Guggenheim Frontier Markets ETF (FRN)
	Vietnam	Market Vectors Vietnam ETF (VNM)
	Diversified frontier markets	Templeton Frontier Markets Fund (TFMAX)
	Frontier markets	MSCI Frontier Markets 100 Index ETF (FM)
	Africa and Middle East	T. Rowe Price Africa & Middle East Fund (TRAMX)
	Diversified frontier markets	HSBC Frontier Markets Fund (HSFAX)

Table 6.3 Global Developed Market Performance: 1970–2013

Equity Index	Mean Annual Return	Standard Deviation	Correlation with United States
United States	11.17%	15.48%	1.00
EAFE	11.08%	17.20%	0.62

value is 0.64 for EAFE, and the high is 0.72 for the United States. The relatively strong performance of U.S. stocks has been used by U.S. investors as justification for maintaining a home country bias. Why invest in foreign equities when U.S. equities have been superior performers? The answer of course is the diversification potential offered by foreign equities. Unfortunately, the correlation of the developed markets with one another is very high, and this tends to diminish the diversification potential associated with foreign investment. The correlation between U.S. equities and the EAFE is 0.62, which is quite high but still offers some diversification potential. Rather than accepting the view that U.S. investors gain little by diversifying into foreign equities, the following sections investigate the effects that monetary conditions have on foreign market performance. Furthermore, we consider the possibility that emerging markets hold more investment promise than do foreign developed markets.

Monetary Conditions and Developed Market Stock Performance

In earlier chapters we presented overwhelming evidence that U.S. monetary conditions play an instrumental role in the performance of U.S. securities. We now investigate the role that the Federal

Table 6.4   Global Developed Market Performance by Monetary
Environment: 1970–2013

Index	Mean Return (Standard Deviation) by Monetary Conditions		
	Expansive	Indeterminate	Restrictive
United States	16.17%	9.67%	7.95%
	(16.48%)	(15.26%)	(14.69%)
EAFE	13.24%	12.54%	7.26%
	(19.33%)	(16.33%)	(15.94%)

Reserve and U.S. monetary conditions play in foreign equity markets. Table 6.4 reports the return performance (mean return and standard deviation) for the two indexes listed in Table 6.3; performance is reported for each of the three alternative monetary environments.

The data reported in Table 6.4 indicate that the monetary-conditions-based return patterns that we identified in U.S. equity markets prevail in much of the world. World equity markets generally prosper under expansive monetary conditions but languish under restrictive monetary conditions. Thus, the simple strategy of rotating out of U.S. stocks and into foreign equities would have produced greater transactions costs, increased risk, and resulted in a lower return; it would have been an overall disaster of a strategy move.

The similarity in patterns between the U.S. index and the EAFE index is supported by two underlying factors. First, the Federal Reserve has tremendous influence throughout the global economy because it controls the purse strings of the largest global economy. Since the major financial markets are globally integrated, Fed policy changes have global ramifications. Second, the monetary policies of developed countries' central banks are frequently synchronized as a result of commonality in those countries' economic interests.

The similarity in return patterns, however, is disappointing, as it would have been comforting if foreign equities could have served as a safe haven for U.S. investors when the Fed shifted to a restrictive policy. The performance data reported in Tables 6.3 and 6.4 offer little evidence to motivate U.S. investors to shift funds to the foreign developed markets. The performance data are simply uninspiring. However, before abandoning the foreign developed markets, we evaluate individual country performance. Perhaps one or more of the countries on an individual basis can offer investment inspiration.

And the Winning Country Is . . .

We next evaluate the individual performance of 17 foreign developed markets, using return data from 1970 through 2013. Evaluating individual country performance provides a more complete picture of the merits of investing in foreign equities. Table 6.5 reports the performance data for the U.S. stock market and 17 foreign markets that are ordered alphabetically. The performance data are derived from returns that are based on an investment valued in U.S. dollars. Thus, the reported data represent the performance in a way that is relevant for a U.S. investor. Box 6.1 details the role that changes in currency value play in determining the success or failure of investing in securities outside the United States.

Table 6.5   Performance of Developed Markets by Country: 1970–2013

Country	Mean Annual Return, %	Standard Deviation, %	Return-to-Risk Ratio	Correlation with U.S. Returns
Australia	12.21	24.35	0.50	0.56
Austria	11.15	23.59	0.47	0.35
Belgium	13.42	20.62	0.65	0.53
Canada	11.54	19.79	0.58	0.75
Denmark	14.61	19.73	0.74	0.48
France	12.57	22.77	0.55	0.57
Germany	12.47	22.19	0.56	0.55
Hong Kong	20.12	34.93	0.58	0.40
Italy	8.88	25.93	0.34	0.40
Japan	11.39	21.39	0.53	0.36
Netherlands	13.78	19.44	0.71	0.67
Norway	14.86	27.47	0.54	0.54
Singapore	15.00	28.64	0.52	0.53
Spain	11.92	23.82	0.50	0.47
Sweden	16.21	24.36	0.67	0.56
Switzerland	13.03	18.38	0.71	0.57
United Kingdom	12.43	22.10	0.56	0.58
United States (S&P 500)	11.17	15.47	0.72	1.00

Note: We limited Table 6.5 to the 18 developed countries that reported return data for the entire period 1970–2013.

Box 6.1   Total Return from a Foreign Investment

When an investor purchases a foreign asset, that investor is actually taking a stake in two assets: the asset itself and the associated foreign currency. Therefore, the investor does best when both the foreign asset and the currency of the foreign country appreciate in value. In many cases, investors in foreign assets are unaware of their exposure to the foreign currency because the financial institution that executes the trade makes the appropriate currency conversions behind the scenes.

Let's look at an example to illustrate the two separate return components. Assume a U.S. investor makes a large investment in the stock of a Brazilian coffee producer. The firm pays no dividend, and so the investor is banking on an increase in stock price. During the year, much to the U.S. investor's delight, the Brazilian coffee producer's stock price advances by 20%. Should the U.S. investor purchase that new Mercedes with her newly gained bonanza? Not so fast. The answer depends on the performance of the Brazilian real relative to the U.S. dollar. If during the year the real depreciated by 20% relative to the dollar (i.e., it took 20% more reals to purchase a U.S. dollar), the investor earned no profit on the investment. After the investor converted her reals back to dollars, she would be exactly where she started.

Of course, the best of all worlds for an investor is when the stock price in the local currency advances and the foreign currency appreciates relative to the dollar. In that case, the investor wins on both counts. In our example, suppose the stock price advanced by 20% and the real appreciated by 20%. The investor would realize a gain on both the asset and the foreign currency. In this example the gain would be more than 40%. You can't simply add the percentage

(continued)

gains together; instead, you need to multiply 1 plus the percentage gain on the stock by 1 plus the percentage gain on the currency:

$$(1 + 0.20) \times (1 + 0.20) - 1 = 0.44, \text{ or } 44\%$$

If this happens, the investor may just call the local Mercedes dealer and schedule a test drive after all.

The bottom line is that when investing in a foreign asset, an investor needs to consider the merits of the asset as well as predict movements in the value of the foreign currency. For example, an investor hearing the buzz about Russia's growth potential may have decided to invest in the Russian stock market in October 2013. On October 23, 2013, the MICEX Index, an index composed of the 50 most liquid Russian stocks, stood at 1504.48. At the same time, it took 31.7158 Russian rubles to buy a U.S. dollar. On March 14, 2014, the MICEX Index stood at 1248.56 and the ruble-to-dollar conversion ratio was 36.6326 to 1. The investor would have lost 17% on the depreciation in the stock value. To add insult to injury, the investor would have to convert his rubles into U.S. dollars, which would further add to his loss, producing a total loss of over 28%. This investor should have ignored the buzz and said *nyet* to Russia.

The Best and the Worst

The performance data in Table 6.5 show that Hong Kong produced the highest annual return over the 44-year sample period, with an incredible average return of 20.12%. Although the annual return of the Hong Kong market was very attractive, its risk was not. The

Hong Kong market reported a standard deviation of 34.93%, which was far higher than the volatility of any other country. In fact, the Hong Kong market exhibited a level of volatility that was more than twice the level of the U.S. market. Overall, the Hong Kong market reported a moderate return-to-risk ratio of 0.58. Italy reported by far the lowest average return yet reported the fourth highest risk level. Thus, Italy's return-to-risk ratio was a dismal 0.34.

On the basis of their return-to-risk ratios, the best performing foreign developed countries were Denmark (0.74), Switzerland (0.71), and the Netherlands (0.71). The strong ratios reported for these three countries can be attributed to the fact that each one reported very solid average annual returns with risk levels that were well below average. The U.S. market exhibited one of the highest return-to-risk ratios (0.72); however, this strong value was due almost entirely to the U.S. market's very low volatility. Somewhat surprisingly, the U.S. market fared relatively poorly on a purely return basis but was far superior to other developed markets on a risk basis.

The correlations reported in Table 6.5 show considerable dispersion across the countries, ranging from a low of 0.35 for Austria to a high of 0.75 for Canada, the U.S. neighbor to the north. The relatively high correlation between the United States and Canada is perhaps not surprising in light of the close geographic proximity of the two countries and the fact that Canada is the largest trade partner of the United States. Researchers have found that geographic variables help explain equity market linkages. In particular, the number of overlapping opening hours and the sharing of a border tend to increase cross-country stock market correlation.[1] Box 6.2 lists the top 10 trading partners of the United States.

Box 6.2   Top Trading Partners of the United States

You would expect that economic ties between countries would affect correlations between market returns. Table 6.6 lists the top 10 trading partners of the United States in 2013 on the basis of the percentage of total trade that was with the United States.

Table 6.6   Top Trading Partners of the United States: 2013 (dollar amounts in billions)

Country	Exports	Imports	Total Trade	Percent of Total U.S. Trade
Canada	$300.3	$332.1	$632.4	16.4
China	$122.0	$440.4	$562.4	14.6
Mexico	$226.2	$280.5	$506.6	13.2
Japan	$65.1	$138.5	$203.7	5.3
Germany	$47.4	$114.6	$162.1	4.2
South Korea	$41.6	$62.2	$103.8	2.7
United Kingdom	$47.4	$52.6	$100.0	2.6
France	$32.0	$45.3	$77.3	2.0
Brazil	$44.1	$27.6	$71.7	1.9
Saudi Arabia	$19.0	$51.8	$70.8	1.8

Source: U.S. Census Bureau, http://www.census.gov/foreign-trade/statistics/highlights/top/top1312yr.html.

The Canadian economy is strongly tied to the health of the U.S. economy, as about 75% of all Canadian exports go to the United States.[2] How coincidental that 75% is also the correlation between the two countries' stock returns. Although the two correlations are related, their equality is a coincidence and shouldn't be extrapolated to other countries. Believe it or not, Mexico's economy is even more dependent on the U.S. economy as nearly 78% of Mexico's exports in 2012 went to the United States.[3] By contrast, only 16.7% of Chinese exports are to the United States.[4] The old cliché "When America sneezes the world catches a cold" is very apt for countries with close economic ties to the United States.

Being a Good Neighbor

If you are a U.S. investor, you may think that investing in the Canadian stock market is the neighborly thing to do. The data in Table 6.5, however, suggest that such thinking would be financially unwise. Canada has a moderate return-to-risk ratio of 0.58, which is exactly equal to Hong Kong's ratio. The Hong Kong equity market, however, would be a much better investment for a U.S. investor because of its much lower correlation with U.S. stocks. Remember from our earlier discussion that a security's diversification benefit is inversely related to its correlation with your portfolio (i.e., lower correlation offers better diversification potential). Thus, U.S. investors should weigh a security's performance and its correlation before making an investment decision. On the basis of this broader assessment, there are several countries in Table 6.5 that appear to be superior choices to Canada.

How Do Countries Perform Relative to
U.S. Monetary Conditions?

As our previously presented evidence has made abundantly clear, one should avoid judging the investment value of a security before evaluating its performance across monetary conditions. With that in mind, Table 6.7 reports the performance (average return and

Table 6.7 Developed Country Stock Performance by Monetary Environment: 1970–2013

Country	Mean Annual Return (Standard Deviation) by Monetary Conditions, %		
	Expansive	Indeterminate	Restrictive
Australia	12.89 (25.27)	20.84 (22.28)	1.57 (25.50)
Austria	4.51 (26.15)	18.70 (23.64)	9.00 (20.62)
Belgium	18.04 (24.33)	10.14 (17.56)	12.65 (19.93)
Canada	12.36 (22.12)	10.05 (17.54)	12.46 (19.92)
Denmark	11.14 (21.53)	15.75 (19.83)	16.71 (17.73)
France	13.18 (23.42)	10.47 (20.55)	14.39 (24.62)
Germany	13.58 (24.40)	13.13 (21.65)	10.60 (20.59)
Hong Kong	26.99 (30.47)	17.89 (32.93)	15.92 (40.91)
Italy	9.60 (27.54)	9.07 (25.13)	7.95 (25.36)
Japan	14.62 (23.23)	13.49 (21.73)	5.79 (19.00)
Netherlands	16.82 (21.73)	12.27 (19.00)	12.53 (17.54)
Norway	4.81 (29.42)	20.24 (23.45)	18.58 (29.62)

Country	Mean Annual Return (Standard Deviation) by Monetary Conditions, %		
	Expansive	Indeterminate	Restrictive
Singapore	17.07 (31.45)	16.01 (27.71)	11.78 (26.88)
Spain	10.42 (26.76)	16.73 (23.80)	7.86 (20.60)
Sweden	17.35 (27.51)	15.31 (23.83)	16.13 (21.66)
Switzerland	16.74 (19.12)	13.98 (18.32)	8.26 (17.74)
United Kingdom	16.24 (26.85)	16.04 (20.84)	4.49 (17.87)
United States (S&P 500)	16.17 (16.48)	9.67 (15.26)	7.95 (14.69)

standard deviation) for each of the 18 developed countries by Fed monetary environment.

As our evidence indicates, there is no shortage of strong investment alternatives when monetary conditions are expansive. It seems that almost all asset classes have excelled when Fed policy has been easy, with especially exceptional performance shown by small-value stocks, mortgage REITs, and cyclical stocks. The strong performance during easy policy periods is also true of the majority of developed equity markets as 10 of the 17 foreign countries reported their highest return when U.S. monetary conditions were expansive. Furthermore, seven of the foreign developed markets actually reported higher returns during expansive conditions than the return from the U.S. market. The problem has been identifying securities that perform well when monetary conditions are indeterminate; even more problematic is identifying superior performers when Fed policy is restrictive.

The Miracle on Ice

People commonly refer to the U.S. men's Olympic hockey team win over Russia as the "Miracle on Ice." From a U.S. investor's perspective, the Miracle on Ice may very well be the performance of the Scandinavian countries. The data in Table 6.7 identify several countries that prospered when Fed policy was indeterminate or restrictive, but there is one group of countries that stands out. In particular, the Scandinavian countries (Denmark, Norway, and Sweden) report extremely strong stock performance in both indeterminate and restrictive monetary periods. For example, the average annual return for these three countries is 17.10% during indeterminate periods and 17.14% during restrictive periods. There are several other countries, such as the Netherlands, France, Hong Kong, and Singapore, that offer attractive returns when monetary conditions are not expansive, but they do not match the outstanding performance of the Scandinavian countries (see Box 6.3).

Box 6.3   Scandinavia: What's in the Water?

What is special about Scandinavia? None of the Scandinavian countries in the exhibit use the euro as their currency, and so they aren't integrated into the bigger European Union. More important, each country can exercise its monetary policy independently and thus match its policy to its individual funding requirements.

Table 6.8 provides data on the Scandinavian countries (and the United States for comparison) on three important economic variables.[5,6]

Table 6.8   Data on Scandinavian Countries

Country	Percent of Total Exports to United States	Public Debt as a Percentage of GDP	Gross National Savings Rate as a Percentage of GDP
Denmark	6.6	47.0	24.1
Norway	5.0	30.1	38.2
Sweden	5.5	41.5	25.8
United States	NA	71.8	13.5

As you can see, the Scandinavian countries do not rely on the United States as a significant trading partner.

The Scandinavian countries also have much less public debt as a percentage of GDP than the United States does. Furthermore, they have substantially less debt as a percentage of GDP than the average of the euro area countries, for which the value exceeded 90%.[7] Many readers may question the U.S. number and believe that it should be much higher. The data for the United States exclude debt instruments issued by the Treasury that are owned by other U.S. government agencies. If data for intragovernmental debt were added, gross debt as a percentage of GDP would increase by about one-third for the United States.

Finally, the Scandinavian countries have a much higher gross national savings rate than the United States. Norway, for example,

(continued)

has a gross savings rate that is almost three times that of the United States, and Denmark and Sweden have rates nearly twice as high.

However, the Scandinavian countries are not completely insulated from the U.S. economy and financial system. Narvik, Norway, a town of roughly 18,000 people 140 miles north of the polar circle, lost $18 million ($1,000 for every citizen) in August 2007 after it purchased collateralized debt obligations (CDOs) from Citigroup. The selling brokers represented the securities as being safe to the town officials. Unlike the U.S. government, the Norwegian government didn't believe in bailouts, and Narvik was forced to implement severe budget cuts.

As was noted above, there are numerous foreign country ETFs that allow investors to implement a strategy that targets particular countries or regions of the world. Table 6.2 presents some of the most popular ETFs that are available to investors. In light of the evidence presented above, you may find the following ETFs, which target the Scandinavian region, of particular interest, especially during tight Fed policy periods: iShares MSCI Sweden (EWD), Global X MSCI Norway (NORW), iShares MSCI Denmark (EDEN), and Global X FTSE Nordic Region (GXF). In light of the relatively limited holdings in the individual country Scandinavian ETFs, GXF is frequently advocated because it offers a more diversified exposure to the region.

Emerging Market Stock Performance

Two major advantages are generally advanced to explain why investors should include emerging markets as a component of their foreign market investments. First, emerging markets are viewed as having superior growth potential and thus greater expected stock returns relative to the foreign developed markets. After all, the developed markets were all once emerging markets but have already experienced their accelerated growth phase. Second, emerging markets are subject to unique factors that affect their economic growth and market development. Thus, their stock returns are likely to exhibit relatively low correlations with the equity markets of developed countries. To these two traditional advantages we add another, which is that emerging market countries are likely to exercise more independence in their monetary policies, and therefore, their stock returns are likely to be relatively insensitive to Fed policy shifts, much as we observed for the Scandinavian countries.

Economic Growth of Emerging Markets

With respect to the first advantage of emerging markets (their higher growth potential), Figure 6.1 shows a graph of the GDP growth of developed and emerging countries. The graph shows the history of actual GDP growth from 1980 through 2013 as well as projected growth through 2018.

Figure 6.1 clearly identifies a separation in the GDP growth rates between the emerging and the developed markets that occurred in approximately 2000. On the basis of the graph, the growth rate for both markets generally ranged between 2 and 3% between 1980 and 2000. The post-2000 period shows a stark contrast in the GDP growth rates, however, as the emerging markets rate has hovered around 6% whereas the developed market rate has settled around 2%. Of course the crisis period of 2008 was damaging for both groups of countries. The divergence in GDP growth rates

Figure 6.1 Developed and Emerging GDP Growth

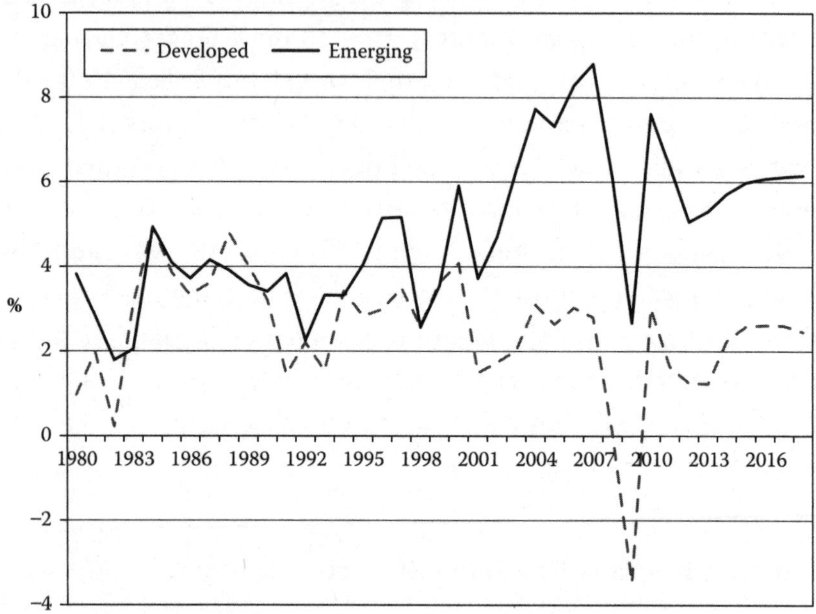

Note: In Figure 6-1, "Emerging" includes both emerging markets and frontier markets.

clearly supports the view that relative to the developed markets, emerging markets offer considerably greater economic growth potential going forward. One would generally expect the greater growth in emerging markets to translate into greater growth in emerging market equity values. However, keep in mind that the greater economic growth of emerging markets has not gone unnoticed by large multinational firms. See Box 6.4 for an illustration of how many large multinationals have been rapidly expanding their operations in emerging markets to take advantage of their greater growth potential.

Box 6.4   Are These Really U.S. Companies?

Being an American-based company does not mean you aren't global. In 2012, 46.6% of all sales for S&P 500 companies were outside the United States.[8] In fact, firms in the energy, healthcare, information technology, and materials sectors each reported that the majority of their sales took place outside the United States.

To give you some perspective, Table 6.9 lists 10 of the largest U.S. companies and the percentage of their 2013 sales that were made outside the United States.

Table 6.9   Percentage of Sales from Outside the U.S. for Selected Companies

Company	Ticker Symbol	Percent of 2013 sales from outside United States
Apple	AAPL	61.3
Chevron	CVX	58.9
Coca-Cola	KO	57.7
Exxon Mobil	XOM	63.7
General Electric	GE	53.0
General Motors	GM	41.4
IBM	IBM	56.0
Johnson & Johnson	JNJ	55.3
Phillips 66	PSX	32.8
Walmart Stores	WMT	28.9

It is clear that these companies' fortunes truly do depend on the health of the global economy. Investors may believe that by

(continued)

investing in U.S. companies they are exposed only to the U.S. economy, but that is not true with these large multinational corporations. The evidence indicates that the biggest multinationals derive a substantial share of their revenue from overseas, with an increasing share coming from emerging countries. In 2013 the Boston Consulting Group polled over 150 executives of the biggest multinational companies and presented the findings in the report titled "Playing to Win in Emerging Markets." The survey found that the multinationals polled derived an average of 28% of their revenues from emerging markets. Prominent firms such as Colgate-Palmolive, Procter & Gamble, Boeing, Kimberly-Clark, General Motors, Coca-Cola, Pepsico, DirecTV, and Caterpillar all reported that in 2012 sales to emerging markets accounted for more than 20% of their total sales.

One firm that showed a steady increase in percentage of sales to emerging markets is DirecTV. Table 6.10 shows that DirecTV was pursuing a strategy of increasing sales in Latin America and the Caribbean. No wonder the firm was an attractive acquisition candidate for AT&T.

Table 6.10   DirecTV Sales (dollar figures in millions)

	2009	*2010*	*2011*	*2012*	*2013*
Total sales	$21,565	$24,102	$27,226	$29,740	$31,754
Total Latin America and Caribbean sales	$2,721	$3,418	$4,916	$6,062	$6,666
Latin America and Caribbean sales as a percentage of total sales	12.6	14.2	18.1	20.4	21.0

The Risk and Return of Emerging Markets

Table 6.11 addresses the two major advantages of emerging markets: the higher potential stock returns and their relatively low correlation with developed markets. In the next section, we address the third proposed advantage: their relative independence from shifts in Fed monetary policy. The performance data for emerging markets are somewhat limited by the lack of return data for an extended period. You should keep this limitation in mind as we compare their performance with that of the developed markets.

The returns reported in Table 6.11 for each of the emerging market indexes exceed the returns generated in developed markets over the corresponding period. The higher stock returns correspond with the greater economic growth generated by emerging market countries. Unfortunately, the higher average returns also correspond with greater risk. The stand-alone risk (standard deviation) is particularly high for the BRIC and African frontier indexes.

Emerging Market Diversification Benefits

The correlations of the emerging markets with the developed market indexes indicate that the emerging markets offer some

Table 6.11 Emerging Market Equity Performance Through 2013

Index	Start Date	Mean Return, %	Standard Deviation, %	Correlation with United States	Correlation with EAFE
Emerging markets	January 1988	14.36	23.67	0.66	0.69
Frontier markets	June 2002	11.96	19.95	0.55	0.63
BRIC	June 1994	12.56	29.22	0.61	0.72
African frontier	January 1996	14.35	28.96	0.15	0.23

diversification opportunities for developed market investors that are centered in both the United States and foreign markets. The frontier markets in Africa appear to offer the best opportunities as the correlations are only 0.15 and 0.23 with the United States and with the EAFE, respectively. The correlations with the broader emerging market indexes are much higher at 0.66 and 0.69 with the United States and with the EAFE, respectively. To provide some context, the average correlation between an individual stock in the Russell 1000 Index and the index itself ranged from under 0.2 to nearly 0.6 through 2012.[9] Correlations are certainly not consistent over time and tend to increase in periods of crisis. Investors learned that lesson particularly well during the financial crisis of 2008, when stocks were moving up and down—mostly down—more in tandem than during "normal" market conditions.

Monetary Conditions and Emerging Market Stock Performance

The data in Table 6.11 offer some evidence that emerging markets have diversification potential relative to general market moves. We next investigate their potential to help diversify or hedge the return patterns that the developed markets display relative to monetary conditions. In particular, the evidence presented above indicates that developed market equities have generally floundered after shifts to a restrictive Fed monetary policy. The performance data in Table 6.12 offer evidence regarding our third identified advantage of emerging markets: their ability to hedge the poor performance of developed market equities during periods of restrictive Fed policy.

Table 6.12   Global Emerging Market Performance by Monetary Environment Through 2013

	Mean Return (Standard Deviation) by Monetary Conditions		
Index	Expansive, %	Indeterminate, %	Restrictive, %
Emerging markets	8.48	17.78	16.53
	(27.30)	(22.98)	(20.47)
Frontier markets	−0.65	10.60	21.43
	(27.17)	(13.83)	(17.82)
BRIC	0.04	18.45	18.62
	(35.88)	(25.80)	(25.14)
African frontier	18.44	0.22	24.38
	(29.96)	(33.02)	(22.64)

Note: Data availability for the indexes begins according to the following schedule: emerging markets, January 1988; frontier markets, June 2002; BRIC, June 1994; African frontier, January 1996.

The Monetary-Related Performance Patterns of Emerging Markets

The performance patterns reported in Table 6.12 are encouraging because they display little resemblance to the patterns reported for the developed markets. Surprisingly, all the emerging market indexes have flourished during periods of restrictive Fed policy. Since restrictive policy periods have been the bane of developed market equities, this finding is particularly welcome. As a case in point, in July 2004 the Fed initiated a restrictive monetary policy, which was followed over the subsequent 12 months by a subpar return of 6.4% for the S&P 500. In stark contrast, over the same time frame, the emerging market index returned 34.9% and the frontier market index returned 88.1%.

Investors should keep in mind our previously presented evidence showing the expansion of many of the most prominent multinationals into emerging markets. This evidence can be used by investors in implementing their reallocation strategies. For example, after a Fed shift to a restrictive monetary policy, an investor may want to reduce her exposure to the developed markets and increase her exposure to emerging market equities. The investor can accomplish the reallocation by purchasing an emerging markets index or by overweighting the stock of multinational firms that have a heavy presence in emerging markets. The first approach offers a direct exposure to the emerging markets, and the second provides an indirect exposure.

Although the volatility for the emerging market indexes is quite high, it is generally not extreme. Some individual emerging countries exhibit extreme stock return volatility; however, the relatively low correlation of the emerging markets with one another greatly reduces the overall risk of the composite indexes. In light of the limited time frame in which the data are available for the emerging market countries and their extreme individual volatility, we do not report the performance data for individual emerging countries. The combination of a short time span and extreme volatility makes it almost impossible to draw robust inferences from such data.

Conclusion

The foreign markets offer both good news and bad news. The good news is that we have identified several foreign countries and regions that perform well when monetary conditions are restrictive. As we have shown repeatedly in earlier chapters, such securities are hard to come by, and so this is certainly a welcome result. In particular, relative to the majority of developed foreign markets, the emerging markets and the Scandinavian countries perform admirably when monetary conditions are either indeterminate or restrictive. We chalk this up to the lack of coordination of those countries' monetary authorities with Fed policy and the relative independence of those countries' economic policies from the United States. The bad news is that the return patterns we observed for the U.S. stock market prevail for the vast majority of foreign developed stock markets. Thus, most of the developed foreign markets offer little relief from the dismal performance generally associated with the U.S. market under restrictive monetary conditions.

CHAPTER 7

HEDGE FUNDS

When people ask me what I do for a living, I generally tell them
"I run a hedge fund." The majority give me a strange look,
so I quickly add, "I am a money manager." When the
strange look persists, as it often does, I correct it to simply,
"I'm an investor." Everyone knows what that is.

*David Einhorn, Greenlight Capital, from a speech
at the Value Investing Congress, November 10, 2006*

In social settings, when the topic of investments comes up, individual investors often say that they are invested in "mutual funds."
The typical response to that declaration is "Me too." However, simply acknowledging that you and your cocktail party acquaintance are
both invested in mutual funds does not imply that you have similar
investments. Mutual funds come in many flavors that vary with
the types of assets held (stocks, bonds, money market securities, or
a combination) and the specific type of each security held (small
stocks, large stocks, technology stocks, etc.). In other words, mutual
funds are a diverse lot that can encompass a variety of assets and
strategies. The same thing can be said of hedge funds.

What Is a Hedge Fund?

What is a hedge fund? Other than knowing that hedge funds generate enormous fees and wealth for their managers, it turns out that the general public has little knowledge about hedge fund operations.[1] When most people hear the term *hedge,* they think of some sort of risk-minimizing activity, as the phrase "hedge one's bets" implies. Are hedge funds investment vehicles that mitigate investor risk? Not exactly. The Chartered Financial Analyst curriculum defines a hedge fund as a "loosely regulated, pooled investment vehicle that may implement various investment strategies." This vague definition offers little clarification but is entirely consistent with the observation that hedge funds are very heterogeneous. Thus, it is difficult to offer a definition for the group as a whole. A common characteristic of hedge funds is that they create portfolios that include combinations of long and short positions in various securities. Many funds also employ a great deal of leverage (borrowed money) to magnify their bets. The features that differentiate one hedge fund type from another are the underlying securities that the funds target and the ratio of long to short positions that they hold (see Box 7.1).

Our main reason for evaluating hedge funds is that they have a structure that offers investors an opportunity to greatly enhance their portfolio performance. In earlier chapters, we identified several security types that exhibit prominent return patterns relative to shifts in Fed policy. For example, we observed that small-value stocks outperform the average stock by a huge margin after an expansive policy shift by the Fed; however, the outperformance of this category of stocks is only modest when Fed policy is restrictive. The question is the extent to which the hedge fund structure will allow an investor to exploit such observations. We explore the exploitation of four of the most prominent return patterns in this chapter; however, once you understand the process, the hedge fund structure will allow you to exploit any return pattern. We begin the chapter by discussing the basic structure of hedge funds to facilitate that necessary understanding, a big part of which involves understanding the idea of short selling a security. Once you gain that understanding, you will be equipped to use it as you see fit.

Box 7.1. Types of Hedge Funds

Long only. These funds operate much like stock mutual funds. These funds purchase shares of stock they think are going to increase in value. The funds often take more diverse stakes across securities and much larger stakes in individual securities than mutual funds are allowed to take.[2] Some long-only hedge funds specialize in certain sectors of the market (e.g., stocks of technology firms), whereas others target particular geographic regions.

Equity long-short. These funds purchase shares of firms they feel are going to rise in value and enter short positions (more on short selling later) in shares of firms they believe are going to fall in value. There are several variations of equity long-short funds, the most common being market-neutral funds. A market-neutral fund balances its bullish positions and bearish positions so that its performance is not dependent on the direction of the overall market.

Relative value (arbitrage). These funds attempt to take advantage of the mispricing of similar types of securities. The concept of arbitrage involves identifying securities with similar risk and reward features and purchasing the underpriced security

(continued)

---

while simultaneously selling the overpriced security. To make a profit, these funds are betting on the securities reverting to their "true" or intrinsic value. One of the most common types of relative value funds is convertible arbitrage funds. These funds purchase the convertible bonds and sell the common stock of the same issuing firm, as they believe that the bonds are systematically undervalued relative to the stock.

Event driven. These funds attempt to take advantage of the potential mispricing that occurs in special situations such as bankruptcies, mergers, and spin-offs. A common event-driven strategy is to buy the shares of the target firm (the one being acquired) in an acquisition and sell the shares of the acquiring firm.

Global macro. This is a catch-all category. Global macro funds have the broadest mandate of any type of hedge fund. These funds will buy and sell stocks, bonds, commodities, currencies, and just about any asset class you can imagine. They typically switch their attention from one asset class to another as perceived opportunities arise.

In contrast to most hedge funds, long-only investment funds enter only long positions. A mutual fund is a good example of a long-only investment fund. Like hedge funds, mutual funds are pooled investment vehicles; that means that shareholders in the fund are all treated the same. An investment fund creates a long position by taking an ownership stake in a security. The ownership stake can be created by purchasing a security or committing to purchase it at a set price at a later date. Creating a short position (short selling) is a less intuitive process as it involves selling a security that the investor does not own. You may wonder how an investor can sell something that is not owned; it turns out that short selling an asset works much like bank lending. When you make a deposit at a bank, the bank may use your money to extend a loan to another customer. In the same way, your investment manager may take your shares and lend them to a customer who has decided to sell the shares without owning them. In a loan transaction, the bank is responsible for making sure a depositor's money is returned when demanded, just as an investment manager is responsible for making sure a client's shares are available when the client wishes to sell them.

What Is the Rationale for Short Selling a Stock?

What motivates a fund manager to enter a short position, that is, to short sell a security? A fund manager creates a short position in a security when he believes the security's price is too high. The manager sells the security with the intention of repurchasing it at a lower price. The client whose shares are borrowed and sold is unaware that the transaction ever occurred. If a client decides to sell her shares and the shares have been borrowed and sold already, the manager will simply borrow shares from another client. During the financial crisis of 2008, many short sellers made substantial gains in financial stocks (see Box 7.2). A fund manager who had the foresight to short sell financial stocks in 2007 was rewarded handsomely when he repurchased the same financial stocks at much lower prices in 2008. Thus, the financial crisis was not a crisis for everyone. However, if the manager had been premature and entered the short position in financial stocks in 2005, the strong performance of financials in 2006 probably would have precipitated the closing of the short position at a significant loss.

As a security's price increases, a short seller accumulates losses and at some point is compelled, either voluntarily or by her broker, to close the position, that is, to purchase the shares to cover the short position. Short sellers gain when prices fall, but they can lose substantial amounts if prices rise unexpectedly. For example, assume that in early 2013 an investor believed that the services offered by the online business rating and review company Yelp represented a short-term fad. To take advantage of that belief, assume the investor shorted 100 shares of Yelp at $19.13 on January 2, 2013, collecting $1,913. The investor would have accumulated a loss of $4,982 if the shares were repurchased (the short position was covered) at the end of 2013 after the stock price had risen to $68.95.

For most investors, the risk/return trade-off of a long position is much more attractive than that of a short position. In particular, the asymmetric payoff that accompanies a short position makes short selling unappealing to many individuals. A long investor's potential loss is limited to the amount invested in the stock. If you buy $10,000 worth of a stock and that stock becomes worthless, you lose only the amount you invested. Although losing your entire investment may seem like little consolation, at least your broker isn't going to call you for a further financial commitment. In contrast, a basic problem with short selling is that an investor's potential loss is unlimited: the loss keeps rising as long as the price increases. In the best scenario, the stock price goes to zero and the short seller's profit matches the original stock price. Thus, the maximum potential gain for a short seller is limited to the price of the stock.

Box 7.2   A Hedge Fund Legend is Born

David Einhorn from Greenlight Capital, whose quote was featured at the beginning of this chapter, made a fortune and burnished his reputation as a hedge fund titan during the financial crisis in 2007 and 2008. Einhorn shorted the investment bank Lehman Brothers in July 2007, when the stock was selling for over $70 per share. The share price steadily declined over the next 10 months to around $35 per share until he publicly announced his short position at a large New York City investment conference in May 2008. On the day of his speech, Lehman's stock closed down $2.44, with its highest volume of the entire month.[3] The public pronouncement of his short position led to Einhorn appearing on radio, on TV, and in the print media explaining his position. He went toe to toe with Lehman management—particularly Lehman's CFO, Erin Callan—publicly debating the firm's valuation and future. Einhorn's chief contention was that he had encountered dubious accounting practices at the firm, specifically that Lehman was incorrectly accounting for illiquid real estate positions.

At the time, many market observers blamed short selling by activist investors such as Einhorn for wreaking havoc and causing extraordinary volatility in the financial markets. This led the SEC and the United Kingdom's Financial Services Authority to take the unprecedented step of temporarily banning the short selling of 799 financial stocks for a period of 10 days starting in late September 2008. The short sellers were largely exonerated by the bankruptcy examiner's report, which alleged that Lehman executives manipulated financial reports, withheld information from its board, and inflated the value of real estate–related assets.

Einhorn has garnered so much acclaim for his role as a short seller that some in the media refer to a stock being "Einhorned" when someone takes a short position and publicly comes out defending that position.[4]

What Makes Hedge Funds So Appealing?

As was noted above, there are many different types of hedge funds, each designed to exploit a particular investment opportunity. Since hedge funds take positions in securities, all hedge funds entail some level of risk. However, relative to the risk of long-only funds, the risk of hedge funds ranges from extremely high to quite low. This chapter focuses on the most popular form of hedge fund, the relative value fund, which seeks to exploit valuation discrepancies through combinations of long positions (for stocks believed to be underpriced) and short positions (for stocks considered overvalued). For ease of exposition, we will assume that the long and short positions are of equal value, but in practice, the relative weighting of the two is one of the features that differentiate hedge funds.

There are a couple of potential major advantages associated with the hedge fund structure. First, a hedge fund can establish positions that are subject to relatively little risk. For example, the manager of a market-neutral hedge fund may enter a long position in Ford Motors stock and a short position in General Motors (GM) stock. Entering such a position is called a paired-trade strategy for obvious reasons. If the general stock market prospers, both Ford and GM are likely to increase in price. What the manager desires is for Ford's stock price to appreciate more than GM's. If the general stock market languishes, both Ford and GM are likely to suffer. However, the manager still gains if GM's stock price falls more than Ford's. Thus, the investment manager is not concerned about the market's direction and bears no risk from a general market move; even if that move is extreme, his only concern is the spread between the price of Ford and that of GM. If the manager enters numerous comparable paired trades in many industries, he will create a diversified portfolio of such hedges. This type of portfolio is subject to substantially less risk than is a long-only mutual fund, since the long-only fund would suffer from a market correction. Second, hedge funds have greater potential to benefit from the investment manager's skill. For long-only funds, the identification of overvalued stocks means the manager takes no action, which means she has no ability to capitalize on her insight. In contrast, a hedge fund manager would capitalize on her identification of an overvalued stock by entering a short position. Since the vast majority of investment funds are long-only funds, there is far more competition to identify undervalued relative to overvalued stocks. Thus, it is logical to assume there are more opportunities for mispricing on the short side and therefore more potential profit opportunities.

An investor wishing to implement a paired-trade hedge fund strategy that is based on Fed policy shifts may proceed as follows. When the Fed shifts to an expansive policy, the fund manager purchases the stock of Ruth's Hospitality Group (RUTH), which operates Ruth's Chris Steak House and other fine dining establishments. At the same time, the manager would short sell McDonald's (MCD) stock. The reasoning for this paired trade is that RUTH is more sensitive to changes in discretionary spending than MCD is. After all, how many people have to give up a visit to McDonalds because of financial troubles? By the way, RUTH also has a much higher beta than MCD (1.19 versus 0.36 in August 2014, according to Yahoo Finance). Similarly, on the basis of a corresponding paired trade, a Fed shift to a restrictive policy would motivate the manager to buy MCD and short RUTH. We hope you can see the merit to this hedge fund example and, more important, are formulating your own paired trades as you contemplate it.

A feature of hedge funds that we have not yet discussed is their loosely regulated nature. Because of this characteristic, hedge funds are generally restricted to institutional investors and high-net-worth individuals. Since 2006, hedge fund advisors operating in the United States have been required to register with the SEC; however, by limiting their ownership to "sophisticated investors," hedge funds are able to avoid strict regulatory oversight. If you are neither an institutional manager nor a high-net-worth investor, do not despair; you can essentially replicate a hedge fund position with relative ease. Unfortunately, we have been unable to devise a scheme that will allow you to capture those enormous hedge fund fees from other investors; however, our approach allows you to avoid paying those enormous fees to someone else.

Rather than evaluating the performance of actual hedge funds (see Box 7.3 for a discussion of the problems with hedge fund return data), we create several alternative hedged portfolios. The portfolios are created to mirror some of the most successful investment strategies that have been identified in prior research. In light of the recognized success of the strategies, hedge fund managers rely on them to varying degrees in executing their own investment techniques. Therefore, by evaluating the performance of hedged portfolios, we offer investors a view of the potential profits available to particular hedge fund approaches.

For each strategy, we first evaluate the strategy's performance without regard to the monetary environment to indicate the general attractiveness of the strategy. We then investigate the potential benefit associated with incorporating monetary conditions as part of the strategy. Our analysis does not consider paired-trade positions because of their unique characteristics and their focus on individual stocks. Obviously, we could create several dozen paired-trade examples that have been extremely successful during previous periods. We offered one example above for illustrative purposes (RUTH and MCD) but will leave additional versions to your creation. Instead, we focus on general hedge strategies that are based on well-recognized patterns in categories of securities, such as small stocks, value stocks, and loser stocks.

Box 7.3   The Problem with Hedge Fund Return Data

Throughout this book we have presented actual market returns from different asset classes. In this chapter, we deviate from that convention and do not use actual hedge fund data for several reasons, as outlined below.[5]

1. *Relatively short time period.* Most hedge fund databases came into existence in the mid-1990s. The relatively short existence of hedge fund data would make comparisons of hedge fund returns to returns from other asset classes problematic.

2. *Selection bias.* The inclusion of the returns for a hedge fund in any database is voluntary. Unlike publicly traded securities, hedge funds are organized as private investment vehicles, and any sort of public reporting is voluntary. In addition, there may be systematic biases regarding those hedge funds which choose to report returns to databases and those which don't report. Specifically, if a hedge fund's returns are good, managers are more likely to decide to report than they are if those returns are poor. Fund managers often "shout from the mountaintop" when their performance is strong and remain silent when their performance is weak.

3. *Survivorship bias.* Many indexes include only firms that remain in operation for a particular period. If funds are excluded because they are no longer in operation, the reported returns of the survivors will have a positive bias. Firms that have performed poorly and folded or have been reconstituted under a different name are not included in many indexes.

4. *Instant history bias.* Related to selection bias, instant history bias is in operation "when an index contains histories of returns that

(continued)

predate the entry date of the corresponding funds into the database and thereby cause the index to disproportionately reflect the characteristics of the funds that are added to the database."[6] This again serves to upwardly bias the reported returns to hedge funds, as funds with good returns are more likely than funds with poor returns to begin reporting results to a data provider. Furthermore, the funds with a strong performance will provide a history of their superior return performance.

5. *Liquidation bias.* Generally, poorly performing funds that are in the process of being liquidated will not report returns. Thus, although these funds may still be in operation, they will stop reporting returns, resulting in an upward bias in the reported returns of the remaining funds.

The bottom line is that because of the private nature of hedge funds, the reported returns of the databases may not be representative of the performance of the average hedge fund.

Exploiting the Small-Firm Premium

The first hedged position we consider is designed to exploit the small-firm premium, which, as we noted in Chapter 2, is the fact that small stocks have generally outperformed big stocks over time. Thus, the position entails a long position in small-cap stocks and a short position in large-cap stocks. Since the two positions are of equal size, the short position in large stocks entirely funds the long position in small stocks. In other words, an investor could use the funds obtained by shorting the large-stock portfolio to purchase the small-stock portfolio, thus leaving a portfolio with no net investment. In finance parlance, the portfolio composed of a long position in small stocks and a short position in big stocks is referred to as a small-minus-big (SMB) portfolio.

To make the SMB investment strategy comparable to a long-only strategy, we assume the investor places the hedged position's value in T-bills and earns the T-bill return. In other words, since the SMB portfolio requires no net investment, it cannot be directly compared with a portfolio that represents a long position. Thus, we make the position "fully invested" by assuming the investor invests the position's value in 1-month T-bills. After converting the SMB position to a fully invested position, we can legitimately compare the performance of the strategy with that of other long-only positions.

The approach we use to convert the SMB hedged position to a fully invested position is a conservative approach as we assume equal allocations to the long side and the short side with the position value invested in 1-month T-bills. Many hedge funds take a more aggressive approach by placing a greater allocation on the long side relative to the short side. In effect, the fund leverages the position by placing a greater portion of the position value in the long asset rather than placing equal values on both sides. By structuring the position to have a long bias, hedge funds are able to leverage (i.e., magnify) the potential outcome of their bets. See Box 7.4 for further discussion of hedge fund strategies.

Box 7.4   Popular Hedge Fund Strategies

Equity long-short strategies that commit equal dollar values to the long side and the short side of the transaction are called market-neutral. But not all long-short strategies are created equal, and

(continued)

not all are market-neutral. In many cases, hedge fund managers intentionally maintain a long bias to leverage or magnify their bets. One of the most common long-short strategies is called the 130/30 strategy. With this strategy, the fund overweights the long side of the position relative to the short side by a ratio of 130 to 30, hence the name. The way to think about the strategy is as follows: a fund manager enters a long position (with a set value) in stocks that she is relatively optimistic about (we'll refer to these shares as bull stocks). The manager then enters a short position in stocks that she is relatively pessimistic about (bear stocks); this short position is 30% of the value of the original position in bull stocks. The manager uses the proceeds from the short position in bear stocks to purchase additional shares of bull stocks, thus leaving the position 130% long in bull stocks and 30% short in bear stocks.

There are other popular variations of the equity long-short strategy that are not market-neutral. Other examples include 150/50 funds, 140/40 funds, and 120/20 funds. Note that since the first number represents the long side and the second number the short side and since the proceeds from the short sales fund the extra investment in the long side, the difference between the two numbers must equal 100.

In July 2009, ProShares introduced the first 130/30 ETF (CSM). In launching the product, Michael Sapir, the chairman and CEO, stated, "We believe that this new ETF will be attractive for investors' 130/30 allocations because it combines a rigorous quantitative investment process developed by two renowned experts with an indexed, lower cost, and liquid investment." Table 7.1 reports performance for CSM over the period 2010–2013.

The performance data in Table 7.1 indicate that the four years from 2010 to 2013 was a very favorable period for both CSM and the

Table 7.1   Performance of CSM and S&P 500: 2010–2013

Year	CSM Annual Return, %	S&P 500 Annual Return, %
2010	14.05	15.17
2011	0.55	1.88
2012	16.68	16.00
2013	35.35	32.36
Mean annual return	16.65	16.35
Standard deviation	12.41	10.81
Return-to-risk ratio	1.34	1.51

U.S. stock market in general; both reported return-to-risk ratios well in excess of 1.0. The evidence indicates, however, that beating the market is a very difficult accomplishment even for "two renowned experts." Perhaps if the experts had access to the material in this book, the fund's performance would have improved.

Has the SMB Strategy Been a Winner?

To form an SMB portfolio, we first rank all firms by their market capitalization; the smallest 20% make up the small portfolio, and the largest 20% the big portfolio. The small-firm premium represents the difference in returns for the two portfolios.[7] By subtracting the big portfolio return from the return to the small portfolio and adding the 1-month T-bill return, we mimic a strategy of entering a long position in small stocks and a short position in big stocks, with T-bills posted as collateral (margin) for the position.

Table 7.2 reports performance data for the fully invested SMB portfolio for the full sample period and two subperiods. For comparison purposes, we also include the performance of the S&P 500. We split the sample period in half to evaluate the consistency of the hedged portfolio over time. As you might expect, investors aggressively pursue investment opportunities once they are revealed. The attention that an identified return pattern receives from investors tends to diminish the future effectiveness of any strategy designed to exploit the pattern. Whether the small-firm premium has suffered this fate since its existence became widely acknowledged in the 1980s is subject to debate.[8]

The full-period performance data reported in Table 7.2 refute the general effectiveness of the SMB strategy. For the full period, the strategy produced a return of about 8.5%, which when compared with the annual return for the S&P 500 of 10.56% over the same period is subpar. Furthermore, the risk of the hedged portfolio (15.29%) is very similar to the general market risk of 15.26%. Thus, relative to the general market, the hedged portfolio strategy produced considerably lower returns with slightly higher risk; this is clearly a strategy one would want to avoid.

Table 7.2 Small-Minus-Big (SMB) Fully Invested Portfolio Performance

	Full Period (1966–2013)	Subperiod 1966–1989	Subperiod 1990–2013
SMB portfolio			
Mean annual return	8.46%	10.50%	6.42%
Standard deviation	15.29%	15.08%	15.51%
S&P 500			
Mean annual return	10.56%	10.86%	10.25%
Standard deviation	15.26%	15.71%	14.82%

The subperiod results show that the SMB strategy was more effective in the first subperiod (first half of the sample period); however, even here the performance was less than spectacular. On the positive side, during the first subperiod, the strategy subjected investors to slightly less risk than the general stock market did; however, it also produced a slightly lower return. During the second subperiod, the performance of the hedged strategy was abysmal, subjecting the investor to more risk and at the same time resulting in substantially lower returns. It would appear that the SMB hedged strategy became much less effective after its widespread recognition in the 1970s; this observation is consistent with Jeremy Siegel's contention that the strategy's effectiveness has diminished over time.

The Small-Firm Premium and Monetary Conditions

We next consider the performance of the SMB fully invested portfolio across monetary environments. Table 7.3 reports performance across the three monetary environments for the full sample period and each of the subperiods. Since the strategy consists of a combination of positions, we also report the percentage of months in which the strategy paid off (i.e., produced a positive return). In our own investing, we are always more comfortable employing a strategy if it produces positive results on a consistent basis. Our advice is to be skeptical of strategies that rely on a limited number of spectacular return months for their success.

Consistent with our previous conjecture that small firms are more sensitive to changes in monetary conditions, we find that the performance of the SMB hedged portfolio differs dramatically across the three monetary environments. The heyday for the hedged strategy was clearly when monetary conditions were expansive.

Table 7.3   Monetary Environment and SMB Hedged Portfolio Performance: Mean Annual Return (Standard Deviation) and [Percentage of Positive Return Months]

Monetary Conditions	Full Period (1966–2013), %	Subperiod 1966–1989, %	Subperiod 1990–2013, %
Expansive	18.31	28.05	11.47
	(14.89)	(15.11)	(14.48)
	[59.89]	[63.38]	[57.43]
Indeterminate	3.00	1.41	4.72
	(14.34)	(15.06)	(13.58)
	[50.24]	[48.62]	[52.00]
Restrictive	5.62	8.14	2.51
	(16.33)	(14.38)	(18.52)
	[55.38]	[59.26]	[50.57]

During the first subperiod of expansive policy, the strategy was spectacular, producing a return exceeding 28% with risk of slightly over 15%. The strategy's return-to-risk ratio during this time frame was a remarkable 1.86. Furthermore, the strategy was remarkably consistent as it produced positive returns in over 63% of the months in which it was applied. Although not nearly as impressively, the strategy continued to perform well during the second subperiod, but only when monetary conditions were expansive. In the latter period, the strategy produced a robust return of 11.47% with relatively low risk of 14.48%, creating a very respectable return-to-risk ratio of 0.79. In addition, the strategy paid off in over 57% of the months in which it was applied.

The SMB hedged strategy performed consistently very poorly during both indeterminate and restrictive monetary periods. Somewhat surprisingly, for the full period, the worst performance occurred during indeterminate conditions, not restrictive conditions. In either restrictive or indeterminate conditions, however, we would have a hard time advocating the use of the strategy.

Overall, on the basis of our evidence, we would argue that the SMB hedged strategy's effectiveness is much more dependent on monetary conditions than it is on the time frame. This is good news for Fed watchers and readers of this book. Knowing when to implement a strategy is generally more important than knowing the strategy's overall success, and now you have insight into when to implement. On the basis of our evidence, an optimal implementation of the hedge strategy calls for an investor to take the following actions, but only when the Fed shifts to an expansive policy: purchase a small-firm portfolio (or small-cap ETF) and simultaneously short sell a large-firm portfolio (or large-cap ETF).

Finally, lest you forget, we defined the small-firm premium on the basis of ranked firms separated into quintiles; previous research, including our own, has shown that the return patterns are more prominent for finer separations, for example, the smallest 10% and largest 10% of firms.[9] Furthermore, as was noted above, a hedge fund manager can magnify the outcome of a hedged strategy by overallocating to the long side of the position (e.g., a 130/30 fund). Thus, the evidence reported here should be viewed as a conservative indicator of the strategy's performance. The same consideration applies for the analyses that follow since we employ the same conservative approach throughout.

Exploiting the Value Premium

The second hedged position we consider is designed to capture the value premium (i.e., the fact that value stocks have historically outperformed growth stocks). Remember, value stocks are the stocks of firms with relatively low price multiples (e.g., low price-to-sales ratios), whereas growth stocks have high price multiples (e.g., high price-to-sales ratios). The portfolio is constructed in the same manner as the SMB portfolio but with the price-to-sales (P/S) ratio as the characteristic of interest. The return to the hedged position is created by subtracting the high P/S portfolio (growth portfolio) returns from the low P/S portfolio (value portfolio) returns; this value is frequently identified as the value premium. Again, we follow the conservative approach and add the T-bill return to the value premium to make the portfolio fully invested. In finance parlance, the hedged position is referred to as a high-minus-low (HML) portfolio.

The performance data in Table 7.4 suggest that the HML hedged position fared much better than did the SMB position over time. For the full period, the hedged portfolio earned a return that is comparable to the market return (S&P 500 return) with a risk level that is somewhat lower. The hedged portfolio, however, was much more effective during the first subperiod, when it produced a return-to-risk ratio of approximately 1. The strategy's effectiveness was diminished considerably in the second subperiod, in which

Table 7.4 High-Minus-Low (HML) Portfolio Performance

	Full Period (1966–2013), %	*Subperiod 1966–1989, %*	*Subperiod 1990–2013, %*
HML Portfolio			
Mean annual return	10.70	12.30	8.84
Standard deviation	14.51	12.31	16.41
S&P 500			
Mean annual return	10.56	10.86	10.25
Standard deviation	15.26	15.71	14.82

it produced a return-to-risk ratio of only 0.5. This observation is consistent with the contention that investors exploited the value premium after the widespread attention it received by researchers during the 1970s and 1980s, which diminished the strategy's subsequent effectiveness.

The Value Premium and Monetary Conditions

Table 7.5 reports performance data for the HML portfolio segmented by the monetary environment and by sample subperiod. Once again, in addition to mean annaul return and standard deviation, we report the percentage of months in which the strategy was successful.

Consistent with the SMB performance pattern, it is obvious that the success of the HML hedged strategy is more reliant on the monetary environment than it is on the time frame.

Table 7.5   Monetary Conditions and HML Hedged Portfolio Performance: Mean Annual Return (Standard Deviation) and [Percentage of Positive Return Months]

Monetary Conditions	Full Period (1966–2013), %	Subperiod 1966–1989, %	Subperiod 1990–2013, %
Expansive	18.56	20.44	17.23
	(16.45)	(12.88)	(18.61)
	[62.21]	[70.42]	[56.43]
Indeterminate	8.17	11.47	4.51
	(14.12)	(13.26)	(15.01)
	[58.37]	[58.72]	[58.00]
Restrictive	6.48	7.76	4.04
	(12.86)	(10.69)	(15.03)
	[58.97]	[60.18]	[57.47]

Under expansive conditions, the HML hedged portfolio performed well during each of the two subperiods, producing annual returns of 20.44% and 17.23%, respectively. However, unlike the performance for the SMB portfolio, the HML strategy's mean return tailed off very little in the second subperiod. The risk of the strategy did, however, increase in the second subperiod as the standard deviation rose from 12.88% to 18.61% and the percentage of positive return months fell from 70.42% to 56.43%. Thus, the HML strategy's performance during the second subperiod was inferior to its performance during the first subperiod. In expansive conditions, the strategy's performance in the second subperiod, however, was vastly superior to its performance during the other two monetary environments.

Overall, we can conclude that outside of expansive monetary conditions, the HML portfolio offered little to be very enthusiastic about, but the strategy's performance was particularly abysmal when monetary conditions were constrained. Once again, the optimal timing for the implementation of the hedge strategy is when the Fed shifts to an expansive monetary policy, and the associated trades are to buy value stocks and short sell growth stocks. Per our previous addenda, the success of the strategy can be magnified by using more extreme classifications of firms (e.g., top and bottom 10%) and applying a strategy that overweights the long side (e.g., 140/40).

Exploiting the Reversal Phenomenon

We next consider a hedged position that is designed to exploit the reversal premium, which, as was indicated in Chapter 3, is based on the superior performance of losers compared with winners. Losers are defined as firms with poor long-term past performance (i.e., firms whose stock price has been beaten down over the last five years). In contrast, winners are firms whose stock price has been pushed up to lofty levels over the last five years. Evidence has shown that the performance of losers has traditionally trounced the performance of winners over subsequent years.

Table 7.6 shows the performance of the fully invested portfolio that is long the quintile of stocks that have the worst long-term (five-year) performance (losers) and short the quintile of stocks that have performed the best over the last five years. Relative to the other strategies, the LMW portfolio (loser-minus-winner portfolio) displays considerable stability across the two subperiods, but once again, the strategy performs better during the first subperiod.

On the basis of Table 7.6, we would have to label the LMW hedged strategy an investment flop. The strategy produces results that are very similar to the general market during the first subperiod but underperforms the market on a return-to-risk basis by a substantial amount during the second subperiod (0.53 to 0.69).

Table 7.6   Loser-Minus-Winner (LMW) Portfolio Performance

	Full Period (1966–2013), %	*Subperiod 1966–1989, %*	*Subperiod 1990–2013, %*
LMW Portfolio			
Mean annual return	10.04	11.03	9.04
Standard deviation	16.25	15.56	16.94
S&P 500			
Mean annual return	10.56	10.86	10.25
Standard deviation	15.26	15.71	14.82

Reversals and Monetary Conditions

We next evaluate the merits of the LMW strategy relative to monetary conditions. As shown in Table 7.7, the monetary environment is the key to the strategy's success. The strategy offers very attractive returns when the monetary environment is expansive. In addition, the superior performance in expansive conditions is surprisingly consistent across both subperiods as the returns are 17.97% and 16.92%, respectively. On the negative side, the strategy does entail considerable volatility during expansive conditions.

Overall, the LMW strategy shows considerable promise, but once again, only if it is applied in expansive conditions. As with the two previous strategies, our evidence indicates that the LMW hedge should be implemented only when the Fed has shifted to an expansive policy. In such circumstances, the strategy performs remarkably

Table 7.7   Monetary Conditions and LMW Hedged Portfolio Performance: Mean Annual Return (Standard Deviation) and [Percentage of Positive Return Months]

Monetary Conditions	Full Period (1966–2013), %	Subperiod 1966–1989, %	Subperiod 1990–2013, %
Expansive	17.36 (19.08) [54.65]	17.97 (18.77) [50.70]	16.92 (19.39) [57.43]
Indeterminate	5.14 (15.80) [51.20]	6.26 (16.31) [50.46]	3.91 (15.31) [52.00]
Restrictive	8.83 (13.71) [59.49]	11.29 (12.08) [61.11]	5.78 (15.53) [57.47]

well; in addition, our previous addenda could be applied to magnify the strong performance. A couple of the strategy's most favorable features are that it produced very strong returns (16.92%) in the most recent subperiod of expansive conditions, and during the same time frame, the strategy's success rate was 57.43%.

Exploiting Both the Small-Firm Premium and the Value Premium

As we noted with the investment style grid, it is common for investors and funds to combine the size characteristic with price multiples to formulate a combined style strategy. We test one of the most popular hedged portfolio formulations, which is designed to simultaneously exploit both the size premium and the value premium. The strategy we create is fully invested and takes a long position in small-value stocks and a short position in big-growth stocks. Thus, the created portfolio is small-value-minus-big-growth (SVMBG) plus the T-bill return. In investigating the SVMBG hedged portfolio, we use the small-value and big-growth portfolios reported on the Kenneth French website.

The performance for the SVMBG portfolio for the full period and the two subperiods is reported in Table 7.8.

In assessing the performance of the SVMBG strategy we have only two words: ho hum. We were excited to combine the two firm features to form the strategy; however, the strategy's performance in the most recent period is a real letdown. Relative to the S&P 500, the strategy offers minimally higher returns with considerably more risk. I hope at this point you are asking, "But what about monetary conditions?" If you aren't asking that question, you haven't been paying attention.

Table 7.8 Small-Value-Minus-Big-Growth (SVMBG) Portfolio Performance

	Full Period (1966–2013), %	Subperiod 1966–1989, %	Subperiod 1990–2013, %
SVMBG Portfolio			
Mean annual return	14.01	16.53	11.48
Standard deviation	21.19	21.20	21.18
S&P 500			
Mean annual return	10.56	10.86	10.25
Standard deviation	15.26	15.71	14.82

Monetary Conditions and the Style Premium

Of course we are going to consider monetary conditions, and of course this is the crucial consideration. By now you shouldn't expect anything else. Table 7.9 presents the performance of the SVMBG strategy across the three monetary environments.

We may be a little biased, but we believe the performance results in Table 7.9 are fabulous. The strategy produces incredible results during expansive periods, and, more important, the incredible results persist during both subperiods (42.64% and 27.54%). You may be asking, But what about those extremely high risk levels (23.99% and 24.96%)? This is where the percentage of positive return months becomes very instructive. Note that the strategy is successful in 64.79% of months during the first subperiod and 63.37% of months during the second subperiod. What this implies is that the large standard deviation values can be attributed to the strategy producing a number of unusually large positive return values. When your portfolio risk is driven by an unusual number of large positive returns, that's when you throw a big party. Remember,

Table 7.9   Monetary Environment and SVMBG Hedged Portfolio Performance: Mean Annual Return (Standard Deviation) and [Percentage of Positive Return Months]

Monetary Conditions	Full Period (1966–2013), %	Subperiod 1966–1989, %	Subperiod 1990–2013, %
Expansive	33.77	42.64	27.54
	(24.59)	(23.99)	(24.96)
	[63.95]	[64.79]	[63.37]
Indeterminate	5.37	5.23	5.53
	(20.28)	(21.33)	(19.16)
	[52.15]	[52.73]	[51.51]
Restrictive	5.80	10.83	−0.38
	(17.73)	(17.82)	(17.57)
	[51.03]	[54.21]	[47.13]

the strategy's amazing results are obtained even without magnifying the returns by refining the sample of firms or using an overweighted hedge structure.

With respect to indeterminate and restrictive periods, we can simply say that the SVMBG strategy is consistently pretty bad. During these periods, the strategy produces subpar returns with above-average risk levels, clearly a losing combination.

How Can You Create a Hedged Portfolio?

As you may have guessed, there are ETFs and ETNs that allow you to capture the return patterns associated with the hedged positions identified above. Unlike mutual funds, which allow investors to take only long positions in the fund, you can enter short positions in ETFs and ETNs. Table 7.10 reports some ETF/ETN positions that would

Table 7.10 Creation of a Hedged Portfolio with ETFs/ETNs

Hedged Position	Return Pattern to Exploit	Long Position ETF/ETN	Short Position ETF/ETN
Small-minus-big (SMB) hedged portfolio	Small-firm premium	Vanguard Small-Cap (VB)	Schwab Fundamental U.S. Large Company (FNDX)
High-minus-low (HML) hedged portfolio	Value-firm premium	iShares Russell 3000 Value (IWW)	iShares Russell 3000 Growth (IWZ)
Small-value-minus-big-growth (style) hedged portfolio	Combination of small-firm premium and value premium	Vanguard Small-Cap Value (VBR)	Vanguard Mega Cap Growth (MGK)

allow an investor to replicate a hedged portfolio. To capture the return from one of the acknowledged return patterns, the investor would purchase the security in the long position column and short sell the corresponding security in the short position column.

Conclusion

In this chapter we reported the performance of several hedge fund strategies that are designed to exploit recognized stock return patterns. We showed that the success of these strategies depends almost exclusively on the monetary environment. Specifically, when Fed policy is expansive, the performance of the strategies is exceptional, but the strategies perform poorly when Fed policy is indeterminate or restrictive. Our most interesting results pertain to a common strategy that is long (i.e., purchases) small-value stocks and short (i.e., short sells) big-growth stocks. We show that when monetary conditions are expansive, the strategy produces phenomenal results even without using the leverage that hedge funds frequently apply to magnify their bets. This same strategy, however, has generally been a dud when monetary conditions are indeterminate or restrictive. Overall, our evidence indicates that there is a lot to get excited about when it comes to hedge funds; however, your excitement level should mirror Fed policy developments.

CHAPTER 8

FIXED-INCOME SECURITIES

These days, with firms such as Google and Apple, everyone takes dynamism for granted. But Mike Milken started out in the 1970s when capitalism was struggling. In those days, there was very little innovation. Along comes Drexel, a firm with a visionary purpose, and suddenly you could get capital.

Kenneth Moelis, head of the investment bank Moelis & Company[1]

In Chapter 1 we considered the performance of two traditional fixed-income securities—long-term Treasury bonds (T-bonds) and short-term Treasury bills (T-bills)—across the three monetary environments. In this chapter we provide a much more thorough analysis of the fixed-income market by considering a broad spectrum of fixed-income securities. We consider bonds from the lowest-risk classifications (Treasury, government, and investment-grade corporates) to the highest-risk classifications (high-yield corporates). We also examine fixed-income securities across the maturity spectrum from the shortest-term money market securities (3-month T-bills) to the longest-maturity bonds (long-term Treasuries).

In this section, we examine the performance of the highest-quality (lowest-risk) classification of bonds. Treasury bonds are issued by the U.S. government and are generally considered to have the lowest default risk of any U.S. security or indeed of any security in the world. The term *default risk* refers to the risk that a security will break its contractual obligation. Of course, for investors, the most critical obligation is the security's specified interest and principal payments. Government bonds are issued by agencies of the federal government such as the Government National Mortgage Association (GNMA or, more popularly, Ginnie Mae). Government bonds are considered to have comparable default risk to a Treasury bond but are sometimes less liquid (i.e., they can be harder to sell quickly at a fair price). The final classification of high-quality bonds considered here is investment-grade corporates. This classification includes corporate bonds that have relatively low default risk (see Box 8.1 for further discussion of investment-grade bonds).

Box 8.1   What Is an Investment-Grade Bond?

Similar to the grades handed out by teachers to students in educational systems, bond rating agencies provide ratings or grades for individual bond issues. Standard & Poor's, Moody's Investors Service, and Fitch Ratings assign ratings to all different types of bonds from sovereign government debt to corporate bonds and even very complex mortgage-backed securities. The purpose of bond ratings is to give investors an idea of a bond's creditworthiness or risk of default. Simply put, creditworthiness is a measure of how likely the lender (the bondholder) is to receive both the promised interest and the principal payments. It should be noted that bond rating agencies are explicit that their ratings are only opinions.

Much like letter grades, bond ratings range from AAA to D, and much like letter grades, bond rating agencies seem to live in the fictional Lake Wobegon, where "all the women are strong, all the men are good looking, and all the children are above average." A bond rating of C is certainly not average. For instance, the definition of a C rating for Moody's is as follows: "Obligations rated C are the lowest rated class of bonds and are typically in default, with little prospect for recovery of principal or interest."[2] That certainly doesn't sound like an average-quality bond. It seems that bond ratings have a bit of grade inflation built into them.

An investment-grade bond is one that is rated BBB– or higher by Standard & Poor's and Fitch or Baa3 or higher by Moody's. Thus, investment-grade bonds include bonds in the four highest quality rating categories; for Standard & Poor's that would be AAA, AA, A, and BBB. The distinction between being investment-grade and being non-investment-grade is extremely important. Some institutional investors have provisions in their investment policy statements that allow them to hold only investment-grade securities. Thus, if a certain institutional investor holds a security that is downgraded from investment-grade to below investment-grade, the investor is forced to sell the holding.

In general, the lower the bond rating, the higher the bond's yield to maturity. That is, to induce investors to purchase riskier bonds, issuing firms and institutions must be willing to offer higher yields. This is also why bond issuers want bond rating agencies to give them the highest grades possible. For all bond issuers—federal, state, and municipal governments as well as corporations—the difference of one bond rating category can mean millions or even billions of dollars of difference in interest costs.

(continued)

Credit ratings are determined by a combination of quantitative and qualitative considerations. Just as you probably feel that there was a teacher who assigned you an inappropriate grade, sometimes credit ratings agencies seem to fail with their ratings. For instance, just one year before the Russian government debt default of 1998, Russian debt was rated BB– and Ba2 by Standard & Poor's and Moody's, respectively. Even more egregious was the performance of credit rating agencies with respect to mortgage-backed security ratings during the financial crisis of 2008. Many mortgage-backed securities with AAA ratings defaulted, and investors ended up receiving a fraction of what they paid for the securities.

It is ironic that before the financial crisis many mortgage-backed securities carried triple-A ratings considering the fact that triple-A ratings on corporate debt are nearly extinct. As of June 2014, only three U.S. companies had triple-A ratings by Moody's and Standard & Poor's: Johnson & Johnson, Exxon Mobil, and Microsoft. Of the three, Fitch rates only Johnson & Johnson as triple-A.[3] Even Warren Buffett's Berkshire Hathaway lost its triple-A rating from Standard & Poor's in 2010.[4]

The Performance of Investment-Grade Bonds

Table 8.1 reports the performance of the three categories of high-quality bonds across the three monetary environments. In examining bond performance, it is important to differentiate the actual return on a bond investment from that bond's promised return. In this chapter, the mean returns we report are derived as an average of actual bond returns. A bond's promised return is

Table 8.1　High-Quality Bond Performance by Monetary Environment: 1973–2013

Bond Classification	Bond Issuer	*Mean Annual Return and (Standard Deviation) by Monetary Environment*		
		Expansive	*Indeterminate*	*Restrictive*
T-bonds	U.S. Treasury	6.98% (5.72%)	9.07% (4.95%)	6.27% (5.28%)
Government bonds	U.S. government agency	7.33% (5.48%)	9.06% (4.83%)	6.05% (5.24%)
Investment-grade bonds	Large, financially sound U.S. corporation	8.97% (7.49%)	10.05% (6.82%)	5.01% (7.38%)

represented by its yield to maturity (YTM) and is, roughly speaking, the annual return an investor would earn if the bond was purchased and held to maturity. Actual returns are generally considered more appropriate for evaluating bond performance because bonds are frequently sold before maturity. For example, investors purchasing 20-year bonds frequently hold those bonds for 1 year or less.

The performance data in Table 8.1 show that all three categories of bonds performed best during indeterminate periods. Incredibly, bonds reported both their highest return and their lowest risk when monetary conditions were indeterminate. Compared with the return differences we reported earlier in this book, the return differences here may seem somewhat muted; however, the relatively low volatility in bond returns (the standard deviations are approximately one-third the volatility of stocks) supports the practical relevance of the differences. Remember, consistency in returns is a crucial consideration for investors.

The second best performance for the bond categories occurred during expansive monetary periods, and the worst performance occurred when monetary conditions were restrictive. For example, in February 2001 the Fed adjusted both policy rates downward, thus shifting to an expansive monetary posture; over the next 12 months, investment-grade bonds returned 7.94%. Subsequently, in July 2004 the Fed increased policy rates, thus shifting to a restrictive posture; over the next 12 months investment-grade bonds returned 5.77%.

Although it may seem odd that indeterminate periods had the best performance, it's possible that this observation mirrors inflation pressures. Inflation is a huge threat to a fixed-income investor because it eats away at the investor's return; in this case the return occurs in the form of a payment of a fixed size. When monetary conditions are restrictive, the Fed is in an inflation-fighting mode, which means that inflation is a credible current problem. When monetary conditions are expansive, it means the Fed is applying an easy money policy, which investors may view as creating a climate for future inflation troubles. During indeterminate periods, there are no clear inflation signals either way.

Interestingly, the best-performing bond class during expansive periods was investment-grade bonds; however, they were by far the worst performers when conditions were restrictive. T-bonds did best when conditions were restrictive. Under indeterminate conditions, there was not a clear-cut winner as investment-grade bonds had the highest return but also had considerably higher risk. Although this is not considered here, investors need to also consider tax effects when evaluating the merits of a fixed-income investment or for that matter any investment. See Box 8.2 for a discussion of some broad tax implications of bond investments.

Box 8.2   What About Taxes?

Most investors are aware that bonds issued by municipalities (state and local governments) receive favorable tax treatment. The income from municipal bonds is exempt from federal income taxes, and in most cases investors are also able to avoid paying state and local income taxes on municipal bond income. Investors can avoid state and local income taxes on municipal bond income by purchasing bonds from their own local municipalities. That is why investment companies package municipal bonds by state [see, for example, the Vanguard Massachusetts Tax-Exempt Fund (VMATX) or the USAA Virginia Bond Fund (USVAX)].

In contrast, the tax benefit of Treasury securities is sometimes overlooked. The income from Treasury securities is taxed at the federal level but is exempt from taxes at the state and local levels. In a high-income tax state such as California, which has a top marginal rate of 13.3%, the difference between gross return and net return can be substantial. The tax benefit of securities that are exempt from state taxation relative to those which are not, however, eludes residents of states such as Florida and Texas that have no state income tax.

To compare the after-tax rate on taxable and nontaxable bonds, investors should compute the tax equivalent yield. That is, you take the tax-exempt yield and "gross it up" for the effect of the tax exemption. Suppose you are a resident of California, are in the top marginal income tax bracket (13.3%), and purchase a T-bond with a 4.8% yield. What is the tax equivalent yield on the bond?

$$Tax\ equivalent\ yield = \frac{Tax\ exempt\ yield}{1 - marginal\ tax\ rate}$$

$$= \frac{0.048}{1 - 0.133} = 0.0554 = 5.54\%$$

(*continued*)

Thus, a taxable bond would have to pay 5.54% to make it "equivalent" to its nontaxable peer that is paying 4.8%.

Continuing the example, suppose you are in the 28% marginal tax bracket at the federal level and decide to invest in a bond issued by the state of California with a 4.2% yield. As was stated earlier, by purchasing a municipal bond, a bondholder can avoid federal taxes as well as state and local taxes. To approximate the combined tax equivalent yield you simply add the effective state tax rate to the federal tax rate and use the sum as your marginal tax rate. The approximate combined marginal tax rate is 28% + 13.3%, a total of 41.3%. The tax equivalent yield is

$$Tax\ equivalent\ yield = \frac{Tax\ exempt\ yield}{1 - marginal\ tax\ rate}$$

$$= \frac{0.042}{1 - 0.413} = 0.0716 = 7.16\%$$

With both fresh produce and municipal bonds, it pays to buy local.

Fed Policy and the Performance of High-Yield Bonds

Although high-quality bonds are the dominant bond category by value, high-yield bonds tend to attract the majority of press coverage. High-yield bonds are generally referred to by their more popular designation *junk bond,* or in some cases they are referred to as *speculative bonds.* The term *junk bond* was coined by the financial media in an effort to create a catchier term to reference these instruments. Obviously, an investment manager advocating the purchase of these instruments for a client's portfolio is likely to go with the designation high-yield bonds rather than junk bonds. See Box 8.3 for a discussion of the junk bond market. In this section we consider how monetary conditions relate to the performance of high-yield bonds and default-free bonds.

Box 8.3   The Birth of a Market

Junk bonds have been around as long as bond ratings have been handed out. However, before the 1980s, the majority of junk bonds were issued as investment-grade bonds; they became junk bonds only when the fortunes of these companies took a turn for the worse and the bonds were downgraded to junk status. The financial markets are full of colorful terminology, and the junk bond market is no exception. Bonds that were originally issued as investment-grade and have fallen to junk status are known as fallen angels.

The leveraged buyout (LBO) craze of the 1980s was largely financed with original-issue junk bonds, that is, bonds that by design were issued at below investment grade. Leveraged buyouts are deals in which a buyer borrows money and uses it to purchase a target firm. The world's most famous LBO is the approximately $25 billion takeover of RJR Nabisco by the private equity firm Kohlberg Kravis Roberts in 1989. This deal was immortalized in the book *Barbarians at the Gate* and the movie of the same name.

Table 8.2 reports the performance for the junk (high-yield) bond index and for comparison purposes also reports the performance of the T-bond index over the same time frame. Return data for the high-yield bond index are available starting in July 1983, and therefore all the analyses in this chapter that use the high-yield index

Table 8.2   Performance of High-Yield (Junk) Bonds Versus T-Bonds: July 1983–2013

	Mean Annual Return (Standard Deviation), % and [Percent of Positive Months]			
		Monetary Environment		
Index	Full Period	Expansive	Indeterminate	Restrictive
High-yield	9.46	12.40	7.58	8.50
	(8.58)	(11.17)	(7.82)	(5.67)
T-bonds	7.30	6.48	8.10	7.22
	(4.89)	(5.71)	(4.53)	(4.32)
Junk premium	2.17	5.92	−0.52	1.28
high-yield less T-bonds	(9.62)	(12.69)	(8.20)	(6.85)
	[56.00]	[58.20]	[49.60]	[61.50]

Note: Data for high-yield bonds are available starting in July 1983.

begin in July 1983. Performance data are reported for the full sample period and separately for each of the three monetary environments. We also report the mean return difference between the two indexes (we reference it as the junk premium), the standard deviation of the return differences, and the percentage of positive monthly return differences. The return difference can be thought of as the return to a hedged position that is long high-yield bonds and has a short position of an equivalent value in T-bonds. This hedged position requires no net investment (other than the margin one would be required to post). If you think about the difference in two return series as being a hedged position, you are thinking like a hedge fund manager.

The performance data in Table 8.2 indicate that for the full period, the average return to high-yield bonds substantially exceeded the return to T-bonds (9.46% versus 7.30%). It is this spread in performance (2.17%) that entices investors to allocate a portion of their fixed-income portfolios to junk bonds. The much higher volatility of high-yield bonds, however, is the factor that constrains investors from making junk bonds the majority of their fixed-income allocation. At 2.17%, the hedged position performs reasonably well, but there is relatively high uncertainty associated with the strategy. The standard deviation of the hedged strategy is higher than that of either index individually; however, the strategy does generate a positive return in 56% of months.

The most interesting data in Table 8.2 are the disparate return patterns for the high-yield index across the three monetary environments. Relative to indeterminate and restrictive monetary periods, the performance of high-yield bonds is dramatically better during expansive conditions. Furthermore, the return spread between high-yield bonds and T-bonds at 5.92% is enormous during expansive periods, is small during restrictive periods (1.28%), and, incredibly, is negative during indeterminate periods (−0.52%). This indicates that the greater reward that investors achieve for assuming the risk of holding junk bonds can be attributed almost entirely to the outstanding performance of those bonds in expansive monetary conditions. The very large and fairly consistent (it is positive in over 58% of months) junk premium during expansive periods is an attractive factor for hedge fund managers. Remember that hedge funds can lever/magnify a return premium by overweighting the long side of a hedged position. I'm sure that a hedge fund manager looking at these results would state, "There's big money to be made in that junk."

We offer an example that is based on an investor who used Fed policy shifts to initiate an investment in a fund that targeted the junk premium. We base the example on the three most recent monetary periods that existed for consecutive seven-month periods. For instance, an expansive monetary period started when the Fed shifted both policy rates downward in August 2009. By the time the Fed shifted rates again seven months later, an investor holding a fund targeting the junk premium would have earned 13.2%. An indeterminate environment was initiated in January 2011, when the Fed's two policy rates contradicted each other; seven months later an investor who held a junk premium fund would have earned only 2.00%. Finally, in February 2012, the Fed shifted both policy rates upward, creating a restrictive environment; by the time the restrictive environment ended seven months later, an investor targeting the junk premium would have earned 5.16%.

Overall, the evidence in Table 8.2 indicates that there is no incentive to hold junk bonds when monetary conditions are indeterminate. Furthermore, in restrictive conditions, junk bonds have surprisingly little risk, which makes their somewhat higher return only moderately appealing. The performance of junk bonds across the three monetary environments roughly mirrors the performance of the stock market. This observation is consistent with investment managers using junk bonds as an alternative approach to gain exposure to stocks. See Box 8.4 on the use of junk bonds to achieve stock market exposure.

For investors interested in getting an exposure to high-yield bonds, there are several alternative investment vehicles. Mutual funds offering high-yield exposure include Loomis Sayles Institutional High Income Fund (LSHIX) and TIAA-CREF High Yield Fund (TIHYX); ETFs offering the same exposure include iShares iBoxx $ High Yield Corporate Bond Fund (HYG) and SPDR Barclays Capital High Yield Bond (JNK).

Box 8.4   Not All Bonds Are Created Equal

Many investors believe that there are bonds and there are stocks and never the twain shall meet. There are some investors, however, who believe that high-yield bonds should be considered a potential substitute for common stock. Douglas Peebles, chief investment officer and head of fixed income investments at AllianceBernstein, puts the issue this way: "Instead of thinking about how much of their bond exposure they should allocate to high yield, we think investors should ask how much equity exposure they should allocate to high yield."[5] Peebles notes that high-yield bonds have characteristics that differentiate them from investment-grade bonds, yet those features align them with common stock. Specifically, relative to investment-grade debt, the return to high-yield bonds is more strongly linked to the business results and fundamentals of the underlying firms. In addition, Peebles contends that high-yield bond prices are generally less sensitive to changes in market interest rates than are their investment-grade counterparts.

Table 8.3 reports performance data and correlations to provide the data necessary to perform a valid assessment of the comparability of the three securities' performance.

As was noted previously, the attraction to high-yield bonds is based on their higher returns relative to investment-grade bonds. On the basis of the returns in Table 8.3, high-yield bonds offer a return premium of 1.22% relative to investment-grade bonds while underperforming stocks by 2.16%. Although investors generally view high-yield (junk) bonds as high-risk holdings, the standard deviations indicate that their high-risk status is entirely dependent on the comparison group. High-yield bonds subject investors to somewhat higher risk than do investment-grade bonds (8.58% versus 5.75%);

(continued)

Table 8.3   High-Yield Bonds, Investment-Grade Bonds, and Stocks: July 1983–2013

Security	Mean Annual Return	Standard Deviation	Return-to-Risk Ratio	Correlation With Investment-Grade Bonds	S&P 500
High-yield bonds	9.46%	8.58%	1.10	0.53	0.58
Investment-grade Bonds	8.24%	5.75%	1.43	1.00	0.29
S&P 500	11.62%	15.22%	0.76	0.29	1.00

however, they are a much lower-risk option than stocks (8.58% versus 15.22%). Overall, the return-to-risk ratios indicate that high-yield bonds compare favorably as an investment alternative with both investment-grade bonds and stocks.

Finally, the correlations in Table 8.3 support the view that high-yield bonds are more similar to common stock than to investment-grade bonds. The correlation between the returns to high-yield bonds and stocks is 0.58, whereas high-yield bonds exhibit a correlation of only 0.53 with investment-grade bonds. Thus, high-yield bond prices track fluctuations in the equity market more closely than they do fluctuations in high-quality bond prices.

On the basis of an overall assessment of the data in Table 8.3, we believe there is evidence to support the contention that high-yield bonds merit consideration as a substitute for common stock. Therefore, we conclude that one person's junk bond is another person's stock treasure.

Fed Policy Shifts and Bond Performance by Maturity

Our earlier analyses considered the impact that monetary conditions have on the relationship between bond quality and return patterns. In the following section we investigate the influence that monetary conditions have on the relationship between bond maturity and bond performance. Fixed-income investors also frequently examine the relationship between the yield to maturity (YTM) on bonds (their promised return) and their time to maturity. See Box 8.5 for a discussion of bond maturities and YTMs.

Box 8.5   What Is the Yield Curve?

The yield curve is a graph that shows the relationship between bond yield to maturity (YTM) and time to maturity (TTM). As was indicated previously, YTM represents a bond's promised return, and roughly speaking, it is the annual return an investor will realize if the bond is purchased and held to maturity. In constructing the yield curve, YTM is plotted on the vertical axis and TTM on the horizontal axis.

The reason the yield curve holds such allure for fixed-income investors is that it depicts the consensus view of market participants' expectations regarding future interest rates; that is, it is a barometer for future interest rates. The shape of the yield curve is constantly changing to reflect changes in interest rate expectations. An example yield curve created from Treasury yields reported on August 18, 2014, is shown in Figure 8.1.

In August 2014, investors in 2-year T-bonds would have expected to earn an annual return of 0.44% over the next 2 years, whereas

(continued)

Figure 8.1   Treasury Yields Reported on August 18, 2014

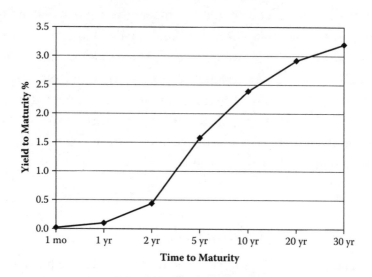

investors in 30-year T-bonds would have expected to earn 3.20% per year over the next 30 years. Why would any investor accept an annual return of 0.44% when he or she could earn 3.20%? The answer is that investors expected interest rates to increase considerably in the future, quite likely because of the anticipation of a Fed shift to a restrictive policy posture in the not too distant future. Therefore, investors were willing to accept the lower returns in the near term to be able to take advantage of the higher-return bonds that were anticipated to be available two years later.

Thus, if you are engaged in conversation with someone and that person states, "I think interest rates are going to rise," if the yield curve appears as it is in Figure 8.1, the appropriate response is, "Well, duh, so does virtually every other investor in the world." The financial markets do not reward investors who have the consensus view because that view is already priced into the market. To receive a reward from the financial markets, two things are necessary. First, your view has to differ from the consensus, and second, you must be right. For example, in January 2011, the yield curve was much steeper than it is now because the consensus view was that interest rates would increase sharply in the near future, and bond prices reflected that view. Instead, rates fell substantially during 2011, producing a substantial gain for investors who took positions that contrasted with the consensus view.

Short Maturity or Long Maturity: Which Is Best?

Table 8.4 reports performance for short-term (3-month and 1-year) T-bills, intermediate-term T-notes (10-year notes), and long-term T-bonds (30-year bonds).[6]

The performance results in Table 8.4 for the full period show a steady progression in returns as maturity is extended. The

Table 8.4   Performance of Treasury Securities by Maturity: January 1973–2013

	Mean Annual Return and (Standard Deviation), %			
		Monetary Environment		
Treasury Index	*Full Period*	*Expansive*	*Indeterminate*	*Restrictive*
3-month T-bill	5.56	4.87	5.71	6.06
	(1.14)	(0.93)	(1.16)	(1.98)
1-year T-bill	6.18	6.02	6.86	5.61
	(2.02)	(1.74)	(1.99)	(2.29)
Intermediate-term	7.78	7.07	10.09	6.00
T-note (10-year note)	(7.98)	(8.71)	(7.75)	(7.47)
Long-term T-bond	8.10	7.18	9.82	7.15
	(12.29)	(14.07)	(10.88)	(11.92)

progression in returns corresponds with a comparable pattern in standard deviations, and this reflects the greater risk associated with longer-maturity securities. See Box 8.6 for further discussion of bond maturity and bond risk.

Box 8.6 Which Has Greater Risk, Junk Bonds or Long-Term Treasuries?

Aren't securities issued by the federal government risk-free? As we noted in Chapter 1, Treasury securities are free of default risk but not interest rate risk. However, we suspect that if you asked most investors which investment entails greater risk, an investment in junk bonds or an investment in long-term Treasuries, the emphatic and overwhelming response would be that the junk bond investment has greater risk. Table 8.5 reports performance data for the two alternatives so that their performance can be directly compared.

Table 8.5 Performance of Junk Bonds and Long-Term T-Bonds: July 1983–2013

Security	Mean Annual Return	Standard Deviation	Return-to-Risk Ratio
High-yield bonds	9.46%	8.58%	1.10
Long-term T-bonds	8.89%	12.55%	0.71

Remarkably, an investment in long-term T-bonds subjects investors to far greater risk than does an investment in junk bonds (12.55% versus 8.58%). Furthermore, the high-yield bonds have a higher mean return. Putting the return and risk together, we see from the return-to-risk ratios that high-yield bonds dominate long-term T-bonds. Why would any investor purchase long-term T-bonds? The obvious answer is that the data in Table 8.5 do not consider the tax advantage of T-bonds.

The evidence in Table 8.5 clearly indicates that the risk of long-term Treasuries dwarfs the risk of junk bonds. Why are so many investors oblivious to this point? We believe the answer is that investors focus their attention on default risk rather than interest rate risk, probably because of the scrutiny and attention that bond ratings receive. Interest rate risk is measured by a statistical measure called duration that indicates a bond's sensitivity to changes in interest rates. Bond ratings are bandied about by the financial media constantly, but when have you ever heard the financial media reference a bond's duration?

Maturity Return Premium and Monetary Conditions

In considering performance across monetary periods, your first impression may be that there was no material difference in short-term (3-month T-bill) returns across the monetary periods. After all, the return difference is only about 1%. Before drawing that conclusion, it is important to consider the certainty of the returns as represented by the standard deviations. Although the difference in mean returns is relatively small, the lack of volatility (i.e., the certainty) in the returns makes the observed difference more reliable. In fact, statistical tests confirm that the return difference across the monetary environments for the 3-month T-bill is the most reliable difference among the four securities in Table 8.4.

Finally, comparing the returns of the longest-maturity security with those of the shortest-maturity security suggests a consistent positive return premium across the monetary environments. The premium is quite small during restrictive periods at 1.09% (7.15 – 6.06), is fairly prominent during expansive conditions at 2.31% (7.18 – 4.87), and is very large during indeterminate periods at 4.11% (9.82 – 5.71). These values clearly merit additional investigation, which is what we do in our next analysis.

Table 8.6 reports a couple of key characteristics of the difference between the return to long-term T-bonds and the return to 3-month T-bills. We call this return difference the maturity premium. As was noted previously, it is important to evaluate the consistency of a return pattern before making a final assessment of the pattern's legitimacy.

Table 8.6 Maturity Return Premium, Long-Term Versus Short-Term Treasuries: January 1973–2013

		Mean Annual Return (Standard Deviation) and [Percent of Positive Months]		
			Monetary Environment	
Index	*Full Period*	*Expansive*	*Indeterminate*	*Restrictive*
3-month T-bill	5.56	4.87	5.71	6.06
	(1.14)	(0.93)	(1.16)	(1.98)
Long-term T-bond	8.10	7.18	9.82	7.15
	(12.29)	(14.07)	(10.88)	(11.92)
Maturity premium	2.54	2.31	4.11	1.09
long-term bond less	(12.16)	(13.91)	(10.76)	(11.82)
short-term T-bill	[52.00]	[52.20]	[54.90]	[48.80]

At 2.54%, the maturity premium for the full period is rather enticing. You can think of the premium as the return to a portfolio that takes a long position in long-term T-bonds and a short position of equal size in 3-month T-bills. Thus, the strategy requires no net investment. Of course, an investor would have to post margin (collateral) as backing for the position. Purely on the basis of returns, a fixed-income strategy that requires no net investment and allows an investor to generate an annual return of 2.54% is very attractive. However, the moderately high standard deviation and the moderately low percentage of months in which the strategy is successful raise some concern about the strategy's reliability.

Once again, the most interesting aspect of the performance reported in Table 8.6 revolves around monetary conditions. When the Fed shifts policy rates upward (i.e., during restrictive conditions), the maturity premium is small and relatively inconsistent. The premium is only marginally more attractive after the Fed lowers policy rates (i.e., during expansive conditions). The 4.11% maturity premium in indeterminate conditions is an attractive outcome, and it is further promoted by the observation that the strategy's success rate is 54.9%. The size and general consistency of the maturity premium in indeterminate conditions has to be especially alluring to hedge funds since they can lever (magnify) their bets by overweighting the long side of a strategy.

We are pleased with the performance results in Table 8.6 because they run somewhat contrary to the general pattern displayed by equity securities. The strong maturity premium in indeterminate periods contrasts with the moderate performance of most equity classes in those conditions. When one is building a portfolio, the more diversity of asset return patterns that can be incorporated, the better the final result. As you have come to expect, there are ETFs that will help in your effort to build maturity diversity in your fixed-income portfolio, and remember, ETFs allow you to establish both long positions and short positions. ETFs that offer exposures to bonds of various alternative maturities include Guggenheim BulletShares and iSharesBond. In addition, Guggenheim offers a high-yield variation of its BulletShares.

Conclusion

In this chapter we considered two basic features of bonds: default risk and time to maturity. We investigated how these characteristics influence bond performance and, furthermore, how bond performance interacts with these bond features and with monetary conditions. Our findings offer some interesting and useful relationships for investors interested in establishing a fixed-income exposure. On the basis of our evidence, fixed-income investors should target high-yield bonds when monetary conditions are expansive and target long-term bonds when conditions are indeterminate. The identified diversity of performance across monetary environments offers attractive reallocation opportunities. For example, establishing a hedged position, especially a levered position, to exploit the junk premium when monetary conditions were expansive and reallocating to exploit the maturity premium during indeterminate conditions would have provided a fund manager with phenomenal results.

CHAPTER 9

INVESTMENT STRATEGIES

> To reduce risk it is necessary to avoid a portfolio whose securities are all highly correlated with each other. One hundred securities whose returns rise and fall in near unison afford little more protection than the uncertain return of a single security.
>
> *Harry Markowitz, recipient of the*
> *1990 Nobel Prize in economics*[1]

In this chapter we combine the material presented in previous chapters to consider alternative comprehensive investment strategies. As you might expect, each of these comprehensive strategies is predicated on shifts in Fed monetary policy. Specifically, monetary conditions serve as the basis for determining the appropriate portfolio composition and identifying the appropriate timing for a shift in portfolio weights. In earlier chapters we alluded to potential trades that investors could make to take advantage of return patterns. Now we are ready to forge ahead to see the outcomes that are possible from using monetary conditions to implement a comprehensive investment strategy.

It is common in the investment industry for advisors to recommend static allocations for investors. For example, an advisor may recommend that an investor allocate his or her portfolio along the lines of 25% bonds, 25% large-cap U.S. equities, and 10% to each of U.S. small-caps, foreign developed market equities, emerging market equities, real estate, and commodities. For investors who are relatively risk averse, a more conservative allocation may be more appropriate, and those investors would weight bonds, large-cap U.S. equities, and equities of foreign developed markets more heavily. In comparison, investors with relatively high risk tolerance probably would prefer a more aggressive allocation and thus would assign those three asset categories less weight.

Designing a Dynamic Investment Strategy

We believe the appropriate weights to be applied to alternative asset classes depend on both the investor's level of risk aversion and, more important, the existing monetary environment as identified by Fed policy shifts. Our earlier findings show that the best allocation after a Fed shift to an expansive policy posture is clearly a subpar allocation when the Fed is applying a restrictive monetary policy. We investigate the alternative allocations with two goals in mind. First, on the basis of the benefit of hindsight, we show the potential performance for an investor who implements a dynamic allocation strategy guided by Fed policy shifts. Second, we evaluate the composition of the portfolio in each monetary environment to establish the types of securities that are optimal in alternative monetary conditions.

We consider two allocations that are fairly simple in their design and construction. The two allocations are not presented as definitive recommendations but are meant to offer a rough representation of each strategy's potential. We recommend that investors apply unique twists in constructing a portfolio that best matches their individual preferences.

In constructing our two allocations we select securities from two alternative investment sets. An investment set includes the types of securities that are feasible investment vehicles for the investor. For a variety of reasons, investors limit their portfolios, either by choice or by mandate, to particular investment sets (i.e., types of securities). For example, an equity fund manager is constrained to invest the vast majority of fund assets in common stock, whereas a global-macro hedge fund manager is free to select across a broad array of securities. In light of the constraints that investors face in making their security choices, we consider two alternative investment strategies that are based on fairly broad investment sets.

Finally, it is worth pointing out in advance that neither of our allocations includes fixed-income securities (money market securities and bonds). This is not because we are opposed to fixed-income securities but merely reflects the fact that the returns to fixed-income securities are relatively invariant to the monetary environment. By far the biggest return patterns exist across the alternative equity classes and commodities, and so that is where we focus our attention. However, we strongly recommend that investors supplement their portfolios with fixed-income securities. Furthermore, we recommend reviewing the information in Chapter 8 when one is establishing a fixed-income position.

We start by considering a basic investment set that is limited to common stock of U.S. firms. This constraint actually provides considerable flexibility as it includes a number of alternative classifications of common stock. From earlier chapters, we find that monetary conditions influence the success of investments in common stocks categorized by firm size, price multiple, past stock performance, and industry/sector. Our evidence shows that there is substantial variation in performance across the various equity types, with performance being closely tied to monetary conditions. The return patterns are consistent with our theory that monetary conditions influence the success of alternative types of firms. There are firms that prosper when money is readily available and spending is relatively unconstrained (i.e., when Fed policy is expansive). Other firms do relatively well when money is harder to come by and spending is somewhat constrained (when monetary policy is restrictive). When monetary conditions are indeterminate, there is no clear direction regarding the availability of money, and thus there is less dispersion in performance across equity types.

Monetary Conditions and the Best Performing Equities

On the basis of the returns observed in previous chapters, Table 9.1 provides a summary of the top five performing stock categories in each of the three monetary environments. The equity classes are ranked by mean return from highest to lowest in each environment.

In expansive environments, the top performing equity classes include firms that generally prosper during periods when funds tend to be more readily available. Small firms that have somewhat depressed stock prices and that have been beaten down tend to flourish on a relative basis when money is more readily available because these firms are able to access much-needed capital. Expansive conditions also offer the greatest benefit to the firms that are most reliant on consumer spending for their earnings, that is, firms that manufacture and sell discretionary products to consumers. Overall, the top equity classes during expansive periods include cyclical firms with above-average risk levels.

Table 9.1   Top Five Equity Classes by Performance in Expansive, Indeterminate, and Restrictive Monetary Environments: 1966–2013

Panel A. Expansive Conditions

Equity Class	Mean Annual Return, %	Standard Deviation, %
1. Small-value	44.04	26.23
2. Past performance losers	30.16	24.49
3. Apparel	28.45	23.62
4. Retail	27.03	19.30
5. Autos	25.42	25.20

Panel B. Indeterminate Conditions

Equity Class	Mean Annual Return, %	Standard Deviation, %
1. Energy	15.35	18.33
2. Consumer goods	14.95	16.96
3. Financials	14.55	18.74
4. Food	14.39	15.09
5. Average past performers	14.39	15.06

Panel C. Restrictive Conditions

Equity Class	Mean Annual Return, %	Standard Deviation, %
1. Energy	11.47	21.11
2. Consumer goods	8.36	15.46
3. Utilities	7.77	13.51
4. Food	7.00	15.10
5. Steel products	6.93	25.23

During indeterminate monetary periods, the top five performers consist of a compilation of average firms. The five equity classes consist of firms with average risk levels and moderate reliance on discretionary spending. The inclusion of average past performers best exemplifies the makeup of this group. The stock performance of average past performers over the last five years was just average; they neither prospered nor languished.

During restrictive monetary periods, the best performers were firms that offer necessities. These firms have relatively little reliance on disposable income. They generally have below-average risk levels and are generally considered defensive firms.

The Performance of an Equity Rotation Strategy Guided by Monetary Conditions

On the basis of the equity classes reported in Table 9.1, we designed a rotation strategy that is guided by monetary conditions. The strategy assumes the following positions relative to the three monetary environments. In each of the three monetary environments, the strategy takes equal weights in each of the five equity categories that were top performers in the respective environment. That means that when the Fed initiates an expansive monetary environment by lowering policy rates, the portfolio consists of 20% in each of the following equity types: small-value, losers, apparel, retail, and autos. In indeterminate conditions the Fed's signals are contradictory as it is lowering one policy rate and raising the other. In this environment, the portfolio invests 20% in each of the following equity types: energy, consumer goods, financials, food, and average past performers. Finally, when the Fed increases policy rates and shifts to a restrictive monetary environment, the portfolio consists of energy, consumer goods, utilities, food, and steel products. Our rotation offers a broad distribution across securities because each index is composed of numerous individual stocks; this ensures that our results are not driven by the extreme performance of a small number of securities.

In assessing the success of the equity rotation strategy, we compare its performance with that of the S&P 500; thus, the S&P 500 is viewed as a general benchmark for the strategy. In addition, we add a new performance measure to our analysis that we have not yet discussed: alpha. In this situation, positive alpha months represent the percentage of months in which the rotation strategy earned a rate of return that exceeded the return to the S&P 500, that is, the percentage of months in which the strategy beat the market. See Box 9.1 for a more complete discussion of alpha.

Box 9.1   What Is Alpha?

You frequently hear the term *alpha* bandied about in the investment world. Managers claim that they are alpha producers, and investors try to identify those managers who can truly generate alpha. There is even a popular website called Seeking Alpha that provides articles on investing ideas and strategies. Most investors know that alpha is a good thing and want to identify it, but what exactly is alpha?

Suppose you are at a cocktail party and find yourself in a conversation with two people who are comparing notes on the performance of their investment advisors. The first individual proudly proclaims, "My advisor had a banner year, as my portfolio returned 20%." That was met with the tepid response "I think I should switch advisors because I only earned 14% last year." Should the second individual

(continued)

---

get on his cell phone and fire his advisor? On an absolute return basis it is easy to determine which advisor had the better year: we all know that a 20% rate of return is markedly higher than 14%. But what kind of risk did each manager assume to earn those returns? Is the 20% truly better performance in light of the risk profile of each manager? That is the essence of alpha; accurately assessing portfolio performance.

Alpha is simply a measure of excess return, that is, return above that which is expected for a particular risk level. Suppose, for instance, that the advisor who returned 20% took on substantial risk and that other portfolios with similar risk levels earned an average of 22%. We would say that the manager had negative alpha of 2%. In contrast, let's suppose that the manager who earned a 14% rate of return did so with a much lower risk level. Perhaps other portfolios with a similar risk level earned only 12%. We would say that this manager had a positive alpha of 2%.

But how do we determine the return that is expected for a particular risk level? We apply a model to calculate expected return. The model most commonly used in the investment industry is the capital asset pricing model (CAPM) developed in the mid-1960s by Stanford University professor William F. Sharpe. CAPM defines risk as beta, or volatility relative to the market. See Box 5.3 for a discussion of beta.

How Much Alpha Did Equity Rotation Produce?

The performances of the equity rotation strategy and its benchmark (the S&P 500) are reported in Table 9.2. The table also reports the percentage of months in which the rotation strategy beat the benchmark. In practical terms, the benchmark represents the return an

Table 9.2   Performance of Equity Rotation Strategy and S&P 500: 1966–2013

Portfolio	Mean Annual Return	Standard Deviation	Return-to-Risk Ratio	Positive Alpha Months
Equity rotation	17.42%	16.26%	1.07	59%
S&P 500	10.56%	15.26%	0.69	NA

investor who simply purchased an S&P 500 index fund would earn. In contrast, the rotation strategy represents a dynamic strategy that is readjusted on the basis of shifts in Fed policy. When both of the Fed's policy indicators point toward easy money, the strategy holds 20% in each of the top five performance categories reported in Panel A of Table 9.1. When both Fed indicators signal tight money, the strategy holds 20% in each of the top five performance categories reported in Panel C of Table 9.1. Finally, if one Fed policy indicator signals tight money and the other signals easy money, the strategy holds 20% in each of the top five performance categories reported in Panel B of Table 9.1.

The returns reported in Table 9.2 support your patience in making it to this point in the book. The equity rotation strategy represents a practical application of the compilation of equity return patterns we identified in earlier chapters. That is, we took the key findings from our investigation of stock returns and monetary conditions and formulated a fairly simple rotation strategy. The performance data for the rotation strategy offer a composite view of the potential from executing an equity rotation strategy guided by monetary conditions. Fortunately, you can now clearly see that your time has been rewarded; the equity rotation strategy is a huge success.

Over the 48-year period, the rotation strategy produces an average annual return of 17.42% versus the market average of 10.56%. That translates into a return premium of over 6.8% per year, every year, for 48 years. Incredibly, the return premium is produced with only a minimal increase in risk. The dominance of the rotation strategy relative to the market is supported by the huge difference in return-to-risk ratios: 1.07 versus 0.69. That is a real drubbing. Finally, the positive alpha months indicate that the strategy beat the market in 59% of months, and this further supports the strategy's superiority.

Although the performance data reported in Table 9.2 are extremely encouraging, you may be wondering about the success of the strategy over time. How successful was the strategy in the early years versus the later years? Is it still a good strategy? Were there periods when the strategy underperformed its benchmark (the market) by significant amounts? To be successful, an investment manager has to outperform the benchmark portfolio and do so on a relatively consistent basis. As is discussed in Box 9.2, such an accomplishment can be a significant undertaking for an investment manager.

Box 9.2   Where's the Alpha?

In addressing the question "Where's the alpha?" we will start with another question. Academic studies show that professional money managers consistently generate alpha, correct? Unfortunately for the active management industry, the answer is a resounding no. Professional money managers actually consistently underperform their benchmarks and are thus considered negative alpha generators.

This really shouldn't come as a surprise. First of all, the proverbial deck is stacked against money managers beating the market. In 1980, institutional investors controlled 34% of the total market

---

value of U.S. stocks. That percentage increased to 67% by 2010.[2] It is difficult to beat the market when you are the market.

Second, most institutional money managers diversify their holdings to limit their risk. Managers don't want big negative returns in one or two securities to ruin their returns. After all, the goal of a manager is often to gather assets and keep them under management (as most are compensated with a percentage of the assets under management), not necessarily to beat the market. In other words, managers want to generate high enough returns to keep their clients happy so that they can maintain the lucrative relationship and continue to collect management fees. But diversification also means that the big winners a manager holds in the portfolio don't necessarily result in high portfolio returns because the gains are diffused across numerous holdings.

Third, investment managers charge much larger management fees than do passively managed index funds. According to the Investment Company Institute, actively managed equity funds charge annual fees of 92 basis points (0.92%) of the assets under management.[3] Thus, the average actively managed fund has to earn nearly 1% more than its benchmark to outperform the market, and that is just for mutual funds. Many hedge funds charge fees of 2% of assets under management and 20% of accumulated profits. Hedge funds have to outperform by substantial amounts to provide alpha to the investor.

A final reason for their underperformance is that money managers often have some portion of their funds in cash. For an investment manager, holding some cash is a necessity to meet shareholder redemption needs, pay transactions costs, and make dividend and

(continued)

capital gain distributions to shareholders. In typical market environ-ments, cash underperforms the asset class of choice, for example, equities. This is what fund managers refer to as cash drag on portfolio returns. The benchmark index, in contrast, is always fully invested.

In light of all the disadvantages of active money management, many investors have decided that if you can't beat the market, you should join it. There is a trend toward investing in index funds and effectively abandoning the search for alpha. Indexing as a strategy has grown in popularity over the last 15 years. At the end of 2012, according to the Investment Company Institute, equity index funds represented 17.4% of mutual fund total assets, up from only 8.7% in 1998. It is worth noting that these equity index funds charged an average fee of only 13 basis points (0.13%).

Figure 9.1 shows plots of the performance of our rotation strategy versus a market indexing strategy, that is, a buy-and-hold strategy in the S&P 500. The plots allow us to consider the consistency of the rotation strategy's relative performance over time. Thus, the figure allows us to answer questions about the reliability of the strategy and its general usefulness across time. Following the common approach taken by mutual funds, we plot the cumulative value of $10,000 invested in each portfolio at the beginning of the sample period, Janu-ary 1966. We apply a log scale to the vertical axis to allow for a clearer visual interpretation of the growth in relative portfolio values.[4]

Illustrating Alpha for the Equity Rotation Strategy

The plots in Figure 9.1 show clearly that the rotation strategy has been an overwhelming success. Over the period 1966–2013, a

Figure 9.1 Value Accumulated from a $10,000 Investment in the Rotation Strategy vs. the Benchmark: 1966–2013

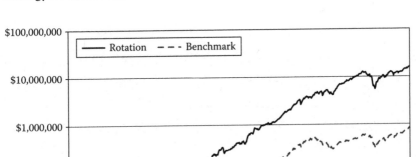

$10,000 investment that was allocated according to the rotation strategy grew to an astounding total value of $20.732 million. In contrast, the same investment in the S&P 500 grew to only $889,110. Incredibly, the rotation strategy produced a final value that was over 23 times greater than the final benchmark value. We believe that this difference in value would cover the extra transactions costs of the rotation strategy and even provide a little extra compensation for the hassle of rotating portfolio holdings.

Another extremely attractive aspect of the rotation strategy is that it outperforms on a very consistent basis. As was shown above, the strategy beat the market in 59% of months. Furthermore, the plots in Figure 9.1 show that the strategy's success was consistently distributed over time. From the beginning of the sample period to the very end, the extra accumulated value from the rotation strategy

Table 9.3   Accumulated Values for Equity Rotation Portfolio and Benchmark by Decade

Portfolio	1970	1980	1990	2000	2010
Rotation	$15,130	$86,378	$577,070	$6,214,486	$14,818,358
Benchmark	$11,766	$26,359	$96,630	$488,952	$568,401
Difference	$3,364	$60,019	$480,440	$5,725,534	$14,249,957

Note: The values in the table are from Figure 9.1 and are reported at the end of each respective year.

continued to expand. Table 9.3 puts actual numbers on the accumulated value premium by reporting the values for the two portfolios at the end of each decade.

A market indexer would have been very pleased with this performance over time. The $10,000 investment in the S&P 500 index grew steadily throughout each period: from $10,000 at the start of 1966, to a value of $11,766 by the end of 1970, to $26,359 by the end of 1980, and so forth. The growth in the final decade, however, was somewhat diminished as the value grew from $488,952 to only $568,401. Many people referred to this period as "the lost decade" because of the poor performance of the stock market. I'm not sure we would go that far, but the decade clearly didn't multiply the portfolio's value the way other decades did.

Although the indexer would have been pleased with this performance, the investor following the rotation strategy would have been downright ecstatic. The rotation investor's value grew tremendously during each decade, expanding its dominance over the benchmark consistently over time. The total value from the rotation strategy more than doubled even during the lost decade.

Caveats for Consideration

Before proceeding, we feel it is imperative that we reiterate that although the equity rotation strategy was a smashing success, our purpose is not to offer it as a definitive recommendation. We present the strategy as an example of the potential of a rotation approach guided by monetary conditions. Investors have unique situations and should design their portfolios to match their unique circumstances. We believe it is important to explicitly recognize a few major limitations of our equity rotation strategy. First, note that the strategy includes only U.S. equities; it is not designed or constructed as a comprehensive portfolio. For example, we would advise investors to allocate a portion of their portfolio to fixed-income securities. Figure 9.1 shows that some fairly significant dips in portfolio value occurred over time. Such dips can cause ulcers, wrinkles, and considerable stress, some of which could have been mitigated with a more diversified portfolio. Chapter 1 and Chapter 8 provide helpful information about the monetary environment and the performance of fixed-income securities that should clearly be part of any comprehensive portfolio. Second, a well-balanced portfolio should include exposures to alternative assets such as real estate and commodities. Alternative assets are excluded entirely from the equity rotation strategy. Third, in implementing any strategy, an investor would be wise to have exposure to foreign securities. The equity indexes included in the rotation strategy are composed entirely of U.S. equities. Box 9.3 indicates that appropriate selection of ETFs will allow investors to easily establish a foreign exposure. For example, many equity ETFs have a global composition. Finally, the rotation strategy has a very simplistic design that equally weights five equity classes. More aggressive investors may want to apply greater weights to the few asset classes that have stronger monetary-based return patterns.

In contrast, relatively conservative investors may want to spread their investments across a broader set of equity securities. Also, investors could easily modify the strategy by altering its implementation. For example, to take advantage of the observation that small firms excel in expansive conditions, investors could purchase equal-weighted ETFs in expansive environments.

Box 9.3   Overwhelmed by Choice

Let's say you have decided that your portfolio would benefit from an exposure to the pharmaceutical industry. In addition, you would like to establish an exposure to foreign pharmaceutical firms. Now you need to decide which ETF to purchase. As in the cereal aisle at the grocery store, there are many choices of specific sector ETFs, and choosing an appropriate one may seem like a daunting task. You would be mistaken to assume that they are all virtually the same and that you need only go to your favorite fund family. Sector ETFs can differ on many dimensions: the number of holdings, the weighting scheme, the size of the companies held, and the global nature of the holdings. Table 9.4 presents a sampling of pharmaceutical ETFs as an example of the diversity of holdings across the various sector ETFs.

You can see that three of the funds are almost exclusively invested in U.S.-based firms, whereas the other two have nearly equal exposures to U.S. and non-U.S. firms. Most of the ETFs are invested almost exclusively in very large companies; in fact, the RBS ETF has "Big Pharma" in its name. One of the departures from the concentration in big firms is the SPDR S&P Pharmaceuticals index. In this ETF, the behemoth Johnson & Johnson with a market cap of

Table 9.4   Five Prominent Pharmaceutical ETFs

Ticker	Name	Percent in U.S. holdings	Size of Stocks	Number of Stocks	Weights	Annual Returns, % 2012	Annual Returns, % 2013
DRGS	RBS Global Big Pharma	50	Large	16	Equal	11.37	44.23
IHE	iShares US Pharmaceutical	92	Large	39	Nonequal	13.88	40.59
PJP	Invesco PowerShares Pharmaceuticals	95	Large	30	Nonequal	24.51	55.69
PPH	Market Vectors Pharmaceutical	53	Large	26	Nonequal	12.98	36.66
XPH	SPDR S&P Pharmaceuticals	94	All	34	Equal	10.91	60.80

$277 billion has the same weight as the microcap VIVUS, Inc., with a market cap of only $612 million.

Two of the five ETFs equally weight their holdings, whereas the other three have dramatically different weightings of firm constituents. For instance, IHE holds over 13% of its portfolio in Johnson & Johnson, whereas Furiex Pharmaceuticals and Prestige Brands Holdings each constitute less than 1% of this portfolio.

The number of stocks held is also quite different across the five ETFs. RBS Global Big Pharma equally weights 16 holdings, whereas iShares US Pharmaceutical has nonequal weightings in 39 different stocks.

(continued)

All these variations lead to dramatic performance differences. In 2012, the group had a range of returns from a low of approximately 11% to a high of slightly over 24%. In 2013, the range was from approximately 37% to nearly 61%. It is worth noting that XPH had the low return in 2012 and the high return in 2013. This can be partially explained by the fact that small firms performed significantly better than large firms in 2013.

Suffice it to say that it pays to research a particular sector fund before investing. A sector ETF may provide you with a significant foreign exposure or virtually none. It is wise to look before you leap.

How About Rotating with Alternative Assets and Foreign Equities?

The results in earlier chapters clearly establish that alternative assets should be included in an investment portfolio. As you may recall, the evidence indicates that commodities offer returns that compare favorably with those of common stocks; however, the huge benefit associated with commodities is their diversification potential. Chapter 4 highlights two separate and crucial diversification benefits associated with commodities. First, commodities exhibit relatively low correlation with the major asset classes: stocks and bonds. Thus, commodities offer an attractive hedge against general moves in security prices. Specifically, in a diversified portfolio, the commodity allocation serves as a potential insurance policy. If a negative economic event causes the prices of traditional securities to decline, there is a good chance that commodity prices will increase and thus offset some of the damage inflicted on the portfolio. Second, monetary conditions influence the returns of commodities very differently from the way they influence the returns of the traditional assets. Unlike stocks and bonds, commodities perform well when monetary conditions are restrictive but perform poorly when conditions are expansive. Thus, commodities have the potential to hedge the negative effect that restrictive Fed policy generally has on the traditional asset classes. Overall, the evidence suggests that commodities have the potential to offset the negative market performance induced by restrictive monetary policy and the adverse market moves induced by negative macroeconomic events. Real estate offers some of the same diversification benefits as commodities, but to a much lesser extent. In particular, equity REITs have some of the same hedging potential as commodities since they perform relatively well during periods of restrictive Fed policy, which are periods during which most equity securities flounder.

Chapter 6 presents the case for including foreign stocks in an investor's portfolio. Consistent with other asset classes, the evidence shows that the benefit of including a foreign exposure is conditional on the monetary environment. Similar to the performance of alternative assets, some foreign equities have very attractive performance patterns. Specifically, the stocks of emerging market firms and the stocks of Scandinavian firms perform relatively well in restrictive monetary environments. We attribute this unique performance pattern to the relative independence of these countries' monetary and economic policies from those of the average developed country. Thus, these foreign equities, like alternative assets, offer a potential hedge against the adverse market performance associated with periods of restrictive Fed policy.

Composition of the Expanded Rotation Portfolio

We next consider the performance of a rotation strategy that supplements the initial equity rotation strategy by adding alternative assets and foreign equities to the investment set. This second rotation strategy follows the same format as the first strategy in that it invests in the top five performing assets in each monetary environment. Each available asset class is allocated an equal weight in the portfolio—20%—when all five asset classes are available.[5] On the basis of data availability for the alternative assets and foreign equity indexes, we begin the sample period in 1970 for this rotation strategy. The composition of the expanded rotation strategy portfolio in each environment is reported in Table 9.5.

In comparing Tables 9.1 and 9.5, the data indicate that during expansive monetary periods the portfolio's composition remains intact; it is exactly the same in Table 9.5 as it was with the first equity rotation strategy (Table 9.1). That is, the same five asset classes are the top five performers for both investment sets. In indeterminate conditions, there are two new top performers (two foreign equity indexes). Finally, during restrictive periods four of the five entries are new, with energy being the only common entry in Tables 9.1 and 9.5. This clearly establishes that the major benefits of the alternative asset classes come from their unique properties during indeterminate and restrictive monetary periods. As we noted in Chapters 4 and 6, some of the alternative assets and some foreign equities tend to exhibit strong performance outside expansive monetary periods, which is contrary to most other asset types. Thus, the evidence suggests that these securities merit a prominent allocation in periods when Fed policy is constrained to any degree (i.e., when at least one of the Fed's policy indicators signals tight money).

Performance of the Expanded Rotation Strategy

The performance for our second rotation strategy is reported in Table 9.6. Note that as a result of the data availability issues that were identified above, we start the sample period in 1970.

Table 9.5   Top Five Asset Classes by Performance in Expansive, Indeterminate, and Restrictive Monetary Environments: 1970–2013

Panel A. Expansive Conditions

Asset class	Mean Annual Return, %	Standard Deviation, %
1. Small-value	44.04	26.23
2. Past performance losers	30.16	24.49
3. Apparel	28.45	23.62
4. Retail	27.03	19.30
5. Autos	25.42	25.20

Panel B. Indeterminate Conditions

Asset Class	Mean Annual Return, %	Standard Deviation, %
1. Emerging markets	17.78	22.98
2. Scandinavian countries	17.10	18.01
3. Energy	15.35	18.33
4. Consumer goods	14.95	16.96
5. Financials	14.55	18.74

Panel C. Restrictive Conditions

Asset Class	Mean Annual Return, %	Standard Deviation, %
1. Commodities (GSCI)	17.66	21.51
2. Scandinavian countries	17.14	19.19
3. Emerging markets	16.53	20.47
4. Energy	11.47	21.11
5. Equity REITs	9.77	15.47

Note: Performance data were measured over the period 1970–2013, with the following exceptions: equity REITs started in 1972, and emerging markets started in 1988. We choose to start in 1970 rather than 1966 because in restrictive conditions, only one of the five top asset classes (energy) was available starting in 1966.

Table 9.6 Performance of Expanded Rotation Strategy and S&P 500: 1970–2013

Portfolio	Mean Annual Return, %	Standard Deviation, %	Return-to-Risk Ratio	Positive Alpha Months, %
Expanded rotation	19.96	17.25	1.16	60
S&P 500	11.17	15.48	0.72	NA

As you may have predicted, the performance of the expanded rotation strategy is phenomenal. The strategy generates an annual return of approximately 20% for 48 consecutive years versus the market average of 11.17%. The return premium above the market is an amazing 8.8% per year. At this point, you might be saying, "But what about the risk?" The strategy subjects investors to a moderate amount of additional risk, and so the extra return doesn't come free. Good catch, but we advise you to take note that the percentage of positive alpha months is 60%. The strategy beats the market in an incredible 6 out of every 10 months. Therefore, the higher standard deviation can be largely attributed to unusually large positive return premiums for the expanded rotation strategy. Investors love that kind of risk.

Illustrating Alpha for the Expanded Rotation Strategy

Before labeling the expanded rotation strategy the crème de la crème, we believe an examination of the strategy's temporal consistency is warranted. Therefore, we follow our previous approach of plotting the accumulated value of a $10,000 investment in the expanded strategy versus the S&P 500 (benchmark). The plots are shown in Figure 9.2.

Figure 9.2   Value Accumulated from a $10,000 Investment in the Expanded Rotation Strategy vs. the Benchmark: 1970–2013

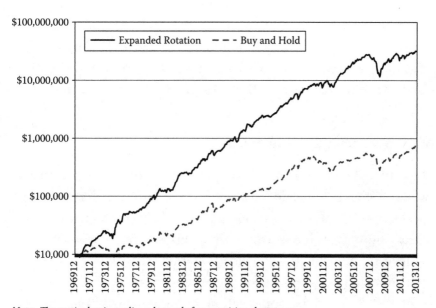

Note: The vertical axis applies a log scale for expositional purposes.

The plots in Figure 9.2 confirm the consistent superiority of the expanded rotation strategy. You may have been tempted to say, What's the big deal with the expanded rotation strategy? It increases the annual return only from 17.42% to 19.96%, a little over 2.5%. (See Table 9.2 and Table 9.6) Is it really worth the extra hassle of investing in alternative assets and foreign equities for a mere 2.5%? When you see the final difference in accumulated value, you will know that it is definitely worth it. The $10,000 investment in the expanded rotation strategy grows to over $32 million versus $786,205 for the market. On the basis of the expanded rotation strategy, the accumulated portfolio value is over 40 times higher than the value accumulated with a market indexing strategy. Furthermore, the expanded rotation strategy had four less years to work than the first rotation approach we presented. If we add those four years and assume that the expanded strategy produced comparable returns over those four years, the portfolio value grows from slightly over $32 million to almost $69 million. I hope that motivates you to initiate your investment strategy without any further delay. Make sure to finish the book, but then get to it.

Rotation Strategy Dominance by Decade

To clarify the growth over time, Table 9.7 shows the accumulated value of the two portfolios (expanded rotation and benchmark) by decade. We also report the difference in accumulated values to clearly show the value sacrificed by a market indexer compared with an investor applying the expanded rotation strategy.

The accumulated values for the expanded rotation strategy highlight the tremendous appreciation in value across time and the consistency in the strategy's superior performance. The strategy begins in 1970 with $10,000, which grows to $127,985 by the end of 1980, to $909,130 by the end of 1990, and so forth. Even during the

---

Table 9.7　Accumulated Values for Expanded Rotation Strategy and Benchmark by Decade

Portfolio	1980	1990	2000	2010
Expanded rotation	$127,985	$909,130	$8,524,498	$26,286,251
Benchmark	$23,308	$85,446	$432,361	$502,614
Difference	$104,677	$823,684	$8,092,137	$25,783,637

Note: The values in the table are from Figure 9.2 and are reported at the end of each respective year. As a result of data availability, performance is measured starting in 1970.

---

last decade, 2000–2010, the portfolio value from the expanded rotation strategy more than tripled. In stark contrast, the growth in the benchmark (S&P 500) during each decade was subpar relative to the rotation strategy's growth. The benchmark's performance over the final decade was especially disappointing, which corresponds with the reference to this period as the lost decade.

After evaluating all the evidence regarding the expanded portfolio, we can confidently declare that the expanded rotation strategy is the crème de la crème. Although the strategy is not intended to be a definitive recommendation, it certainly serves as a great example of what's possible.

In constructing our two rotation strategies, we relied on only five asset classes in each of the three monetary environments. We excluded many assets from our rotation strategies because of data limitations or to simplify the analysis. In the next three tables, we provide a much more comprehensive list of top performing securities by monetary environment. Furthermore, for your convenience, in Tables 9.8, 9.9, and 9.10 we separate the securities by asset type.

Table 9.8   Top Performing Asset Classes in Expansive Monetary Conditions

Equity Classes	Small-value stocks, small-cap stocks, value stocks, past performance losers, cyclical stocks
Equity sectors	Retail, apparel, autos, durable goods, construction, business equipment, fabricated products, transportation
Foreign country equities	EAFE, United Kingdom, Far East, Asia
Real estate	Mortgage REITs, equity REITs
Fixed-income	High-yield (junk) bonds
Commodities	Precious metals, livestock

Table 9.9   Top Performing Asset Classes in Indeterminate Monetary Conditions

Equity Classes	Mid-cap stocks, large-cap stocks, value stocks, big-value stocks, average past performers
Equity sectors	Energy, consumer goods, food, financials, chemicals, utilities, precious metal miners
Foreign country equities	EAFE, Scandinavian countries, Asia, Far East, United Kingdom, BRIC countries
Real estate	Equity REITs, composite REITs
Fixed-income	T-bonds, investment-grade bonds, long-term T-bonds, intermediate-term bonds
Commodities	Composite commodity index, precious metals, energy, agriculture, livestock

Table 9.10   Top Performing Asset Classes in Restrictive Monetary Conditions

Equity classes	Defensive stocks, mid-cap stocks, blend stocks, past performance losers
Equity sectors	Energy, utilities, food, precious metal mining, consumer goods, financials
Foreign country equities	Emerging markets, Scandinavian countries, Canada, BRIC countries
Real estate	Equity REITs, composite REITs
Fixed-income	Short-term T-bills
Commodities	Composite commodity index, industrial metals, energy, agriculture

Why You Might Be Skeptical

For purposes of full disclosure, we now offer justification for why you should be skeptical of the performance of the two rotation strategies. We follow that discussion with reasons you should be encouraged by the performance of the rotation strategies.

Factors That Support Skepticism

1. The strategies suffer from substantial hindsight bias. The securities included in the rotation strategies were selected after we observed their superior performance. Of course you can get positive results when you know which securities are going to perform well.
2. The performance data for the rotation strategies do not include transactions costs. Reallocating portfolio weights would require the payment of considerable trading costs.

Factors That Validate the Rotation Strategies

1. The strategies are based on sound economic reasoning. We believe it is wise to be very skeptical of strategies that claim to beat the market. When executing our own investment strategies, we apply considerable skepticism before investing. That's why throughout this book we have been careful to explain the economic rationale behind the observed return patterns. If a strategy does not make sense, you shouldn't blindly throw your money at it. The positive performance we identify is consistent with rational economic explanations in all cases.
2. The strategies produce substantial performance premiums in spite of their simplistic design. We constructed the portfolios by limiting our investment sets to broad asset classes that were composed of value-weighted securities, and then we

equal-weighted the asset classes within the portfolios. By selecting more refined asset classes (e.g., retailers and apparel manufacturers of higher-end products rather than comprehensive groups that included all types of retailers and apparel manufacturers), an investor can more fully exploit the strategy. Remember, the strategy is based on identifying firms that are most (and least) reliant on aggregate disposable income or discretionary spending. For example, retailers of staple products would have less sensitivity to discretionary spending levels than would retailers of luxury products. We're confident that readers of this book will be able to greatly enhance portfolio performance by carefully selecting securities.

3. The strategy takes a diversified approach rather than targeting the very best categories. Although the strategies include only five asset classes, each of those classes consists of numerous individual securities. For example, the small-value portfolio consists of dozens of individual stocks, and so that portfolio by itself would be fairly well diversified.

4. Although the transactions costs involved in executing the rotation strategies would be significant, they wouldn't be exorbitant. As we have noted throughout the book, the use of ETFs can reduce the costs of trading individual securities, and so reallocating a portfolio becomes less costly. In addition, transitions in Fed policy from one environment to another environment are fairly infrequent, and so the reallocation events would be fairly limited. The Fed in general does not want to throw the financial markets into a tailspin, and so it changes policy fairly infrequently.

After considering the factors supporting skepticism versus those supporting validation, you can decide how you want to proceed. Personally, we think the evidence is heavily stacked in favor of validation.

Conclusion

We designed this book so that each chapter would build anticipation of the crescendo represented by this final chapter. We hope we were successful in laying the groundwork so that the rotation strategies presented in this chapter have had their optimal effect. No matter how you decide to use the information presented in this book, there are a couple of major themes we hope you will take away from our efforts. First, we hope we have convinced you that Fed policy decisions are crucial to the performance of the security markets and, more important, that being aware of Fed policy shifts is crucial for investors in implementing an effective investment strategy. We rely on two monetary policy indicators in identifying monetary policy environments; however, we encourage you to consider other indicators. We have a lot of confidence in our method of defining monetary environments, but we are continuously considering alternative measures to refine our approach. Just as the Fed is continually changing its procedures, we believe it is incumbent on us to stay current. Being a Fed watcher is not only a hip thing to do, it is also an integral part of a successful investment strategy. Second, we hope that we have motivated you and equipped you with the tools necessary to implement an investment strategy. The sooner you get started with your strategy, the more successful you will be.

CONCLUSION

The Federal Reserve receives tremendous attention through-out the financial world and is commonly regarded as the most powerful of global financial institutions. Our empirical evidence serves to reinforce this assessment as we show that returns for virtually all security types are strongly linked to Fed monetary policy changes. Given the Fed's enormous influence on the financial markets and based on the army of researchers it hires to compile and analyze information, a logical question is: Why not use Fed signals to your advantage? This book presents an easy-to-follow roadmap that allows both novice and professional investors to identify shifts in Fed policy and take the appropriate investment actions.

The success of our proposed investment strategy is supported by a comprehensive evaluation of the benefits associated with using Fed policy shifts to select investments. Our analysis includes separate evaluations of U.S. equities (of several different types), foreign equities (of both emerging and developed markets), fixed income securities, real estate, and commodities. Based on the cumulative evidence presented throughout the early chapters, we present a comprehensive investment strategy that showcases the benefits of using Fed policy to guide investment decisions. Remarkably, over the past 48 years, we show that the strategy produces a cumulative wealth enhancement that exceeds a passive investment in the U.S. stock market by more than 40 times. By following the strategy, a $10,000 investment would have grown to over $32 million over the approximately five-decade period.

The investment strategy is based on viewing the Fed as the entity that controls the purse strings for the economy. When the Fed opens the economic purse strings, money flows more freely, encouraging investors, consumers and firms to increase spending. During these "easy money periods," the availability of money and greater consumer spending is particularly beneficial to firms that rely heavily on discretionary spending and those firms that typically have trouble accessing capital. For example, easy money is welcomed by small firms that have trouble obtaining financing and firms that produce or sell durable or luxury products. In contrast, when the Fed tightens the purse strings, the best performing asset classes tend to be alternative assets and the equities of firms that have ready access to funds and are relatively insensitive to levels of consumer spending. For example, commodities, certain types of real estate and the equities of defensive stocks tend to do well during tight money periods.

Our comprehensive assessment serves to demystify Fed policy and provide a rationale as to why market participants should monitor the Fed and its actions. Along the way, we provide guidance for investors on navigating the investment landscape and avoiding common pitfalls. The book offers investors practical advice using easy-to-understand terminology that can be applied by the casual investor or the seasoned investment professional. Unique to this book, the investment guidance is based on widely publicized Fed policy actions and relies at its core on sound economic principles. Let the Fed be your guide!

WHY INTEREST RATES MATTER

It all comes down to interest rates. As an investor, all you're doing
is putting up a lump-sum payment for a future cash flow.

Ray Dalio, founder, Bridgewater Associates

In the Introduction we established the power of the Federal Reserve
to affect various aspects of the financial markets. Of particular interest to many investors is the Fed's influence on the level of interest rates
in the economy. But why are interest rates more closely monitored by
investors than virtually anything else? This Appendix briefly outlines
the four key ways in which interest rates influence asset prices. These
are not separate and distinct influences but are all interconnected and
part of the same story. First and foremost, interest rates are critical
inputs to the valuation process and affect the value of all assets. Second, interest rates affect the level of business profits. All else equal, as
interest rates rise, business profits fall because firms pay higher interest
expense. Third, many investors use margin—borrowed money—to buy
stocks and other assets. An increase in interest rates lessens the appeal
of borrowing on margin. Fourth, there is a simple substitution effect
that accompanies an interest rate increase as the attractiveness of newly
issued securities (with higher promised payments) rises relative to the
desirability of other securities.

Basic Valuation

Unlike the buyers of assets such as homes and cars, the purchasers of financial assets are a notoriously unsentimental lot. Investors don't get a lot of psychic income from the purchase of financial assets. They don't brag to their neighbors about their position in Apple or engage in conspicuous consumption of Berkshire Hathaway bonds. Investors simply want to acquire more future purchasing power in exchange for the current purchasing power they deny themselves. It really is no more complicated than that.

Present Value

Although investors want to acquire more future purchasing power than their current purchasing power, one can't simply compare dollars to be received at different points in time. If I pay $100 today for something and get $150 back at some future point in time, is it a good deal? The answer to that question is, "It depends." Specifically, it depends on when I receive those future dollars. Do I get them in 1 year or in 10 years? Are they spread out over time, or do they come in a lump sum? How risky is the return? Is it a certain payment, or is there some element of risk involved?

Comparing dollars today to dollars to be received at a future time is akin to comparing dollars to Japanese yen or British pounds. We can certainly compare dollars to yen or pounds, but we must convert the currencies into a common currency to get a true comparison. The conversion mechanism with dollars to be received at different points in time is referred to as *present value,* and it is the basis for modern finance and most valuation theories.

Simply stated, present value is the fundamental principle that a dollar received today is worth more than a dollar received tomorrow.

Similarly, a dollar to be received tomorrow is worth more than a dollar received in two days. The rationale is that a dollar received today can be invested to earn interest and will be worth more at a later date. Mathematically, the present value of an amount of money to be received at a future point—let's say a year from now—if the appropriate interest rate is i is shown in the following equation:

$$Present\,Value = \frac{Future\,Value}{(1+i)}$$

Thus, the present value of a dollar to be received in one year if the interest rate is 5% is as follows:

$$Present\,Value = \frac{\$1.00}{(1.05)} = \$0.9524$$

What this means is that if the appropriate interest rate is 5%, you should be indifferent between receiving $0.9524 today and receiving $1 in one year. The theory is that you could invest the $0.9524 at 5% and have exactly $1 in a year.

Carrying out the example further, the present value of a dollar to be received in two years is calculated by dividing by $(1 + i)$ twice, or $(1 + i)^2$:

$$Present\,Value = \frac{\$1.00}{(1.05)^2} = \$0.9070$$

Again, this means you should be indifferent between receiving $0.9070 today and receiving $1 two years from today. The theory is that you could invest the $0.9070 and earn $0.093 in interest over those two years.

The key contribution of present value is that you now have converted amounts of money to be received at different points in time into a common currency: today's dollars. This allows you to add them together as they are now in common units. Therefore, if someone offers to pay you $1 one year from now and another $1 in two years, how much should you be willing to pay if the appropriate interest rate is 5%? The answer is as follows:

$$Present\,Value = \frac{\$1.00}{(1.05)} + \frac{\$1.00}{(1.05)^2} = \$0.9524 + \$0.9070 = \$1.8594$$

Valuing Stocks and Bonds

Why are we exposing you to a crash course in present value? In theory, the value of any investment asset—stock, bond, option contract, futures contract, real estate investment, or gold—is equal to the present value of all future cash flows from that asset. In the case of stocks, those future cash flows are dividends and whatever the sales price is when the investor sells the stock. For bonds, the future cash flows are the periodic interest (or coupon) payments and the principal value. The interest rate that you apply to come up with a present value is often referred to as a *discount rate*. The Fed discount rate, which we discussed in the Introduction, is a special type of discount rate that is set by the Fed on its loans to member institutions. A discount rate is appropriately named because the dollar amount to be received in the future is discounted (made less) to arrive at a present value. In general terms, the value of any asset is calculated as follows:

$$Value = \frac{CF_1}{(1+i)} + \frac{CF_2}{(1+i)^2} + \frac{CF_3}{(1+i)^3} + \ldots + \frac{CF_N}{(1+i)^N}$$

For example, suppose a company has issued a bond that pays three annual, end-of-year interest payments of $80 and promises to return the principal value of the bond of $1,000 in three years. What should you be willing to pay for that bond? If the appropriate discount rate to apply to this investment is 6%, the value of the bond is calculated as follows:

$$Value = \frac{\$80}{(1.06)} + \frac{\$80}{(1.06)^2} + \frac{\$1,080}{(1.06)^3} = \$75.47 + \$71.20 + \$906.79$$
$$= \$1,053.46$$

Once you have estimated the future cash flows and the appropriate discount rate, valuation is a very simple middle school–level math problem. What makes valuation difficult and makes it part art and part science—and leads some investors to believe that an asset is overvalued when others believe it is undervalued—is both the estimation of the future cash flows and the estimation of the appropriate discount rate. That is, determining the inputs for the valuation model is the tricky part. For most bonds, the estimation of the cash flows is pretty straightforward as the interest payments and principal are stated. However, what isn't specified is what the appropriate discount rate should be. For stocks, in addition to the need to specify an appropriate discount rate, the cash flows to a stockholder aren't specified in advance. In fact, the cash flows to the ultimate holder of the stock are the future dividend payments, which need to be estimated to arrive at a current valuation.

Let's return to our bond that makes three annual payments of $80 and returns to the investor the principal value of $1,000 in three years. We found out if the discount rate was 6%, the bond was worth $1,053.46. What happens to the value if the discount rate increases to 8%? This can happen because interest rates in the market sometimes rise. The value of the bond is as follows:

$$Value = \frac{\$80}{(1.08)} + \frac{\$80}{(1.08)^2} + \frac{\$1,080}{(1.08)^3} = \$74.07 + \$68.59 + \$857.34$$
$$= \$1,000.00$$

If the discount rate increases from 6% to 8%, the bond falls in value by $53.46, or by a little over 5%. Because you are discounting the cash flows to a present value, as the discount rate rises, the present value falls. This is precisely why the holders of financial assets are so keenly interested in (fixated on?) interest rates: as interest rates rise, all else equal, the prices of financial assets with fixed cash flows fall.

With stocks, the holder of a share of stock is entitled to the cash flows from the stock. That generally involves a combination of dividends and the price at which the stock is sold. In theory, the price someone should pay for a share of stock is the present value of all future dividends as that is the only cash flow to the ultimate holder of a share of stock. Thus, theoretically, the value of a share of stock is equal to the present value of all future dividends. That is,

$$Stock\,Value = \frac{D_1}{(1+i)} + \frac{D_2}{(1+i)^2} + \ldots + \frac{D_N}{(1+i)^N} + \ldots$$

This doesn't look like an equation that can be easily solved as there are an infinite number of terms. But if we make a simplifying assumption—specifically, that the dividends grow at a constant rate (g) forever—the equation mathematically simplifies and becomes

$$Stock\,Value = \frac{D_1}{i-g}$$

This equation is called the Gordon Growth Model, named for the economist Myron Gordon, who originally published this relationship in 1959.[1] This model is a staple of undergraduate and graduate business school finance programs and a central part of the curriculum for the prestigious Chartered Financial Analyst (CFA) Program. Every equity analyst on Wall Street is conversant with the Gordon Growth Model, although some may not know it by that name. It is often referred to as the constant growth dividend model.

If we have a stock that pays a current annual dividend of $3, dividends are expected to grow at 5% per year, and the appropriate discount rate is 10%, the theoretical value of a share of stock is calculated as follows:

$$Stock\ Value = \frac{D_0(1+g)}{i-g} = \frac{D_1}{i-g} = \frac{\$3(1.05)}{.10-.05} = \$63$$

Note the sensitivity of the stock value to changes in the appropriate discount rate. If the appropriate interest rate increased by 1%, the theoretical stock value would fall to $52.50 (a price decrease of 16.7%), as shown in this equation:

$$Stock\ Value = \frac{D_0(1+g)}{i-g} = \frac{\$3(1.05)}{.11-.05} = \$52.50$$

Similarly, if the appropriate interest rate decreased by 1%, the theoretical stock value would rise to $78.75 (a price increase of 25%):

$$Stock\ Value = \frac{D_0(1+g)}{i-g} = \frac{\$3(1.05)}{.09-.05} = \$78.75$$

As you can see, the theoretical stock value is very sensitive to changes in the interest rate. The key takeaway for investors is that the theoretical value of a share of common stock is positively related to the level of dividends and the growth rate of dividends and is negatively related to the interest rate or discount rate in the denominator of the equation.

More on the Discount Rate

The discount rate applied to any asset can be thought of as containing two components: (1) a risk-free component that compensates the investor for the time value of money and (2) a risk premium that compensates the investor for the perceived riskiness of the cash flows:

$$Discount\ Rate = Risk\ Free\ Rate + Risk\ Premium$$

The discount rate that investors apply to U.S. government securities compensates them only for the pure time value of money as U.S. government securities have no default risk.[2] To hold securities that are riskier than U.S. government securities, investors must expect to earn a rate of return above the risk-free rate. That is, they must expect to earn a risk premium. The greater the risk of a security is, the higher the risk premium investors expect. Investors in IBM bonds, for instance, demand a higher rate of return—and thus the cash flows are discounted at a higher rate of return—than investors in U.S. government bonds. Similarly, investors in IBM stock demand a higher rate of return than investors in IBM bonds because the returns to IBM stockholders are riskier than the returns to IBM bondholders. Thus, the discount rate for IBM stock is higher than that for IBM bonds.

To carry the analysis further, venture capital investors committing funds to a young upstart company will demand a much larger risk premium than they demand from investing in the more established and lower-risk IBM. Part of the return expected from the investment by a venture capital investor is a pure time value of money return, but a large portion of the return is due to the substantial risk premium.

There are several theoretical models that enable investors to estimate a discount rate on a risky security. One of the most prominent models is the capital asset pricing model (CAPM) developed by Nobel laureate and Stanford University professor William Sharpe. The model posits that the appropriate discount rate is equal to the risk-free rate plus a market risk premium that is related to the volatility of the stock's returns relative to the market.

The same basic valuation model involving calculating the present value of future cash flows can be applied to any potential investment, including alternative investments such as real estate,[3] hedge funds, commodities, precious metals, private equity, and structured products. For instance, the value of a rental property can be calculated as the present value of the rental receipts minus the costs of owning the property, specifically required maintenance costs and property taxes (where CF equals the cash flow from the investment):

$$Value = \frac{CF_1}{(1+i)^1} + \frac{CF_2}{(1+i)^2} + \ldots + \frac{CF_N}{(1+i)^N}$$

This equation looks very similar to the general valuation equation. In fact, it is identical. The key element here is that in valuing real estate, the cash flows can change dramatically over time and some of those changes can be related to interest rates. For example, if interest rates rise because of rising inflation, the owner of the real estate property may be able to pass along some of the effects of rising interest rates by raising rents. In this case, as i increases in the denominator (causing the value of the investment to decline), CF will increase in the numerator (causing the value of the investment to rise). That is why real estate is sometimes referred to as an asset that provides a hedge (or protection) against inflation.

Final Note on Interest Rates and Valuation

In summary, interest rates play a key role—perhaps *the* key role—in valuing the majority of financial assets. That is why movements in interest rates—and expected changes in interest rates—are the most closely monitored macroeconomic variable by investors. Investors closely monitor Federal Reserve actions because of the impact those actions have on market interest rates and the subsequent valuation of investment assets.

Business Profits

Business profits are affected by changes in interest rates in two ways. First, the demand for discretionary products often rises and falls with changes in interest rates. The aggregate amount of consumer spending is dramatically influenced by changes in interest rates. As interest rates rise, consumer spending typically falls in the aggregate. Demand for new automobiles or new home construction often declines precipitously as interest rates rise. Rising interest rates make the new product much more expensive to purchase as autos and homes are generally purchased with a combination of equity and borrowed funds and consumers often shy away from incurring debt when the cost of debt rises. Although it is true that rising interest rates and rising inflation affect all industries, industries selling big ticket items that require the consumer to incur significant debt are especially vulnerable to increases in interest rates. Companies selling lower-cost items such as tobacco and food products are less susceptible to changes in demand for their products that result from changes in market interest rates. People may choose not to buy new cars when interest rates rise, but they still need to eat. However, irrespective of the influence on product demand of changes in interest rates, the profitability of businesses themselves is influenced by changes in interest rates as a result of the fact that businesses often borrow money to fund a portion of asset purchases and the cost of ongoing operations. As interest rates rise, borrowing costs (the cost of debt capital) rise. Additionally, as the cost of debt capital rises, the cost of equity capital rises. All else equal, as interest rates rise, a firm's cost of capital rises and its profitability falls. This can be seen by looking at a simplified firm income statement:

Revenues
Less: Cost of goods sold
Gross profit
Less: Selling, general, and administrative expenses
Earnings before interest and taxes
Less: Interest expense
Earnings before taxes
Less: Taxes
Net income

Margin Buying

Not all asset purchases are made with cash. Often investors borrow money to buy many different types of assets, including financial assets. People are most familiar with residential real estate transactions involving a mortgage in which the buyer puts up a small amount of equity and borrows the rest, effectively using the asset itself (the home) as collateral. We all intuitively realize that the lower the mortgage interest rate is, the more attractive the environment is to take out a mortgage loan. In fact, lenders often talk about how much more home you can buy when rates are low, emphasizing the amount of the monthly payment for a particular size of loan.

Homeowners aren't the only group that uses debt to acquire assets. Investors often borrow money from their brokerage firms to purchase financial assets in a margin account. Margin accounts require investors to put up a certain amount of equity and allow them to borrow the rest. Margin requirements were first established in response to the crash of 1929, when a comprehensive series of regulations were enacted with the intent to create a stronger and less volatile financial system. Federal Reserve Board Regulation T sets margin requirements for stock investing and is another example of the Fed's power to influence markets. Although the Federal Reserve has the power to set margin requirements, it has not used it to actively regulate stock market credit. Since 1940, the initial margin requirement has been as high as 100% and as low as 40%. However, the last change in the margin requirement was made in 1974.[4] Initial margin requirements are currently 50%, and maintenance margin requirements are 33%.[5] What this means is that if investors are going to purchase $10,000 worth of stock, they can put up $5,000 in cash and borrow the other $5,000. The stock itself serves as collateral for the loan. To protect the lender, if the stock falls in value and the value of the collateral in the account falls below 33%, the lender will require a further infusion of cash into the account. If the borrower is unwilling or unable to put more cash into the account, the lender will sell the position to liquidate the debt. See Box A.1 for an example of how a margin account operates.

Box A.1   Example of a Margin Account

Suppose you want to buy 100 shares of Merck at a price of $50 per share. The current initial margin requirement is 50% of the purchase amount, and the maintenance margin is 33%. Instead of buying the shares with $5,000 in cold, hard cash, you can spend $2,500 and borrow the other $2,500 from your brokerage firm in a margin account. Your position in Merck would appear as follows:

Total value (100 shares @ $50/share)	$5,000
Less: Margin debt	$2,500
Total equity	$2,500

If the value of Merck rises to $60 per share, your position in Merck will be as follows:

Total value (100 shares @ $60/share)	$6,000
Less: Margin debt	$2,500
Total equity	$3,500

In this case the position in Merck has increased in value by 20% (from $5,000 to $6,000), yet your return is 40% (from $2,500 to $3,500), double the return (ignoring borrowing costs) from the pure cash position.

However, the old adage is that leverage (or borrowing) is a double-edged sword. Suppose the value of Merck falls to $40 a share. Your position in Merck will then be as follows:

Total value (100 shares @ $40/share)	$4,000
Less: Margin debt	$2,500
Total equity	$1,500

In this case, instead of suffering a 20% loss in your position (from $5,000 to $4,000), you have suffered a loss in equity of 40% (from $2,500 to $1,500). The current percentage of equity in the position is now down to 37.5% ($1,500/$4,000).

(*continued*)

If the value of Merck falls to the point at which the total equity is less than 33% of the total value of the position, your brokerage firm will require you to put up additional cash to boost the value of the collateral. If you don't comply with the margin call, the position will be sold, the loan will be paid off, and you will receive any remaining cash proceeds.

Margin interest rates are based on the broker's call rate: the interest rate charged by banks on loans made to broker-dealers. The broker's call rate varies depending on general economic conditions and credit conditions in the financial markets. When the Fed is establishing an expansive monetary policy environment, general interest rates are typically low, and this includes the broker's call rate. Table A.1 provides a brief history of the broker's call rate. It is clear that the broker's call rate progressively declined during the financial crisis that began in 2007 and remained low through the various Fed quantitative easing programs.

Although margin interest rates vary somewhat from brokerage firm to brokerage firm, they generally fall within a very tight range. The specific margin interest rate typically charged by a firm is the broker's call rate plus some percentage markup. It is a good idea for stock investors who use margin to comparison shop for brokerage firms.

A cautionary tale can be drawn from the turn of the last century, as an increase in margin debt was evident in early 2000 and contributed to the bursting of the dot-com bubble. A prescient article appeared in the *Wall Street Journal* less than a month before the Nasdaq meltdown that occurred on March 10, 2000.[6] The article pointed out that margin debt had increased by 36% in a four-month period and warned that "the extra debt has been taken on primarily

Table A.1   Broker's Call Rate: June 2006–November 2013

Dates	Broker's Call Rate, %
6/29/2006–9/17/2007	7.00
9/18/2007–10/30/2007	6.50
10/31/2007–12/10/2007	6.25
12/11/2007–1/21/2008	6.00
1/22/2008–1/29/2008	5.25
1/30/2008–3/17/2008	4.75
3/18/2008–4/29/2008	4.00
4/30/2008–10/7/2008	3.75
10/8/2008–10/29/2008	3.25
10/30/2008–12/15/2008	2.75
12/16/2008–11/15/2013	2.00

Source: WSJ.com.

by a small portion of investors who trade fast-moving technology stocks." Less than a month later the Nasdaq fell dramatically, and its high has not been approached in the intervening 14 years.

Not surprisingly, historically low margin rates have indeed encouraged stock market investors to purchase stock on margin. We have certainly witnessed a dramatic increase in the amount of margin borrowing over the last few years. Figure A.1 shows that the amount of margin debt has more than doubled since January 2009. Some observers, notably Nobel laureate Robert Shiller, have called for the Fed to change margin requirements in response to stock market speculation.[7] He advocates that the Fed increase market interest rates to curb such speculation during times of, as he puts it, irrational exuberance.

Figure A.1   Margin debt in $ millions, 2001–2013

Source: *www.nyxdata.com.*

A low interest rate environment coupled with investors becoming increasingly confident in the economic environment has fueled dramatic increases in margin borrowing. We would remind you that none other than Warren Buffett has cautioned investors to "be fearful when others are greedy and greedy when others are fearful." One measure of greed in the marketplace is the amount of margin borrowing. In essence, speculation can be fueled by low interest rates.

Attractiveness of Newly Issued Securities

As with any good or service, investors comparison shop when choosing investment assets. Interest rates play a key role in determining the attractiveness of already existing securities trading in the secondary markets versus securities newly issued in the primary markets. This is most readily apparent in evaluating the attractiveness of fixed-income securities.

As was shown earlier in this Appendix, the value of a bond is the present value of future cash flows. If market interest rates rise, all else equal, the value of all plain vanilla fixed-income instruments trading in the market will fall—some more than others, of course.[8] Similarly, if market interest rates fall, the value of all plain vanilla fixed-income instruments trading in the market will rise.

For instance, consider a 10-year bond with an annual coupon (or interest rate) of 6%. If the appropriate discount rate for this bond is 6%, the bond will trade at par value. For a $1,000 par value bond, the appropriate price of the bond will be exactly $1,000. Let's assume that market interest rates rise and the appropriate discount rate for that bond rises to 8%. The price of the bond will fall to $865.80. The bond price falls because newly issued bonds (issued at par value of $1,000) with the same risk level will have a coupon rate of 8%, providing the investor with a higher annual cash flow. If an investor can earn 8% annually on a newly issued bond, previously issued bonds are less attractive and investors will be willing to pay a lower price for those bonds. The bonds must trade at a substantial discount from par value to provide the same return as newly issued par bonds.

The discount rate applied to both stocks and bonds is also influenced by changes in the riskiness of the issuer. For instance, if a firm's economic prospects are diminished by a forecasted negative outlook for demand for its products, investors will require a higher rate of return on those securities to invest in the securities of that firm. Therefore, although overall interest rates may not necessarily rise, if the prospects for an individual firm decrease, its securities become less attractive and must be offered at a reduced price to induce investors to purchase the securities.

In the aggregate, all types of financial assets—stocks, bonds, real estate, and so on—compete with one another for investors' dollars. If interest rates rise and the yields on bonds rise, all else equal, the attractiveness of bonds rises and the attractiveness of other assets, including stocks, falls. This is the main reason a low interest rate environment favors stock market investors and penalizes bond market investors. If I have funds to commit and bond yields are high, the bond market looks pretty attractive to me. Why invest in stocks when I can earn high returns in bonds, a less risky asset class? To be induced to invest in the more risky asset classes, including stocks, I must expect to earn relatively high returns. As investors move money from the stock market to the bond market, they bid bond prices up and stock prices down.

One of the ways investors can get a rough measure of the relative valuation of stocks versus bonds is to compare the earnings yield of the stock market to the yield on Treasury securities. The earnings yield on stocks is simply computed by dividing the earnings on a stock index (say, the S&P 500) by the price of the index. In early 2014, this measure stood at approximately 5.76%. An investor in 10-year U.S. Treasury bonds was earning a yield to maturity of around 2.86% at that time.[9] Thus, the gap between the earnings yield on stocks and that on government bonds was only 2.9 percentage points. As the gap shrinks, the attractiveness of stocks falls and the attractiveness of bonds rises.

Conclusion

Interest rates—more specifically, changes in interest rates—have a pervasive influence on the value of all investment assets. As we have discussed in this Appendix, interest rates are key inputs into the valuation models for all assets. As interest rates rise, demand for many products falls and company revenues decline. As interest rates rise, the cost of doing business for companies rises, leading to lower profits. Many investors purchase assets by borrowing money, that is, on margin. As interest rates rise, the cost of margin debt rises and the attractiveness of borrowing money on margin diminishes, leading to a drop in demand for marketable securities. When the demand for marketable securities falls, the price of those securities also falls. Finally, as interest rates rise, the attractiveness of previously issued assets falls as new assets are issued with higher expected returns.

NOTES

Introduction

1. "The Challenge of Central Banking in a Democratic Society." Remarks by Chairman Alan Greenspan at the Annual Dinner and Francis Boyer Lecture of the American Enterprise Institute for Public Policy Research, Washington, D.C., December 5, 1996, http://www.federalreserve.gov/boarddocs/speeches/1996/19961205.htm.

2. Steven Russolillo, "Irrational Exuberance, 17 Years Later," *WSJ.com*, December 5, 2013.

3. Casey Ichniowski and Anne E. Preston, "Does March Madness Lead to Irrational Exuberance in the NBA Draft? High-Value Employee Selection Decisions and Decision-Making Bias." NBER Working Paper No. 17928, issued March 2012.

4. See http://www.coldhardfootballfacts.com/content/the-irrational-exuberance-august-football/7405/.

5. Peter Rowe, "Craft Beer at a Crossroads," *San Diego Union Tribune*, November 14, 2012.

6. Binyamin Applebaum, "Fed Prepares for Change in Policy, and in Policy Makers," *New York Times*, September 12, 2013.

7. "The Federal Reserve Surprises Everyone by Changing Nothing," *The Economist*, September 21, 2013.

8. See http://www.people.com/people/archive/article/0,,20127261,00.html.

9. See http://www.npr.org/2013/08/29/216839752/seth-meyers-prime-time-political-parody.

10. See http://www.thedailyshow.com/watch/tue-january-31-2006/the-daily-show-s-irrationally-exuberant-tribute-to-alan-greenspan.

11. Jason Buckland, "Highest-Paid Public Speakers: Alan Greenspan," *MSN Money Canada*, October 20, 2011, http://money.ca.msn.com/savings-debt/gallery/highest-paid-public-speakers?page=3.

12. "Bernanke Earns Big Bucks in First Post-Fed Speech," *NBCNews.com*, March 5, 2014, http://www.nbcnews.com/business/economy/bernanke-earns-big-bucks-first-post-fed-speech-n44746.
13. Jeffry Bartash, "Fed's Fisher Sees No Reason to Slow Bond Taper," *MarketWatch*, February 3, 2014.
14. "Fed's Lockhart: Stocks in Correction Mode," *Reuters*, February 5, 2014.
15. Joseph M. Besette and John J. Pitney Jr., *American Government and Politics: Deliberation, Democracy and Citizenship*. Cengage Learning. January 1, 2010, p. 578.
16. Quoted in *Six Crises* (1962) by Richard Nixon and Quotation number 18611 in Post-Presidency.

Chapter 1

1. Martin Zweig, *Martin Zweig's Winning on Wall Street*, New York, Warner Books, 1994, pp. 42–43.
2. Adam Shell and Matt Krantz, "Wall Street Cowers as Fed Hints at Stimulus Pull-Back," *USA Today*, June 21, 2013.
3. As an aside, the certainty of outcome was some of the appeal of the returns Bernard Madoff was offering investors. The returns weren't particularly large, but they were very consistent. The fact that they were fictitious is another story.
4. Howard Simons, "Are the S&P 500 and Dow Jones Really in a Period of Disconnection?" *Minaynville.com*, February 19, 2014, http://www.minyanville.com/business-news/markets/articles/Dow-Industrial-SandP-500-Disconnects-Are/2/19/2014/id/53759.
5. Kenneth M. Washer and Robert R. Johnson, "An Intuitive Examination of Downside Risk," *Journal of Financial Planning*, vol. 26, no. 6, June 2013, pp. 56–60.
6. The average October return during indeterminate periods stands out relative to the other observations. It just so happens that the top three monthly returns during our 48-year sample occur in October, and all three observations occur during indeterminate funding conditions. Those "monthly" returns are 16.78%, 11.37%, and 10.88% in October 1974, October 1982, and October 2011, respectively. This is somewhat like rolling three sixes in a row; it is surprising but not unheard of. Without an economic rationale for the observation, we are going to label it as pure chance. If, however, the pattern continues, we will start looking for an economic explanation. Don't be too shocked if in a few months you see a paper titled "What Explains the October Surprise?"
7. Marc R. Reinganum, "The Anomalous Stock Market Behavior of Small Firms in January: Empirical Tests for Tax-Loss Selling Effects," *Journal of Financial Economics*, vol. 12, no. 1, June 1983, pp. 89–104.
8. Sam Mamudi and Jonathan Burton. "Money Market Breaks the Buck, Freezes Redemptions: Reserve Primary Fund Stung by Lehman Collapse, Investor Withdrawals," *MarketWatch.com*, September 17, 2008.
9. The debt ceiling crises of 2011 and 2013 were really political grandstanding, and most analysts agree that the U.S. government will not default on its sovereign

debt. Denmark and the United States are the only democratic countries in the world where the legislature has to approve increases to the debt separately from the budget. It is astounding that during the debt crisis in 2011 that resulted in the downgrade of U.S. debt by Standard & Poor's, Treasury security prices actually rose because of a flight to quality by investors. The very debt that was being downgraded rose in value. That indicates how strongly the market believes that the United States will not default on its debt.

10. Gary P. Brinson, L. Randolph Hood, and Gilbert L. Beebower,"Determinants of Portfolio Performance," *Financial Analysts Journal*, vol. 42, no. 4, July–August 1986, pp. 39–44.

Chapter 2

1. This reminds us of the quote attributed to U.S. Senator Everett Dirksen: "A billion here, a billion there, and pretty soon you're talking real money."
2. Marc R. Reinganum, "Abnormal Returns in Small Firm Portfolios," *Financial Analysts Journal*, vol. 43, no. 2, March–April 1981, pp. 52–56.
3. Edward Dyl and John Schatzberg, "Did Joe Montana Save the Stock Market?" *Financial Analysts Journal*, vol. 45, no. 5, September–October 1989, pp. 4–5.
4. It may appear to be minor, but note that a 3.4% annual return difference compounded for 10 years is nearly 40%. A 40% difference is economically significant to any investor.
5. There are several forms of earnings per share that commentators, analysts, and investors utilize in calculating P/E ratios. When a P/E ratio is quoted, it is important that you understand what definition of earnings the individual is using. Most frequently, the P/E ratio is based on earnings over the trailing 12 months (TTM), in which case it is referred to as a *trailing P/E*. In contrast, the P/E ratio may be calculated on the basis of forecasted earnings over the next 12 months, in which case it is referred to as a *forward P/E ratio*.
6. Benjamin Graham and David L. Dodd, *Security Analysis*, 6th ed., New York: McGraw-Hill, 2009, p. xi.
7. Sanjoy Basu, "Investment Performance of Common Stocks in Relation to Their Price-Earnings Ratios: A Test of the Efficient Market Hypothesis," *Journal of Finance*, vol. 32, no. 3 (June), 1977, pp. 663–682.
8. In this discussion and throughout the book, we use the term *mutual fund* to refer to open-end mutual funds. There are also closed-end mutual funds; however, they tend to be relatively specialized funds and are much less common than the open-end form.

Chapter 3

1. Warren E. Buffett, "2008 Letter to Berkshire Hathaway Shareholders," February 27, 2009, p. 15.
2. In economic terms, in any distribution of data, most observations will be concentrated near the mean and fewer and fewer observations will be located in the far ends, or "tails," of the distribution. Events appearing in the tails of the

distribution are often referred to as two- or three-sigma events. In this case, *sigma* refers to the standard deviation, and a *two-sigma event* appears two standard deviations from the mean of the distribution.

3. Charlie Munger, "The Psychology of Human Misjudgment," speech at Harvard Law School, June 1995, http://www.joshuakennon.com/the-psychology-of-human-misjudgment-by-charlie-munger/.

4. Have you ever wondered why very few talking heads forecast market stability or claim that a security is fairly valued? The answer is that moderate voices don't generate sufficient interest and subsequent airtime. You have to espouse a dramatic viewpoint to be heard. Some well-known individuals have made nice careers out of taking very extreme negative positions. Marc Faber and Nouriel Roubini come to mind. Faber publishes the *Gloom Boom & Doom Report,* and the media consistently refer to Roubini as Dr. Doom. Apparently, pessimism sells.

5. Overconfidence in our abilities isn't limited to our investing activities; 64% of Americans rate themselves as above-average drivers, according to a survey by Allstate. Only 29% were willing to say the same about their friends. The survey found that 56% of respondents had been involved in a car accident, but only 28% said the accident was their fault. It seems that many believe we live in the fictional Lake Wobegon, a place where all the children are above average.

6. To make matters even worse, many of these margin purchases were made with money borrowed through home equity loans on real estate values that later suffered their own bubble.

7. Werner F. M. DeBondt and Richard Thaler, "Does the Stock Market Overreact?" *Journal of Finance*, vol. 40, no. 3, July 1985, pp. 793–805.

8. Jonathan Burton, "Capital Ideas Revisited," *Investment Advisor*, May 2000.

Chapter 4

1. See Frank Newport, "American Dream of Owning Home Lives On, Even for Young," *Gallup Economy*, April 19, 2013, and Lydia Saad, "US Stock Ownership Stays at Record Low, *Gallup Economy*, May 8, 2013.

2. Nathaniel Popper, "Gold, Long a Secure Investment, Loses Its Luster," *New York Times*, April 10, 2013.

3. The first REIT was formed in 1963. Before the formation of REITs, only wealthy individuals and corporations had the financial wherewithal to invest in large real estate projects such as shopping malls, healthcare facilities, hotels, and office buildings. In 1960, Congress passed the Real Estate Investment Trust Act. This legislation exempted these companies from corporate income taxes if certain criteria (such as the distribution of a large portion of income) were met.

4. "The Basics of REITs," *REIT.com*, http://www.reit.com/REIT101/REITFAQs/BasicsOfREITs.aspx.

5. In addition to the types of REITs listed in Table 4.3, there is one REIT, Gladstone Land Corporation (LAND), that owns farmland in Florida and California. In light of the increased interest in farmland as an investment, we believe you probably will see more farmland REITs in the future.

6. See Gary Gorton and K. Geert Rouwenhorst, "Facts and Fantasies about Commodity Futures," *Financial Analysts Journal*, vol. 62, no. 2, March/April 2006, pp. 47–68, who find that during the period 1959–2004 the returns to commodity-based equities were more closely correlated with the S&P 500 Index (0.57) than they were with a commodity futures index (0.40). One possible explanation for the relatively low correlation between commodity-based equities and commodity futures is that commodity-producing companies frequently engage in strategies to hedge exposure to commodity price changes.

7. "First Trust Launches Actively Managed Commodity ETF," *Zachs.com*, October 27, 2013.

8. Chris Dietrich and Steven Russolillo, "Adios, Stock Correlation!" *WSJ.com*, March 14, 2012.

9. Obviously, Buffett was referring to the benefits of diversifying merely for the sake of diversification. As of March 2014, Berkshire Hathaway, which is Buffett's firm, held equity interests in over 50 different firms, including Dairy Queen, Wells Fargo, Coca-Cola, Geico, Burlington Northern, and Goldman Sachs.

10. Noah Buhayar, "Buffett Mocking Gold Sidesteps Slump as He Bets on Stocks," *Bloomberg.com*, April 17, 2013.

Chapter 5

1. Jason Zweig, "Why Investors Need to See the Light and Slow Down," *Wall Street Journal*, August 29, 2009.

2. See, for instance, Geoffrey Frieson and Travis Sapp, "Mutual Fund Flows and Investor Returns: An Empirical Examination of Fund Investor Timing Ability," *Journal of Banking and Finance*, vol. 31, no. 9, 2007, pp. 2796–2816.

3. Sam Stovall, *Standard & Poor's Guide to Sector Investing*, New York: McGraw-Hill, 1995.

4. Gerald R. Jensen and Jeffrey M. Mercer, "New Evidence on Optimal Asset Allocation," *Financial Review*, vol. 38, no. 3, August 2003, pp. 435–454.

5. We thank Kenneth French for making the data available at the following website: http://mba.tuck.dartmouth.edu/pages/faculty/ken.french/data_library.html.

6. Mark Hulbert, "Why 'Boring' Stocks Have an Edge Over 'Exciting' Ones," *Wall Street Journal*, June 7, 2013.

7. Robert Lenzner, "Warren Buffett's Idea of Heaven: I Don't Have to Work with People I Don't Like," *Forbes*, October 18, 1993, p. 43.

8. Andrew Bary. "What's Wrong, Warren?" *Barron's*, December 27, 1999.

9. The risk measures (standard deviations) are largely consistent across the monetary environments, and therefore we choose not to report them for brevity's sake. For example, mining, steel products, business equipment, and autos have the four highest standard deviations for the overall period and also have the four highest standard deviations for expansive and indeterminate periods. During restrictive periods, mining and steel products have the two highest risk levels; however, autos and business equipment have lower risk than several other sectors. Thus, autos and business equipment have performed poorly during restrictive

periods, but at least their performance has been consistently poor. Overall, since the risk ranking for the sectors is generally preserved across each of the three monetary environments, there is little information added from including the standard deviations by monetary environment.

10. Gerald R. Jensen, Robert R. Johnson, and W. Scott Bauman, "Federal Reserve Monetary Policy and Industry Stock Returns," *Journal of Business Finance & Accounting*, vol. 24, no. 5, June 1997, pp. 629–644.

11. Burton Malkiel, *The Random Walk Guide to Investing*, New York: Norton, 2007.

12. There are two prominent methods of calculating an average: the geometric average and the arithmetic average. The arithmetic average is the most common approach and is the one with which most people are familiar. In dealing with investments, however, it is necessary to use the geometric average in calculating the accumulated wealth from a buy-and-hold investment strategy.

Chapter 6

1. See Thomas J. Flavin, Margaret J. Hurley, and Fabrice Rousseau, "Explaining Stock Market Correlation: A Gravity Model Approach," *The Manchester School*, vol. 70, issue S1, 2002, pp. 87–106.

2. Simeon Hymand and Karl Cates, "The Proportion of Canadian Exports That Go to the U.S.: 75%," *Bloomberg.com*, August 1, 2012, http://www.bloomberg.com/portfolio-impact/2012-08-01/the-proportion-of-canadian-exports-that-go-to-the-u-s-75-.html.

3. "U.S. Relations with Mexico: Fact Sheet," U.S. Department of State, September 5, 2013, http://www.state.gov/r/pa/ei/bgn/35749.htm.

4. *The World Factbook*, Central Intelligence Agency, https://www.cia.gov/library/publications/the-world-factbook/geos/ch.html.

5. All data are from *The World Factbook*, Central Intelligence Agency, and are based on the year 2013, https://www.cia.gov/library/publications/the-world-factbook/geos/ch.html.

6. Gross national saving is derived by deducting final consumption expenditure (household plus government) from gross national disposable income and consists of personal saving, plus business saving (the sum of the capital consumption allowance and retained business profits), plus government saving (the excess of tax revenues over expenditures) but excludes foreign saving (the excess of imports of goods and services over exports). That is a mouthful, but all you really need to know is that a negative number indicates that the economy as a whole is spending more income than it produces, thus drawing down national wealth (dissaving). The higher the number as a percentage of GDP, i.e., the more efficient the economy is at saving.

7. Eurostat Newsrelease, "Euroindicators," January 22, 2014, "Euro Area Government Debt Down to 92.7% of GDP, EU28 up to 86.8% of GDP."

8. Howard Silverblatt, "S&P 500 2012: Global Sales Year in Review," S&P 500 Indexes, McGraw-Hill Financial, August 2013.

9. Matt Jarzemsky and Tom Lauricella, "Stock Break from Herd: Shares Trade in Less Correlation Than in Any Time Since Financial Crisis," *Wall Street Journal*, August 18, 2013.

Chapter 7

1. Operating a successful hedge fund is a very lucrative business. The standard fee structure in the industry is "2 and 20." Hedge fund managers typically charge investors a fee of 2% of assets under management (AUM) annually and in addition are paid 20% of the cumulative profits of the fund. It is, as they say, good work if you can get it.

2. The SEC requires mutual funds to invest at least 80% of their assets in the type of investment suggested by their name. Furthermore, mutual funds cannot invest more than 5% of their assets in the securities of a single firm or own more than 10% of the voting securities of a firm.

3. Matt Phillips, "Lehman and the Shorts: Why Regulators Should Have Listened," *WSJ.com*, March 12, 2010.

4. Julia LaRoche, "David Einhorn: Apparently, Now I'm a Verb," *BusinessInsider.com*, October 3, 2012.

5. For a more complete discussion of various problems with reported hedge fund data, see David A. Hsieh and William Fung, "Hedge-Fund Benchmarks: Information Content and Biases," *Financial Analysts Journal*, vol. 58, no. 1, January–February 2002, pp. 22–34.

6. See Mark J. P. Anson with Donald R. Chambers, Keith H. Black, and Hossein Kazemi, "Chapter 12: Hedge Fund Returns and Asset Allocation," in *CAIA Level I: An Introduction to Core Topics in Alternative Investments*, 2nd ed., New York: Wiley, 2012, p. 339.

7. It is worth noting that there are several alternative methods to derive the small-firm premium. By using quintiles of ranked firms rather than deciles, for example, we utilize one of the more conservative approaches. We base our selection on the fact that quintiles represent the most common approach used in finance, and the use of quintiles is sufficient to identify any significant, systematic return pattern that exists.

8. For instance, Wharton Professor Jeremy Siegel notes in his popular book *Stocks for the Long Run* that the small-firm premium can be attributed largely to the superior performance of small stocks over the 10-year period 1974–1983. During this period, the small-firm premium averaged a whopping 18% annually. The end of this 10-year period roughly coincides with the publication of the academic research that investigated the small-firm effect.

9. For example, see Gerald R. Jensen, Robert R. Johnson, and Jeffrey Mercer, "The Inconsistency of Small-Firm and Value-Stock Premiums," *Journal of Portfolio Management*, vol. 24, no. 2, Winter 1998, pp. 27–36, and Gerald R. Jensen, Robert R. Johnson, and Jeffrey Mercer, "New Evidence on Size and Price-to-Book Effects in Stock Returns," *Financial Analysts Journal*, vol. 53, no. 6, November–December 1997, pp. 34–42.

Chapter 8

1. "Drexel Burnham Lambert's Legacy: Stars of the Junkyard," *The Economist*, October 21, 2010.

2. Moody's Investors Service, *Moody's Rating Symbols & Definitions*, June 2009, p. 8.

3. "And Then There Were Three: ADP Loses Triple-A Rating," *MarketWatch.com*, April 12, 2014. http://www.marketwatch.com/story/and-then-there-were-three-adp-loses-triple-a-rating-2014-04-12.
4. "Berkshire Loses Last Triple-A Rating," *Dealbook.com*, February 4, 2010, http://dealbook.nytimes.com/2010/02/04/buffetts-berkshire-loses-last-triple-a-rating/comment-page-1/?_php=true&_type=blogs&_r=0.
5. http://blog.alliancebernstein.com/index.php/2012/02/14/high-yield-bonds-equity-like-returns-with-lower-risk/.
6. Treasury bills, notes, and bonds differ only in time to original maturity when the securities are issued. T-bills have 1 year or less to maturity, T-notes have 1-year to 10-year maturities, and T-bonds have more than 10 years to maturity.

Chapter 9

1. Harry M. Markowitz, *Portfolio Selection: Efficient Diversification of Investments*, New York: Wiley, 1959, p. 5.
2. Marshall E. Blume and Donald B. Keim, "Institutional Investors and Stock Market Liquidity: Trends and Relationships," University of Pennsylvania Working Paper, August 21, 2012.
3. Investment Company Institute, *2013 Investment Company Fact Book*, 53rd edition.
4. Without applying a log scale to the vertical axis, the red dashed line representing the value of the benchmark portfolio would have appeared as a nearly flat line running from the very left of the figure to its very right. The dashed line would appear just slightly above the horizontal axis.
5. Since the REIT index and the emerging markets index are not available at the start of the period, these indexes are added to the portfolio when they become available. Before their inclusion, the portfolio consists of an equal weighting of the then-existing asset categories. For example, in indeterminate monetary environments, for the years 1970–1987, the rotation portfolio consists of equal weights of Scandinavian countries, energy, consumer goods, and financials (25% in each category).

Appendix

1. Myron Gordon was a professor of finance at the Rotman School of Management at the University of Toronto.
2. Or perhaps virtually no default risk. For purposes of this discussion we will assume that a more rational fiscal policy will be restored in the future. Most financial models are built on the premise that a risk-free security exists and the proxy for this risk-free security is the issues of the U.S. government.
3. It may seem counterintuitive to refer to real estate as an alternative asset, as many individuals have an investment in real estate—equity in their personal residences—and may not hold any stocks or bonds. In this context, finance professionals are generally referring to real estate other than one's personal residence.

4. See Peter Fortune, "Margin Requirements, Margin Loans and Margin Rates: Practice and Principles," *New England Economic Review*, September–October 2000, pp. 19–44.
5. Regulation T merely sets the legal limit for margin loans. Brokers may certainly impose stricter requirements and require a higher percentage of equity. However, to remain competitive most brokerage firms operate at the legal limit.
6. Greg Ip, "Margin Debt Set a Record in January, Sparking Fresh Fears Over Speculation," *Wall Street Journal*, February 15, 2000, pp. C1, C2.
7. Robert Shiller, "Margin Calls: Should the Fed Step In?" *Wall Street Journal*, April 10, 2000, p. A46.
8. We refer to plain vanilla fixed-income instruments because there are some complex fixed-income instruments whose payouts may vary inversely with market interest rates. Investment bankers are a very creative lot and have designed all sorts of exotic financial instruments with complex payouts.
9. See Callie Bost and Whitney Kisling, "Stocks Lose Allure with Highest Valuation to Bonds," *Bloomberg.com*, January 13, 2014, http://www.bloomberg.com/news/2014-01-13/stocks-losing-allure-with-highest-valuation-to-bonds-since-2011.html.

INDEX

ABOUT THE AUTHORS

Robert R. Johnson is the president and CEO of the American College of Financial Services in Bryn Mawr, Pennsylvania. Bob also serves on the board of RS Investments, a San Francisco-based investment management firm that is majority-owned by The Guardian Life Insurance Company. He was formerly Deputy CEO at CFA Institute and was responsible for all aspects of the CFA Program for the majority of his 15-year tenure at CFA Institute. He received the Alfred C. "Pete" Morley Distinguished Service Award from CFA Institute in appreciation of his leadership, stewardship, and outstanding service. Bob has over 70 refereed articles in leading finance and investment journals. He has extensive media relations experience and has been quoted in the *Wall Street Journal, Financial Times, Barron's,* and *Forbes,* among others. He has appeared numerous times on *ABC World News, Bloomberg TV,* and *CNN,* among others. He is a coauthor of *Strategic Value Investing, Investment Banking for Dummies,* and *Tools and Techniques of Investment Planning.* Bob is a CFA charterholder and a chartered alternative investment analyst (CAIA). He holds a bachelor's degree in business administration from the University of Nebraska-Omaha, a master's degree from Creighton University, and a doctorate from the University of Nebraska-Lincoln.

Gerald R. Jensen is a board of trustees professor of finance at Northern Illinois University (NIU) and holds the Jones, Diedrich, Mennie Endowed Finance Professorship. He teaches undergraduate investments courses and is responsible for the NIU student-managed portfolio. At the graduate level, Gerry teaches corporate finance in the regular MBA and the executive MBA program. Gerry is a prolific publisher and has published articles in the leading academic and professional journals including the *Journal of Financial Economics, Journal of Financial and Quantitative Analysis, Financial Analysts Journal* and *Journal of Financial Research*. Gerry serves as an associate editor for the *Journal of Financial Research*. He holds a bachelor's degree from South Dakota State University, a master's degree from Iowa State University, and a doctorate from the University of Nebraska-Lincoln. Gerry was formerly director of the NIU CFA review program, and continues to be actively involved with the CFA Institute as a volunteer and a consultant.

Luis García-Feijóo is an associate professor of finance at Florida Atlantic University. He teaches investments and international finance and he is the Ph.D. program coordinator for the finance department. He also serves as an associate editor of *Financial Analysts Journal.* Prior to joining FAU, he worked as Director, Exam Development at CFA Institute, and was responsible for managing all activities necessary to develop the CFA item set examinations. He was an Associate Professor at Creighton University before joining CFA Institute. Luis has published his research in leading academic and practitioner journals such as the *Journal of Finance, Financial Analysts Journal,* and the *Journal of Portfolio Management.* Luis earned the chartered financial analyst (CFA) designation in 2001 and the certificate in investment performance measurement (CIPM) in 2011. He holds a Ph.D. in finance from the University of Missouri-Columbia. Luis actively served on the board of directors of the CFA Society of South Florida from 2009 through 2014. He is an active volunteer and consultant for the CFA Institute.